FINANCIAL INSTITUTIONS AND
SOCIAL TRANSFORMATIONS

Financial Institutions and Social Transformations

International Studies of a Sector

Edited by

David Knights
Professor of Organizational Analysis
Director of the Financial Services Research Centre
Manchester School of Management
UMIST

and

Tony Tinker
Professor of Accountancy
Baruch College
City University of New York

First published in Great Britain 1997 by
MACMILLAN PRESS LTD
Houndmills, Basingstoke, Hampshire RG21 6XS and London
Companies and representatives throughout the world

A catalogue record for this book is available from the British Library.

ISBN 0–333–67750–1

First published in the United States of America 1997 by
ST. MARTIN'S PRESS, INC.,
Scholarly and Reference Division,
175 Fifth Avenue, New York, N.Y. 10010

ISBN 0–312–17715–1

Library of Congress Cataloging-in-Publication Data
Financial institutions and social transformations : international
studies of a sector / edited by David Knights and Tony Tinker.
p.   cm.
Includes bibliographical references and index.
ISBN 0–312–17715–1 (cloth)
1. Financial institutions.   2. Banks and banking.   3. Financial
services industry.   4. Financial institutions—Social aspects.
5. Banks and banking—Social aspects.   6. Financial services
industry—Social aspects.   I. Knights, David.   II. Tinker, Tony.
HG173.F512 1997
332.1—dc21   97–28030
                                                                      CIP

This book is printed on paper suitable for recycling and made from fully managed and
sustained forest sources.

10   9   8   7   6   5   4   3   2   1
06   05   04   03   02   01   00   99   98   97

Printed in Great Britain by
The Ipswich Book Company Ltd
Ipswich, Suffolk

Contents

Acknowledgement

We would like to thank Helen Dean for secretarial assistance in bringing the book to final completion.

Notes on the Contributors

David Knights is Professor and Head of Organizational Analysis at the Manchester School of Management, UMIST, where he is also Director of the Financial Services Research Centre (FSRC). Recent books include: *Managers Divided: Organisational Politics and Information Technology Management*, (with F. Murray), Wiley, 1994, and *Regulation and Deregulation in European Financial Services*, London: Macmillan, 1997 (with G. Morgan).

Michael Muller is at the Department of Business Education and Human Resource Management University of Innsbruck. He has a PhD from the University of London and an MSc from the London School of Economics. His latest publication is 'Lean Banking und deutsche Arbeitsmarkt-institutionen', Sparkasse, forthcoming.

Andrew Sturdy is a Lecturer in Organizational Behaviour at the School of Management, University of Bath. He has been involved in financial services research in Europe for over ten years, focussing on the context, management and experience of organizational changes. His current research is on the global diffusion of customer service practices in retail banking.

Terry Austrin teaches in the Department of Sociology at the University of Canterbury, New Zealand. He has published articles on the organization of work in the construction, mining and finance industries and is co-author of the book, *Masters and Servants: Class and Patronage in the Making of a Labour Organisation* (with Huw Beynon).

Jon Sundbo is Associate Professor in Organization and Business Administration and leader of the Centre of Service Studies at Roskilde University, Denmark. He has been working in the areas of human resource management, information systems, service organization and management and innovation in services. He has published several articles including: 'The Tied Entrepreneur; On the Theory and Practice of Institutionalization of Creativity and Innovation in Service Firms' (*Creativity and Innovation Management* 1992) and 'Modulization of Service Production and a Thesis of Convergence between Service and Manufacturing Organizations' (*Scandinavian Journal of Management* 1994).

Mark J. Scher is Senior Research Fellow at the Institute of Financial Affairs (Japan), New York office and former editor and publisher of *Japan Financial*

Market Report. This article is based on a chapter from his forthcoming book, *Japanese Governance Structures and the Relational Access Paradigm: The Origins and Practices of Japanese Industrial Groups and Their Main Bank Relationship.*

Michael Shaoul completed his doctorate at the Manchester School of Management, UMIST, in 1992. Thereafter moved to New York to help run a small real estate company that bought and managed properties in the City's Lower East Side and East Village. In addition to his involvement in real estate he recently became a partner in a Wall Street firm.

Christopher Grey is Lecturer in Organizational Behaviour at the School of Business and Economic Studies, University of Leeds. He editor (with Robert French) of *Rethinking Management Education* (Sage, 1996). He is Reviews Editor and Editorial Board member of the journal *Management Learning*, and co-ordinates the ESRC 'Critique and Renewal in Management Education' Seminar Series. His forthcoming critical analysis of post-bureaucracy is to be published by Sage in 1997.

Tony Tinker is Professor of Accountancy at Baruch College, City University of New York. His recent books include: *Social Accounting for Corporations, 1984; Paper Prophets, 1985 and policing Accounting Knowledge, 1995* and he has published numerous academic articles. He is also co-editor of *Critical Perspectives on Accounting* and the *Accounting Forum.*

1   An Industry in Transition: Regulation, Restructuring and Renewal[1]

DAVID KNIGHTS

The very term financial services is indicative of the way in which banking, insurance, credit and the vast range of financial institutions (for example, stock markets, foreign exchange agencies and money markets) associated with the management of money are in a process of transformation. While there remain disputes about where to draw lines around the different activities and divergent financial instruments, the 'packaging' of the major financial institutions within the broad category financial services *cannot* be seen merely as a verbal convenience. It reflects and reproduces a discursive formation which has certain effects upon the construction and development of contemporary social relations (Foucault, 1970).

This introductory chapter to a series of papers on contemporary developments within the financial services examines the changes represented by this reclassification across a range of countries. A number of previously associated yet discrete industries are focused upon with respect primarily to the UK, but then briefly in relation to the parallels and differences in other parts of the world.

What brings these chapters together is not any grand universal and coherent theory of financial services. In our view, there is an abundance of established grand theoretical coherence and consensus in the field of finance and economics against which this book contrasts itself. Accordingly, an alternative, more social and sociological approach to the study of financial services is attempted here. Given the increasing talk in Western economies of welfare crisis and the imputed increased role for the private sector in the provision of various social securities, the switch of theoretical focus is perhaps timely.

A word of caution is necessary, however, for we are not offering a theoretical perspective that can overthrow the hegemony of finance economics in this field. Rather, the book provides a number of different viewpoints on particular developments in a variety of countries, including the three major international financial centres of Britain, Japan and the US. The distinctive feature of this book, then, is its diversity of approach, subject matter and cultural context within which the studies have been undertaken. So, for example, on the one hand, there is a critical analysis of the growth and development of banking in the US and, on the other, a challenge to the traditional finance economic theories of the role of the main or primary bank in Japanese corporate industry. There are two studies of consumer subjectivity in the form of the promotion of suburban subjects and the growth in credit in the UK, respectively and another showing how the sophisticated marketing in French banking captures a growing preoccupation amongst consumers with managing risk through financial media.

This chapter seeks to provide an account of the restructuring and renewal of regulation in UK retail financial services where, it may be argued, some of the most dramatic changes have been taking place. This could and there are some signs that it might serve as a model of 'things to come' in the finance sector in other parts of the world. Within the chapters of this book there are already indications of radical change in the organisation of the retail financial sector in Denmark, Germany and New Zealand, for example. In addition, the harmonisation rules within the European Union (EU) may result in the investor protection legislation in the UK acting as a catalyst to similar developments in the rest of Europe. The US has a very active consumer lobby and regulation could well move closer to the British model as the Glass–Steagall Act is repealed and restructuring/renewal moves in the direction of European bancassurance developments.

While largely concerned simply with describing the developments in the UK, one argument of this chapter is that the proliferation of discourse surrounding the regulatory and deregulatory changes in banking, credit and insurance has been extremely 'good' for business. Despite some short-term suffering from the bad publicity of regulatory sanctions and poor selling practices in the early 1990s, the financial services have a much greater public profile as a result of regulation and reconstruction and the consequent continuous media attention given to the industry. Instead of being peripheral to the everyday concerns of consumers, the financial services are beginning to occupy a more central place in their lives (Knights, 1997). Of course, this is also stimulated by the experience of several years of New Right governments who appear to be unsympathetic to state forms of social security (for example, health, welfare and pensions).

Until the late 1970s in Britain, few practitioners or commentators would have dreamt of banking and insurance let alone credit, mortgages, investment and other financial activities as part of the same industry. Each was seen as a separate sector having its own distinct set of customers, marketing/distribution systems, management skills and regulatory procedures. Banking was as different from insurance as textiles from motor manufacturing. This is not to suggest that relations between banking and insurance were non-existent or that mutual compatibility was absent. Just as motor manufacturers saw the marketing potential in deploying attractive textile designs in place of plastic or leather as car seat covers, so insurance companies perceived the potential in collecting regular contractual premiums through the banking system rather than in the form of physical cash payments.[2] In addition, bank managers have traditionally offered advice on insurance and associated financial matters as part of what they perceived to be a full and 'professional' banking service.

The transformation of the production, distribution and consumption of financial services has continued over recent times as neo-liberal economic policies of deregulation have reinforced the breakdown of traditional boundaries and intensified interindustry and international competition. In Britain the changes in the financial services have been part of a broader political commitment to extend the boundaries of the so-called 'property-owning' democracy beyond mere home ownership. The government has, thereby, sought to incorporate a wider ownership of financial securities, stimulated either directly through offering privatised public corporation shares at discounted prices or indirectly through fiscal incentives to purchase personal equity plans (PEPs) and personal pensions.

This political preoccupation with building the population's financial stake in the national economy was paralleled by the Thatcher regime's economic concerns with, on the one hand, retaining London's importance as an international centre of finance and, on the other, encouraging the services to fill the economic gap left by the decline of manufacturing. Believing the financial services to be bound by restrictive practices, the New Right economic policy has been directed towards shaking the industry out of its self-satisfied and inefficient complacency. This it has attempted by increasing the competition within a framework of regulation that would restrain competitive strategies from stepping beyond the boundaries of an ethical code of some minimal protection for the consumer.

These domestic changes have also coincided with pressures from the EU to establish a single European market and, ultimately, a single currency. This has resulted in further modifications of and will continually transform trading and consumer regulations in financial services, against a more general background of the 'globalisation' of competition and markets (Porter, 1990).

The major specific stimulants to change in Britain have been a product of government intervention. The 'Big Bang' in the City, the Building Societies Act (1986), the Social Security Act (1986) and the Financial Services Act (1986) have each contributed significantly to the reconstitution of a distinct range of business activities to be known as financial services and to a blurring of the boundaries between the separate industries within them. There have, however, been varying responses to these regulatory changes and this opening chapter seeks to document this diversity by examining their distinctive impact on the building societies, banks and insurance companies.

The chapter begins by providing a brief account of the more significant aspects of the new regulatory order before turning to discuss the restructuring in each of the sectors. Here, the building societies, banks and insurance companies are examined, respectively, followed by a more general analysis of the financial services within the new regulatory regime of competition, new technology and the state. Finally, there is a brief section examining some international comparisons as a way of anticipating the various chapters of the book that focus on different aspects of financial services in a variety of countries. In this section it is suggested that many of the changes that the financial services are experiencing are a product of 'crisis talk' surrounding the public provision of welfare and social security as well as political demands for market rather than state solutions to social problems. The conclusion simply reiterates the argument that economic deregulation and political re-regulation will probably be central to the changing character of financial services throughout the world in the early part of the twenty-first century.

REGULATORY CHANGE

The Big Bang

The 'Big Bang' was the only change not directly involving legislation, yet was the most concerned with the problem of restrictive practices. To avoid the threat of legislation following a monopolies and mergers commission investigation of restrictive practices in the City, there was an agreement to abolish the 'closed shop' nature of the stock exchange which prevented new entrants obtaining a licence to trade on the floor.

The principal change was to eradicate the jobber's exclusive role in 'making markets' and allow what is known as 'dual capacity', whereby broking companies 'make markets' as well as sell equities or gilts to clients. The two arms of the business were expected to be kept separate through a system known as the 'Chinese Wall' (Jessop and Stones, 1992). Whether this has been successful is difficult to establish but few scandals in the stock exchange[3] other than those connected with 'insider trading', have been exposed since the change to dual-capacity trading.

Part of the revolution in the City was the development of information technology that would give on-line, real time prices and data as well as promising paperless trading. Although the first attempt at developing such a technology system (TOPIC) failed, technology-facilitated screen trading rendered the stock exchange business more transparent and, therefore, less open to fraudulent practice.

As was intimated above, the UK Government was concerned that restrictive competition in the stock exchange was keeping trading prices high and, thereby, acting as a disincentive to small investors. Despite this, one outcome of the Big Bang has primarily been to benefit the large institutional investors such as insurance, pension and unit trust (mutual fund) companies in terms of reduced commissions for volume business. However, in relation to the government's anxieties about the threat to London's role as an international financial centre, the changes here allowed UK investment banks such as BZW, County Nat West and Midland Montague to provide a comprehensive range of investment and corporate finance services, placing them in a position to compete in world markets. It has also made London one of the most 'open' of the major global financial markets, attracting foreign banks and financial traders from all over the world to establish a role or stake in the City.

Legislation

Clearly regulation under the guise of the Financial Services Act (1986) has raised the profile of financial services significantly and resulted in considerable changes at the distribution end of the business. It has certainly stimulated further intensification of the breakdown of traditional 'demarcation boundaries' (Odih, 1991, p. 18), resulting in major shifts in the relationship between the building societies and insurance companies and closer links between most of the banks and either their own or other insurance companies. The central feature of the Financial Services Act affecting the retail financial services institutions was the insistence under the 'polarisation' rules that the distributors of insurance and investment products were registered either as appointed representatives of a single provider or offered independent advice across the whole range of providers.

All the high street banks retained an independent broking arm to which the more complicated financial advice or up-market customer could be referred but, with the exception of National Westminster Bank (who succumbed later to the trend), they also trained their bank staff to sell products from their own life insurance subsidiaries. In contrast, presumably out of tradition and the feeling that this was the more 'professional' route, the majority of the building societies initially opted for an independent agency status offering financial advice on products from the full range or a panel list of life companies. However, it soon became clear that the 'commission disclosure' rules which ensured transparency in the amount of commission paid to agents for selling life insurance or investment products were to become much more severe for independents than appointed representatives (and tied agents) of a single life company. At this point, most building societies changed to the latter status and this probably stimulated the bank parallel of establishing their own insurance companies. Currently of the largest ten building societies, only the Bradford & Bingley Building Society offer independent financial advice. Because of the volume of mortgage-linked business, the building societies were in a powerful position to secure favourable agency contract terms with the life insurance companies who were competing aggressively to secure tied arrangements, particularly with the bigger institutions that had national branch networks.

RESTRUCTURING IN THE FINANCIAL SERVICES

Banking, insurance and mortgage lending has probably experienced the most intensive period of restructuring in its history over the last few years. Major regulatory changes, oversupply and the search for new markets and profit centres have combined to force previously complacent companies to seek new challenges and to stimulate several mergers, acquisitions and take-overs. This section examines this restructuring from the point of view of each of the three sectors.

Building Societies

The Building Societies Act (1986) enabled the traditional domestic mortgage business of building societies to be extended so they could compete with the banks directly through offering routine money transmission services and unsecured loans, in addition to their traditional mortgage and deposit-taking business (Datamonitor, 1986). Part of the stimulation for this extension of their activities might be seen as a retaliation against the increased competition they had experienced in their traditional markets when the Big Five banks began offering mortgages at competitive rates in the 1970s. The banks entered this market largely in search of new sources of profit at a time when other alternatives (for example, money transmission and lending in less-developed countries) were looking decidedly precarious.

Although merger mania has hit the financial services since these sweeping regulatory changes, this is probably a delayed response to the deregulation of building societies whereby some of them have felt the need to become larger in order to compete on similar terms with the banks. In turn, the banks have sought to buy up building societies to increase their customer base. Many of these mergers and acquisitions have taken considerable time and effort because of the mutual status of some of the players on both sides of the insurance–building society divide. Insofar as demutualisation requires supplementary legislation from parliament and a two-thirds majority of the members to secure its approval, the speed is slow and the cost is high in terms of the sweeteners to the customers whose votes are required. However, the demand for increased resources to compete effectively both internally and internationally makes demutualisation attractive as it provides immediate access to new capital through a public share issue. Abbey National Building Society saw the benefits of this as early as 1987 and, in the process of acquiring public limited company (PLC) status, transformed itself into a fully fledged bank. Like its competitors, it has bought a life insurance company – Scottish Life – rather than remaining in a tied agency relationship with a life provider whom it could not control. From the point of view of life insurance companies, mergers or a take-over of their building society tied agents would provide a more stable relationship between the parties and a guarantee of what, given that contracts can be severed, is otherwise a precarious distribution outlet for its products.

Building societies continued to experience competition in a much 'thinner' market from both specialist mortgage companies (for example, the Household Mortgage Corporation) and, at the top end of the market, from foreign currency loans arranged by professional intermediaries. Very often the new entrants, whether banks or specialists, were taking the 'cream' of the 'up-market' business. By way of retaliation, the building societies had to differentiate their pricing policy (that is, reduce the rates of interest) for the larger and less risky mortgages in order to retain a share of the bigger more profitable business. As the market contracted, the size and visibility of the larger building societies ensured that they retained a competitive advantage over the new entrants who were primarily attracted to the market when the housing boom made mortgages appear to be virtually a risk-free business. However, the competition for market share resulted in heavy discounting for new mortgage business that could only be sustained because the majority of existing customers remained loyal at the non-discounted rates, rather than perpetually switching to whichever lender was offering the lowest discounts.

The most significant development in both banking and the building societies is the quantitative and qualitative extension of their activities in the insurance business. Throughout their history both have acted as agents for insurance business but, with minor exceptions, this has been a peripheral and low-profile activity. Until the recent upsurge in competition, the bank or building society manager would recommend certain insurance contracts either as a protection against loan risks (for example, compulsory property insurance and indemnity policies accompanying mortgage offers) or as part of a 'gentleman-like' (*sic*) professional service to clients. Under this arrangement, the non-compulsory business of the banks and building societies was peripheral to their central activity – so much so that often the manager pocketed the commission of life insurance contracts as a perk of the job. The amounts of business were small largely because such products traditionally have had to be sold and selling was not considered an appropriate mode of behaviour for 'professional' bankers. More often than not, the managers allowed their mortgage-linked life insurance to be arranged by sales persons (for example, brokers and insurance company representatives) from outside the building society or bank, thus depriving the latter even of the potential to secure a fee income or commission on the transaction.

Partly because of a threat to their monopoly of the mortgage market as a result of the competitive challenge of the banks and other specialists, the building societies began extending their insurance interests in the late 1970s. This was further stimulated by the burden of a new government requirement to administer the tax relief on mortgages (that is, the reduction of tax at source on mortgage interest or MIRAS) in 1984. Forced (at their own expense) to communicate with all their customers to inform them of the changes instituted by the government, the building societies simultaneously took the opportunity to market endowment-linked mortgages. Indeed, they went so far as to mailshot all their existing mortgage holders with an offer of switching to an endowment method without the usual administrative fee. This resulted in a considerable expansion in this kind of business involving a large commission income and an increase in the levels of income due to the higher interest charge on the endowment mortgages over the lifetime of each contract.[4]

The experience of this exercise persuaded the building societies to develop and expand their fee-paying, insurance-linked business through extensive mailshots of existing clients, advertising in branches and the media and by training certain counter staff in sales and product knowledge. However, the pressure to seek alternative or expand existing sources of profit in this way cannot be seen as unrelated to the growing competition and concentration within the sector itself. In the period between 1985 and 1990, 71 building societies were involved in mergers and the total number shrank from 167 to 115 (Wright *et al.*, 1991, p. 57).

Banks

The banks had extended their activities in the insurance market in a more aggressive fashion and much earlier than the building societies and did so by establishing separate insurance companies and/or insurance broking arms. So, for example, Barclays Bank, Lloyds Bank and the TSB established their own insurance companies and set up direct sales staff to distribute a wide range of insurance or investment linked products. The banks varied in the degree to which they linked their bank client base with the sales and distribution of their life companies' products. Of all the UK banks, the TSB has moved furthest in the direction of integrating the two sets of activities by having sales representatives of the insurance company located in the branches. This was not achieved, however, without considerable conflict as the distinctive cultures of insurance sales and professional banking clashed (Knights and Morgan, 1991).

The other banks have tended to maintain some distance between professional banking and the sale of insurance-linked products, merely registering their own staff as appointed representatives of the life company although, where retaining an independent advisory arm, passing on direct enquiries for specialist business from the bank. In addition to owning Black Horse Life, which largely distributes through a nationwide estate agency network, in 1990 Lloyds Bank also acquired Abbey Life giving them a two-pronged distribution system in the life insurance market. Then in 1994, Lloyds Bank acquired one of the top ten building societies – Cheltenham & Gloucester Building Society – as part of its strategy of building a comprehensive financial services conglomerate. In 1996 a merger took place between Lloyds Bank and the TSB giving the corporation a leading edge role in the field of bancassurance and making it the third largest UK bank with over 15 per cent of the market share against around 25 per cent each for National Westminster Bank and Barclays Bank (Knights and Odih, 1996b, p. 18).

Of all the banks only National Westminister Bank sought to remain as independent advisers for life and investment products after the Financial Services Act (1986) enforced a separation of independent from tied (that is, single-company) financial advice in 1988 (see below). However, survey evidence of the failure of the customers to detect or be concerned about the difference between independent and tied advice resulted in National Westminister Bank's decision in 1991 to abandon their exclusive reliance on independent financial advice services. They therefore followed the competition in establishing their own life insurance company in conjunction with the Clerical, Medical and General Insurance Company who provided the technical expertise in exchange for a minority shareholding. Just prior to demutualising and assuming full banking facilities, Halifax Building Society broke its tie with Standard Life in order to establish its own insurance company with technical assistance from General Accident.

Insurance Companies

This takes us to the question of where the insurance companies fit into this new financial services jigsaw. Although the profits are generally lower than in the life sector, more subject to international competition and to underwriting catastrophes as a result of major natural disasters, the providers of general insurance (that is, fire, accident, motor and so on) have not been as dramatically affected by economic deregulation and are outside the legislative remit of the Financial Services Act.

It is primarily in the field of motor insurance that competition has recently taken a dramatic turn. This sector of the market has seen a number of new entrants that have bypassed the traditional distribution route of broker intermediaries and sold policies direct over the phone. The most notable example is Direct Line which by 1994 had been able to secure 8 per cent of the market after only a couple of years' trading. Because motor insurance is compulsory, the possibility of competing on price has always been an option, but in the 1960s companies such as Vehicle & General offering discounted premiums grew rapidly only to become insolvent once the claims began to mount. Direct Line have not offered low rates across the board but have tended to 'cherry pick' the lower risk drivers and have reduced the distribution costs dramatically by dealing direct with customers on the telephone.

Few of the other sectors have sought to challenge the composite and specialist insurance companies' domination of this market[5] although the banks and building societies have become much more active as agents in securing such business. On the back of its outstanding success in the motor insurance market, Direct Line has now extended its activities into house insurance, lending, mortgages and investments. Although consumer research shows fewer people would be happy buying such products over the telephone than motor insurance, this may reflect the lack of exposure to the idea rather than any inherent resistance (Noble, 1996). In addition, there has recently developed a bypassing of the intermediary in these lines of business through the direct mail marketing of general insurance on the part of the insurance companies, banks and building societies. While the insurance companies are forced into greater competition as a result of these innovations, it is the insurance brokers who are ultimately threatened by these innovations in direct distribution. They are unable to compete on advertising and direct mail with these bigger and more capital-intensive retailers.

The other major change in insurance is the entry of other retailers such as Marks & Spencer and Virgin, suggesting that some financial service products can benefit from branding in a way that has not been the traditional route to market in this industry. The use of debit or credit cards in retail stores also provides these retailers with excellent personal data on customers through which to target financial products by direct mail. This is probably easier to do with tax efficient products such as PEPs or tax exempt savings schemes (TESSAs) but more difficult with more traditional life insurance products, as Marks & Spencer Financial Services appear to have discovered. Whereas their launch of unit trusts and PEPs was highly successful, their entry into the life insurance market did not have the same impact.

The intensification of the competition in distribution, resulting in particular from bancassurance, also affects the retailing of life insurance, pensions and associated investments. Currently the independent financial advisers (IFAs), the smaller (ex-broker) tied agents and company representatives enjoy a competitive advantage by virtue of their experience of the products, selling and financial skills. They also have a network of well-established clients that is difficult though not impossible to erode. However, as the larger bancassurance retailers train customer service staff in both product knowledge and sales skills, their routine access to a very large client population can clearly be turned into an exploitable advantage in terms of the retailing of a broader range of fee-paying or commission-based (that is, insurance- or investment-linked products) financial services. At present, the banks secure 50 per cent of their gross profits from such fee-paying services (Watkins *et al.*, 1996). This is certainly the field where the banks and building societies are identifying profits to compensate for the provision of 'free banking', money transmission (that is, current account) services which have arisen as a result of aggressive competition for personal bank accounts since the 1970s.

It is partly for this reason that the potential profitability of the provision, as opposed to the mere distribution, of life insurance, investment products and pensions renders the life companies more vulnerable to direct competition from other sectors of the financial services. In the early days of regulation, the cost and training disadvantages of independent advice resulted in a majority of building societies forming tied agencies with independent insurance companies. Thus, for example, Halifax Building Society tied with Standard Life, Nationwide Building Society with GRE and Cheltenham & Gloucester Building Society with Legal & General. However, the potential profits from being a producer as well as a distributor of insurance products soon persuaded the major building societies and banks to establish their own life insurance subsidiaries. All the high street banks have established their own life insurance subsidiaries and those building societies that are transforming themselves into banks (for example, the Halifax Building Society and the Woolwich Building Society) have followed suit as have some of those (for example, the Britannia Building Society) who were, at the time of writing, determined to remain mutual building societies.

Clearly, economic deregulation is affecting financial services in numerous countries throughout the world as neo-liberal regimes (see Chapter 3) extend their market boundaries. We can already see the transformation of retail financial services in New Zealand (see Chapter 5) where the banks have insisted that the staff take a personal responsibility for their own clients to whom they sell various financial products, much like traditionally self-employed life insurance sales people. Changes are also beginning to take place in the US as the financial sector becomes influenced by the bancassurance and other changes occurring in Europe. For example, the Insurance Advisory Board (a research organisation in the US) has recently been investigating UK financial services because they perceive them to be an indicator of the potential and probable future changes in the US (personal communication at the Insurance Advisory Board Executive Retreat, 1995).

While regulatory change is creating a transformation of the financial services across several distinct cultures, as already intimated, demographic fears about the growing ratio of elderly dependants against the working population is stimulating some governments to contemplate a privatisation of welfare. The degree to which the 'crisis talk' is valid varies from country to country. For example, Italy, where the state pension provision is very generous and private sources of provision are extremely undeveloped, has far more serious problems than the UK where the opposite situation prevails. In addition, there is no doubt that the crisis talk is as much a function of New Right political ideology as it is of demographic analysis since the data, by definition, has been available for some years without arousing these concerns. It is easy to slip into presuming that because change is occurring in financial services across several countries, a convergence of the systems and practices is under way.

This is not the case, for different cultures and business systems tend to intervene to prevent it (Whitley, 1992; Morgan and Knights, 1997). Take the example just mentioned of Italy *vis-à-vis* the UK. While Britain has much less serious a problem than Italy both demographically and in terms of the high participation rates in private occupational pensions schemes, the government recently reduced its liability considerably by partially privatising the state pension scheme. Italy, by contrast, which has the lowest rate of labour participation among the Organization for Economic Cooperation and Development (OECD) countries and one of the highest average life expectancy rates leaving it with a much higher dependency ratio than Britain, has intervened only marginally to allow pensioners to work part-time thus encouraging gradual rather than complete retirement at a specific age (Geneva Association, 1996, pp. 8–9). The government had earlier also sought to limit excessive state pension benefits but the population has deeply embedded pension expectations that politically are difficult to displace (Knights *et al.*, 1992) and there are virtually no private pension arrangements of the kind available in the UK and other Western economies.

COMPETITION, NEW TECHNOLOGY AND THE STATE

Competitive Change

The changes that have transpired to reflect and reproduce the complexity which now constitutes the financial services seem clearly to have benefited the larger retail institutions against the smaller because they are able to invest heavily in large sales forces, capital-intensive information technology, advertising and direct mail. It would also seem that the large building societies have secured an advantage over the banks and the traditional retail distributors of insurance products. One advantage they have over the banks is their branch network conveniently located for the shopper, their comparatively low-risk profile due to the asset-backed basis of their mortgage lending and their insistence that low-deposit borrowers purchase indemnity insurance. Their advantage in selling fee-paying, insurance-linked products follows as a result of dispensing much-desired mortgages to customers who buy endowment policies partly because of a psychological feeling of dependence on the lender (Knights *et al.*, 1994). Many of the building societies have moved from their traditions as mutual bodies with only a limited commercial approach to the market-place into organisations operating along aggressively competitive lines to advance their share of both banking and insurance services.

However, generally most of the larger institutions in the financial services market are having to struggle against fairly entrenched organisational cultures that are incompatible with the more competitively structured, deregulated markets in which they now find themselves. Banks have a strong tradition of lifetime employment in which promotion through the ranks was largely a function of the combined effects of the length and loyalty of service, geographical mobility and professional bankers' qualifications. Even a mildly aggressive sales and marketing orientation sits uncomfortably with the 'gentlemanly' (*sic*) professional image associated with traditional banking.

In some respects this culture clash restrains the banks and building societies from too robust an embrace of the new sales-oriented approach and they may thereby avoid stimulating a counter-productive customer sales resistance that could otherwise obtain. Indeed, there are signs of a much more sophisticated approach to selling insurance and investment products within some of the banks and building societies. This involves socially skilled, mature women receptionists qualifying prospects (that is, ensuring that they are appropriately in need of personal financial advice) through carefully designed, 'informal' talk before passing clients onto specially trained sales staff (Kerfoot, 1993).

The life insurance companies might be seen as the best prepared for the new competitive circumstances as they have always existed within a selling environment. However, the ease of their post-war success and ability to rely on a steadily growing market for insurance-related products has left them complacent and self-satisfied. Their divorce from the 'sharp' end of the selling process because of dealing through independent brokers and in relatively comfortable markets leaves them comparatively unprepared for the thrust and bustle of a highly aggressive and competitive market-place. The traditional companies have relied on a self-complacent belief in their own paternalism as moral guardians of their clients' best interests in financial security (Morgan and Knights, 1990), a belief which the present regulations put into question.

In this regard they were not dissimilar from the banks and building societies but there was often a discrepancy between this self-image and the practices which their insurance sales distributors, whether direct employees or independent agents, adopted in securing business. Indeed the 'bad practices' of these sellers was one of the major stimulants for the demand for closer regulation of the sale of insurance-related products under the Financial Services Act (1986). Despite regulation, however, the intensified competition has provoked a major switch of business attention to increasing sales and often this seems to be at the expense of improving the 'professional' approach to the business (Morgan and Knights, 1990). More recently, the legacy of these dubious sales practices has been exposed in a variety of scandals causing the financial services much consternation as well as financial cost in the form of compensation to consumers and fines from the regulators. Even the unit-linked new entrants of the 1950s who imported American techniques of aggressive and competitive selling and marketing are not ideally suited to the new conditions. Although they can readily face up to aggressive competition, their 'pressure' approach to selling life insurance and investments is out of step with the new regulatory regime, which favours an industry based on providing 'professional' advice rather than manipulative selling techniques.

In sum, both conditional and consequent upon the emergence of the category 'financial services' has been a continuous process of intersector competition and collaboration. The competition began first with the major banks beginning to compete with the building societies for what was then seen as the profitable mortgage business in the 1970s. This was stimulated partly by disappearing profits stemming from money transmissions as a result of 'free banking' and other interbank competitive strategies which had been stimulated by the state questioning the cartel-like arrangements in banking in the 1960s (Knights and Morgan, 1995). Expansion in domestic lending was also encouraged as the less-developed countries' debt was beginning to mount and the corporate sector seemed a less healthy source of profit in that period.

The retaliation on the part of the building societies was slow to advance not least because of legislative restrictions. However, once they could offer money transmission services and issue cheque books and credit cards, a competitive battle between the two institutions was unstoppable. Of course much of this was directly intended by the deregulatory stance of the Conservative Government throughout the 1980s but, once begun, it had its own momentum and in the early 1990s the banks appeared anxious about the erosion of their dominant position in the market for retail deposits and money transmissions. Moreover, as the mortgage market declined as a result of high interest rates and the recession, the building societies were increasingly seeking to diversify into traditional banking and insurance services. They also had a less tarnished image (see the recent ombudsman reports on consumer dissatisfaction with the banks; also Lewis, 1990; McGoldrick and Greenland, 1992). Furthermore, partly as a result of the power which can or appears to the house buyer to be exercised in granting a mortgage, building societies found it comparatively easy to expand their life insurance activities with clients despite a fall off in demand for mortgages during the housing slump.

On the other side, both the fall off in demand and the bad debt possibilities, when house prices were no longer rising, diminished the banks' enthusiasm for mortgage business. In addition, the low profitability of money transmission provided them with no financial space to compete with the building societies on price. For the latter, money transmission is a marginal activity and therefore does not have to fully compensate the capital costs of a high street presence which would be there regardless of these new services.

Distribution in an Age of New Technology

At present, there is a revolution in the making for the distribution of financial services as a result of the dramatic improvements in user-friendly personal computer (PC) technology. Until recently the banks have been ambivalent about the extent to which they prefer clients to transact their business through the automated teller machines (ATMs) because of losing face-to-face access where additional fee-paying products can be sold. One solution to this problem of the loss of face-to-face access caused by customers performing their transactions on ATMs outside the bank is to deploy telephone sales staff, who seek to make appointments for sales representatives in the client's home in order to provide financial advice and sell fee-paying products. Displacing the labour-intensive counter work on unprofitable money transmission services continues unabated as banks reduce their operating costs by closing branches. In addition, as the technology has become more sophisticated, ATMs are capable of going beyond mere money transmission transactions to offer fee-earning products. To facilitate this, ATMs are being moved into kiosks or into the banks so that the customers do not feel as exposed as they would on the high street. An alternative or additional solution would be to encourage the use of home PCs for bank transactions as these would be much more conducive to direct marketing, in particular of investment products. Financial services are already being provided on World Wide Web pages on the Internet and, on the assumption that security codes are invulnerable to the hackers, consumers will be able to bank and purchase financial services through the Internet.

While many people have become immune to the selling potential of junk mail, the direct marketing of financial services through information technology (IT) has the potential of allowing customers to ask questions of the product and engage in an interaction through an expert system 'fact find' (that is, a personal financial profile) and best advice programmes of savings, insurance and investment. Clearly the capital costs of such an IT system puts it beyond the reach of any but the largest financial services institutions; there are, however, prototype home banking systems already operating in the Bank of Scotland and TSB and additional expert system programmes can easily be added on to these systems. Computer as opposed to telephone home banking, which has increased enormously, has had a limited take-up largely because of the costs to the customer who is bound to compare it unfavourably with 'free banking' through other media. It is strange, however, that the banks have, until recently, been hoping to subsidise the cost of branches to make banking convenient and even the cost of telephone calls but not provide 'free' computer banking. Because of their greater asset base it would pay the banks to treat this as a competitive advantage and subsidise clients in promoting their use of IT for financial self-management in the home. As one of the earliest users of IT, the banks are ahead of the field in the development of a diversity of IT systems for both administrative processing and the marketing of products.

Financial Self-discipline and the State

Both deregulation and regulation have given a higher profile to the financial services industry which, although on occasion painful in terms of public relations when in breach of the rules and costly in relation to compliance and training, has been beneficial for business. Almost all of the financial service institutions have increased their activities, retailing larger volumes and a proliferation of products or services. In terms of supply, the life insurance companies have probably benefited most as a result of the increased awareness about pensions, equity-based investments and the dramatic increase in mortgage-linked business stemming from building society ties. Throughout its history, the UK life insurance industry has enjoyed several fiscal privileges which have rendered its products attractive as tax-efficient investments and thereby considerably easier to market and sell. In the early 1980s the Thatcher Government entered a brief period in which there was a strong commitment to fiscal neutrality which looked as if it would destroy the tax incentives attached to life products and it did abolish tax relief on life assurance savings. However, the government's other objectives of encouraging individual responsibility, financial self-discipline (Knights, 1988) and equity ownership have reversed the policy on fiscal neutrality and the incentives to purchase financial service products have never been greater.

In the 1980s there were new tax concessions for products such as PEPs, TESSAs and health insurance for the aged. Perhaps of most importance, is that, in addition to the generous tax concessions on pension savings, the government introduced cash rebates for consumers contracting out of the state earnings related pension scheme (SERPS) and transferring to personal or group pensions – a consequence of the Social Security Act (1986). The espoused rationale behind these attempts to 'privatise' parts of the state pension[6] was the increasing dependency ratio (that is, the number of persons dependent on economic redistribution) leading to future potential funding difficulties. Encouraging the population to take personal responsibility for their own pensions, however, not only relieves the government of incalculable future financial burdens but is also compatible with the ideology of removing the dependence of subjects on state welfare and of increasing their financial independence and stake in the national economy. The consequence of these changes was that the financial services sector and, in particular, the life insurance companies enjoyed a bonanza of new business which even the severe economic recession of the early 1990s only marginally restrained.

So far we have concentrated on the changes in the industry but clearly the consumer is also changing alongside and perhaps in response to these transitions in the provision of financial services. However, these changes in the nature of consumption are not so well documented (cf. Morgan and Knights, 1993, 1995; Knights and Odih, 1996).

It is through the exercise of power by producers, distributors and regulators that individuals are transformed into subjects who *secure* themselves by participating in the consumption practices which are a creation of this power. In short, this power has the effect of defining the 'truth' of what it is to be a subject within that set of social relations wherein financial services reflect and reinforce the 'means of consumption' in the pursuit of items of conspicuous consumption, personal security, individualised wealth and independence from the state or the community (Knights, 1997). These various developments have to be seen not only as new configurations of the power of the financial services and the subjectivity of its consumers but also as an outcome and restructuring of the conditions within which these social relations are reproduced. For instance, it can be argued that the changes in financial services reflect more global contradictions and crises in the 'structural' development of contemporary capitalism.

During the boom cycle in the 1980s, the financial services contributed significantly to the dramatic growth of credit and indebtedness. Some of the bankers (for example, Sir Brian Pitman, Chief Executive of Lloyds Bank) admitted to making bad judgements during this period and therefore 'must share the blame for mounting business failures and bad debts' (*Observer*, 23 February 1992). Of course, the banks were only seeking new sources of profitable lending to compensate for the business lost through the less-developed countries' debt crisis. However, in hindsight, they simply replaced one debt crisis with another and, in the process, helped to fuel the Lawson boom and subsequent recession where both institutional and personal bankruptcies or a restructuring of indebtedness had as severe a dampening effect on growth and consumption as the earlier 'credit bonanza' had on expansion.

In their search for ever-increasing profits, financial services companies may have overstepped the mark and lost far more than they gained. However, these failures should not blind us to the sense in which the subjectivity of consumers has been transformed during the period in which a fragmented set of financial institutions have come to share a common identity and be treated as a single industry. Indeed, it may be argued that a consumer of financial services was created and, although the recession of the late 1980s and early 1990s decelerated the pace at which individuals began to be as concerned about their personal investments, insurance and pensions as their cars, the change encapsulates a new level of individualised material self-interest which will be ripe for further exploitation as economies throughout the Western world climb out of almost a decade of recession in the late 1980s and early 1990s.

INTERNATIONAL COMPARISONS

While this introductory chapter has focused almost exclusively on the UK, it has done so because on a number of key issues this is where the most dramatic changes have taken place (Insurance Advisory Board, 1995). This is particularly the case in terms of regulation, restructuring and renewal in the retailing sector where this book has its main focus. The foregoing provides the context of the changing nature of financial services in the UK where the volume of life assurance sales are the highest in Europe and the third highest in the world. If life and investment business were to be seen as the product market within financial services that has the most potential for growth and producer–distributor profitability, then the UK regulatory system may represent a model for the rest of Europe and other parts of the world. However, to what extent are the changes in the UK paralleled elsewhere? As far as can be seen, financial services in other parts of the world are in the midst of a major transformation that contains many of the same elements present in the UK. There is, for example, a process of deregulation, a blurring of the demarcations between banks, insurance companies and mortgage providers and a more marketing and sales-oriented approach to business than previously.

Those countries which are members of the EU are, of course, further stimulated by the aims and objectives of the Single European Market (SEM) to harmonise regulations, increase cross-national trade, produce a single European currency and possibly a quasi-federal system of European government. The realisation of a single market in financial services may be some distance away but companies are conscious of a large and comparatively underexploited market in some European countries.

In addition, mergers, joint ventures and other kinds of cooperative or collaborative arrangements, both national and cross-national, have developed rapidly as companies have positioned themselves to take advantage of a more universal market in European financial services. Once certain national regulations are abandoned or modified to comply more fully with the SEM, the business potential in the financial services should expand dramatically. The most significant of developments, already well under way, are the links between the banks and insurance companies (that is, bancassurance) whereby the latter are able to distribute their products through the former and have access to the large client databanks of the banks.

By comparison with the UK, German banks have a much larger share of the distribution of insurance products but regulation at the production end of life insurance has restrained product innovation such that 70 per cent of German life business is in the form of individual non-profit whole life assurances (Andersen Consulting, 1990, p. 83). Increased competition from other financial services and foreign banks as a result of economic deregulation is resulting in German banks taking a much more aggressive approach to marketing, product development and sales (see Chapter 7; D'Allessio and Oberbeck, 1997). This could lead to greater pressure from consumer groups for investor protection legislation similar to that in the UK. The experiences of distribution and regulation in the UK could well have an export value for Germany and perhaps other parts of the EU.

Some of the greatest changes have been made in Denmark, where holding companies are able to own a diversity of financial service companies (see Chapter 6), for example the three largest insurance companies – Baltica, Hafnia and Topdanmark – are each members of holding companies that have banks within their groups (Andersen Consulting, 1990, p. 112). As yet, however, the deregulation in the financial services does not appear to be accompanied by a new regulatory regime controlling relations at the retail end of the business as in the UK.

CONCLUSION

This chapter has been concerned with documenting a changing context for the financial services, primarily in the UK, as a result of economic deregulation and political re-regulation. There has only been a limited attempt to analyse the conditions and consequences of these changes, although it has been suggested that the New Right in contemporary politics has resulted in various interventions in this field. Yet even in the absence of such strong political influences it is likely that demographic and government debt factors would have stimulated a trend towards encouraging populations to make private provision for various forms of social security. Welfare crisis talk is continually transforming consumers to seek private solutions to their security problems and this would seem even greater in the rest of continental Europe than in the UK. Ensuring that the financial services are properly competitive and adequately regulated might then be the preoccupation of countries throughout the world in the twenty-first century. Before turning to the next chapter, a brief synopsis of each of the chapters follows.

Tony Tinker's chapter, 'The Dialectic of the Value Form: the Social Evolution of Capital Markets in the US', provides a historical context for understanding the growth of banking and financial services in the US. Over recent decades public commentators and analysts of the Western political economies have been increasingly turning from the fatalism and futility of orthodox neo-classical economics to more radical forms of analysis. Ironically, just as Eastern Europe deposes Stalin's caricature of Marx, so another Marx is rising in the West – the one (rare among economists) who explicitly theorised the crises, slumps and disequilibrium-prone tendencies of capitalism. Nowhere are such social instabilities more poignantly revealed than in this chapter's historical review of the US financial services. This is a long history of disruptions to commodity production by the money form of speculations, scams, financial panics, bubbles and so on. It recounts the continual struggle between acquisitive and speculative forces and regulatory attempts to curb and socialise them. This is not a pendulum movement, but an erratic dialectical dispersion that, historically, unravels into an unpredictable series of speculative crises and regulatory attempts to socialise the acquisitive forces. Hence, the corporate migration to low-cost regimes (New Jersey, Delaware, London and the Bahamas), the 'chartermongering' competition by states and nation states to attract new corporate capital and the revolutions in capital market technology, from the anachronistic trading floors of the NYSE and AMEX, to extended trading hours, to electronic exchanges and to the internalisation and internationalisation of (in-house) capital market markets of large securities firms. Today, the accumulation by banking and financial services has not only 'overmortgaged' most sectors of the economy (corporate, consumer, Third World, farming, schooling, residential and so on) in a way that precludes traditional expansionary remedies, it has increased the risk of general financial default and massive transfers in property rights. The chapter concludes with an argument that US state policies have, in effect, 'socialised' the risks of the financial services sector (insurance programmes for house mortgages, farm loans, bank deposits, Third World loans, student loans, savings and loans deposits and so on). The payments associated with these programmes are a primary component of the record US Government deficits in the 1990s. In pursuit of its traditional function of reproducing the conditions of capitalist accumulation, the US now finds itself as a major player in the financial services sector.

The chapter by Christopher Grey, 'Suburban Subjects: Financial Services and the New Right', argues that financial services are a key site in the production and reproduction of an acquisitive, moralistic and individualised form of subjectivity which may be termed 'suburban'. This is explored in the context of New Right discourses about the consumer society in the UK and an analysis of the role of regulation in sustaining liberal capitalist democracy. However, in contrast to Tinker, Grey does not follow a Marxist line of argument wherein regulation is seen as an ideological smokescreen to cover over the cracks of capitalist exploitation. It may have such effects but this does not necessarily falsify the 'truth' claims of the New Right. These can be examined whilst remaining sceptical as to their truth or falsity in any transcendental sense. This, the author proceeds to do by discussing the effects of the New Right 'truth' claims on the subjectivity of the UK population. The regulation of the financial services, instigated by the Conservative Governments of the 1980s, served to extend the conditions under which suburban forms of subjectivity were viable. Thus, the proliferation of 'Charters' in both the Conservative and Labour Party policies reconstituted the politics of citizenship by asserting the universal rights of citizens as consumers and signalled an end to the divisiveness of the Thatcher years and (once more) the 'end of class'. The chapter recounts the numerous ways in which suburban subjectivity is individualised, normalised and disciplined.

Michael Shaoul's chapter, 'The Acrobat of Desire: Consumer Credit and its Linkages to Modern Consumerism', provides an unconventional social examination of the growth and development of credit in contemporary Western economies. The traditional understandings of credit, he argues, typically stress its secondary, passive and facilitative functions – a catalyst that permits the acquisition and consumption of 'real' goods and services. Such constructions have led us to overlook the manner in which the meaning of contemporary notions of credit has been re-endowed in recent social discourse. Central to the paper's argument is the view that the meaning of consumption and credit does not originate in an economistic notion of utility, but in the social and communicative processes in which meanings and aspirations are constructed and attached to purchasing and consuming. This chapter explores the production of modern consumerism with specific reference to consumer credit. It shows how credit, once associated with a profligate attitude towards spending, has been redeemed in modern advertising as a judicious way of spreading the cost of purchases, of attaining a full and happy life, of securing 'freedom', of acquiring the 'best' and 'special' products and in securing a right of passage. While economics continues to treat credit as simply a financial instrument that links depositors and borrowers or the supply and demand for money, this chapter identifies credit as reflecting and reproducing desire and the acrobatic performances that go to make up human consumption and the consumer society.

In his chapter, 'Bringing the Consumer In: Sales Networks in Retail Banking in New Zealand', Terry Austrin suggests that management control in banking is in the process of a dramatic transformation, at least in New Zealand, where his case study research was conducted. As a result of deregulation in the finance sector (a universal feature of all the papers in this volume), Austrin argues that a new system of managing consumer networks means that personal bankers are less controlled by their own internal hierarchies than by the very network of customers to whom they are accountable. However, this is a willing accountability for it is also the source of self-improvement and an active management of employee self-worth and respect. Personal bankers are responsible for their own networks of customers to whom they sell financial products but also service throughout the lifetime of the long-term products that are bought. The commitment to personal customers generates a degree of self-discipline on the part of employees far greater than the impersonal rules of a bureaucratic hierarchy. Personal bankers will even find themselves contacting customers outside of working hours in a way that would never have occurred under the bureaucratic regime. But then building their customer networks is a source of pride and self-esteem as well as a means of autonomy and independence. For if customers are loyal, not so much to the bank but to the employee, the network provides the personal banker with considerable negotiating power. The reskilling of bank employees in these conditions really appears to be a case of empowerment, of perhaps a much more meaningful variety than that emanating from quality management initiatives.

The chapter, 'Financial Services in Transition: an Examination of Market and Regulatory Forces in Denmark and the UK', by Jon Sundbo, with assistance from David Knights, also examines the impact of deregulation in financial services, comparing Denmark and the UK. It raises questions about the extent to which a decline in customer loyalty and inertia in financial services is providing distinct benefits to the consumer. Part of the problem is that price and product transparency is not universal and even where, as in the UK, it is more advanced, its complex nature combined with a comparative degree of consumer indifference erodes its competitive effects. Drawing upon a range of case studies in Denmark and more general research in the UK, the authors examine in turn the changing market conditions, the responses of companies, the reactions of consumers and, finally, the effects of regulation on producer–consumer relations. Besides deregulation and new regulations, financial service corporations have been affected badly by the economic recession. This transition has been extremely difficult to accommodate for an industry that, in enjoying a healthy expansion throughout its history, had become comparatively complacent. Paternalistic in its approach to management, the industry has been dragged into strategic action by the dramatic and disruptive impact of the changes stimulated by economic deregulation, recession and political re-regulation. Yet while financial services are now much more competitive, it is not clear that consumers have benefited economically. Despite much stricter regulations at the point of sale in the UK, for example, scandals demonstrating how consumers have been badly advised (for example, personal pensions) at great economic cost to themselves continue to proliferate. In forcing companies to be more efficient and cost conscious, it may be argued that, so far, the changes have benefited the producers far more than the consumers. Only by strengthening the consumer lobby and the consumer protection regulations will the benefits become more balanced.

Michael Muller's chapter, 'Stability or Transformation of Employment Relations in German Banking', first contrasts the difference between the German bank-based system of finance and the US–UK market system. It then seeks to examine the changing nature of German banking although the author admits the changes not to be as dramatic as in the UK and US. This to a large extent, is because of the structure of German banking where the assets are almost equally divided between the commercial banks at around 30 per cent (dominated by the Big Three, Deutsche Bank, Dresdner Bank and Commerzbank), the public savings banks owned by local authorities at 38 per cent and the cooperative banks (Sparkasse) with 15 per cent of the total assets. According to Muller, the only group that competes in this market-place is the commercial banking sector. The stability of German banking is evidenced by the comparatively high and modestly falling intermediation ratio (that is, the level of financial dependence on the banks of non-financial companies) of 0.84 to 0.75 between 1975 and 1985, in contrast to the US situation where between 1980 and 1990 the ratio fell from 0.52 to 0.37. Despite this, the German banks are diversifying and seeking out new opportunities – expanding their bancassurance activities and fee-earning business and opening up direct banking through the telephone, fax or computer. The main focus of the chapter is to examine the impact of all these changes on employment relations and practices to assess whether there is a convergence towards the more flexible (and, thereby, precarious for employees) systems operating in the US. Based on six case studies of German banks, Muller discusses consultation, pay, training and employment stability and concludes that, while there are signs of some convergence, in particular where new subsidiaries are created to conduct direct banking, on the whole the changes are much less dramatic than in the Anglo-American financial services.

In their chapter 'Marketing the Soul: from the Ideology of Consumption to Consumer Subjectivity', David Knights and Andrew Sturdy write about the role of marketing and market research within financial services in transforming individuals into consumer subjects. They provide a theoretical excursion through some of the recent literature on subjectivity, relating it to issues concerned with marketing, in general and the practices of segmentation, in particular. The chapter focuses largely on how, through developing a detailed databank of knowledge about individual clients or customers, private financial institutions that offer security products are able to enter the soul or capture the hearts and minds of the consumers. Against the background of New Right, neo-liberal politicoeconomic regimes that seek continuous reductions in public expenditure, this places financial services providers in an enviable position. For the free market imposes a level of insecurity on citizens that the state is no longer willing or able to alleviate fully. The consumers, therefore, are pushed or persuaded to purchase social security in the market-place from private financial institutions. The authors argue that this is an instance of governmentality in the Foucauldian sense of governing the subjectivity of individuals through specific power–knowledge relations. Governing subjects is clearly not the sole prerogative of the official state – it is readily distributed to non-governmental institutions though not because of some grand and coherent plan on the part of the politicians.

In his chapter entitled 'The Japanese Main Bank Relationship: Governance or Competitive Strategy?', Mark Scher explores the nature of the main bank in its role as a major creditor and lender of last resort to its clients within Japanese banking's cultural, historical and institutional context and in relation to the governmental institutions that strive to foster economic development through the main bank system. In so doing it discloses some of the myriad formal and informal systems which the main bank uses to structure a profitable and lasting relationship with its client firms, the nature of the direct rewards sought by the banks and how their needs are served by the main bank relationship. In general, the literature to date has tended to emphasise the benefits of the main bank relationship to the corporate enterprise, particularly in terms of the efficiency of capital or when a firm is in financial distress, as well as its benefits to the economic development of society, particularly in times of scarcity of capital. Some agency theorists have proposed the bank as a corporate governor and monitoring agent, not only on behalf of other creditors, but also for other shareholders in the client firm. Such interpretations ignore the bank's own institutional reasons for promoting the relationship. Treating the bank as a 'black box', the literature has largely overlooked how the bank itself benefits as the 'main bank' and the control it wields in determining the limits and terms of the relationship. Many of these benefits revolve around selling on additional profitable services that in other countries cost banks dearly in terms of marketing and sales activities. The 'main bank' role clearly provides privileges for banks that appear not to be available to the same extent outside of Japan.

ACKNOWLEDGEMENT

Tony Tinker assisted with the production of the synopses of the chapters at the end of this introductory chapter.

Notes

1. An earlier version of this chapter was presented at the European Science Foundation's EMOT Workshop on Financial Services, CREP, Paris, 30 September–1 October 1994.
2. This was made feasible only when major employers in the UK began to pay wages and salaries through crediting the employee's bank account rather than through the administratively costly and security risk methods of cash payments.
3. There have of course been major scandals within the general area of financial services, some of which have been picked up largely because of the Financial Services Act (1986) and others of a more international nature (for example, BCCI, Bank of Commerce and Credit International) which clearly go beyond the specific jurisdiction of a nation state's regulatory body such as the Bank of England.
4. This is because the capital on the mortgage is not reduced until the end of the term of the life assurance endowment. Consequently, the interest remains as a percentage of the initial mortgage for the whole of the term rather than reducing with each successive payment by the mortgagee.
5. There has been some erosion of the motor side of business by accident recovery organisations such as the Automobile Association and some of the larger corporations (for example, ICI) underwrite their own insurance cover. In addition, some of the banks (for example, the TSB) do underwrite general as well as life business.
6. The part that was privatised was the proportion of the state pension index linked to inflation and this was more costly to fund than the basic pension which could be directly controlled.

References

Andersen Consulting (1990) *Insurance in a Changing Europe 1990–95* (London: The Economist Publications).

Building Societies Act (1986) (London: HMSO).

D'Allessio, N. and Oberbeck, H. (1997) 'Development Tendencies in the German Banking Industry', in G. Morgan and D. Knights (eds), *Deregulation and European Financial Services* (London: Macmillan), pp. 86–104.

Datamonitor (1986) *Personal Finance Market Report* (London: Datamonitor).

Financial Services Act (1986) (London: HMSO).

Foucault, M. (1970) *The Order of Things: the Archaeology of the Human Sciences* (New York: Vintage Books).

Geneva Association (1996) *The Four Pillars*, vol. 18, June.

Insurance Advisory Board (1995) 'Reinventing the Insurance Relationship', *Annual Executive Retreat*, 10 November.

Jessop, B. and Stones, R. (1992) 'Old City and New Times: Economic and Political Aspects of Deregulation', in L. Budd and S. Wilminster (eds), *Global Finance and Urban Living* (London: Routledge), pp. 174–96.

Kerfoot, D. (1993) 'Clerical Work in Banking', unpublished doctorate, Manchester School of Management, UMIST.

Knights D. (1988) 'Risk, Financial Self-Discipline and Commodity Relations', *Advances in Public Interest Accounting*, vol. 2: 47–69, New York: Jai Press.

Knights, D. (1997) 'Governmentality and Financial Services: Welfare Crises and the Financially Self-Disciplined Subject', in G. Morgan and D. Knights (eds), *Deregulation and European Financial Services* (London: Macmillan), pp. 216–35.

Knights, D. and Morgan, G. (1991) 'Subjectivity and the Labour Process in Selling Life Insurance', in C. Smith, D. Knights and H. Willmott (eds), *The Non-manual Labour Process* (London: Macmillan), pp. 217–40.

Knights, D. and Morgan, G. (1995) 'Strategic Management, Financial Services and Information Technology', *Journal of Management Studies*, vol. 32, no. 2, pp. 191–214.

Knights, D. and Odih, P. (1996a) *The Consumer 2000*, a report published by the Financial Services Research Centre, UMIST, Manchester.

Knights, D. and Odih, P. (1996b) 'A daring raid – the insurers take a piece of the action' *Chartered Banker*, April.

Knights, D., Morgan, G. and Murray, F. (1992) 'Business Systems, Consumption and Change', in R. Whitley (ed.), *European Business Systems* (London: Sage), pp. 198–218.

Knights, D., Sturdy, A. and Morgan G. (1994) 'The Consumer Rules: an Examination of the Rhetoric and "Reality" of Marketing in Financial Services', *European Journal of Marketing*, vol. 28, no. 3, pp. 42–54.

Lewis, B.R. (1990) 'Bank Marketing', in Ennew, C.T., Watkins, T. and Wright, M. (eds), *Marketing Financial Services* (Oxford: Heinemann), pp. 157–77.

McGoldrick, P.J. and Greenland S.J. (1992) 'Competition between Banks and Building Societies in the Retailing of Financial Services', *British Journal of Management*, vol. 3, no. 1, pp. 169–79.

Morgan, G. and Knights, D. (1990) 'The Financial Services Act and its implications for Life Insurance', unpublished report, Financial Services Research Centre, Manchester School of Management, UMIST, Manchester.

Morgan, G. and Knights, D. (1997) (eds), *Deregulation and European Financial Services* (London: Macmillan).

Noble, F. (1996) 'Distribution Technology Project Pilot Phase Report', *FSRC Forum Report*, May.

Odih, P. (1991) 'Consumption Patterns within the Personal Financial Services Market', unpublished paper, Financial Services Research Centre, Manchester School of Management, UMIST, Manchester.

Porter, M. (1990) *The Competitive Advantage of Nations* (New York: Free Press).

Social Security Act (1986) (London: HMSO).

Watkins, J., Drury, L. and Bolton, R. (1996) *People and Performance: a Survey of HR Issues in the Retail Financial Services Sector* (Bristol: University of Bristol/KPMG).

Whitley, R., (ed.) (1992) *European Business Systems* (London: Sage).

Wright, M., Ennew, C. and Wong, P. (1991) 'Deregulation, Strategic Change and Divestment in the Financial Services Sector', *National Westminster Bank Quarterly Review*, November, pp. 51–63.

2 The Dialectic of the Value Form: the Social Evolution of Capital Markets in the US

TONY TINKER

THEORY AND CRISIS

A sure sign of an economy in crisis is when devotees of neo-classical economics plunge into a neo-Marxist Kondratieff wave analysis for insights into the current situation. Desperation reaches panic levels when prestigious conservative publications such as *Barron's* (10 June 1991) join the chorus, as in a lead interview article with the managers of one of the world's largest mutual funds. The article was called 'Apocalyptic Vision'.

Neo-classical anxieties are not misplaced. By the mid-1990s, the US gross national product (GNP) had declined to an annual rate of 2 to 3 per cent. Official unemployment exceeded 8 per cent – double if we include 'discouraged' and forced part-time workers. The US homeless was over 2 million (100000 in New York alone) while apartment vacancy rates stood at an all-time high. Housing starts were their lowest for 10 years and house prices had slumped more than 30 per cent in some parts of the country. And by early 1997, the NYSE index breached the 7000 barrier!

Nowhere was this lacklustre economic performance more in evidence than in the banking and financial services industry. The rolling depressions of the 1980s led to market collapses in gold and silver, less-developed country loans, farm loans and oil patch loans. The 1987 stock market crash was encored, 2 years later, with a precipitous fall in the junk bond market. Drexel, the founder of the junk bond market, is no more and Michael Milken, whose annual salary once topped $200 million, followed on the heels of his one-time collaborator, Ivan Boesky, by plea-bargaining himself into a Californian minimum security (country club) detention centre.

Continental Illinois, the fourth largest bank in the US inaugurated a spectacular series of multibillion dollar institutional failures, including First Republic, Sunbelt Savings & Loans, Refcorp Financing, the National Bank of Washington and the Bank of New England (*Observer*, 8 July 1988; *New*

York Times, 3 March, 1989; *Barron's*, 17 June, 1991). April 1991 saw the closure of Executive Life ($15 billion in assets) a warning of much larger problems in the insurance industry (Equitable Life Assurance, a $60 billion institution, was afflicted with a deeply distressed real estate portfolio) (*Barron's*, 1 October 1990, pp. 10–38; *Fortune*, 6 May 1991, pp. 60–2).

Commercial banks were in acute difficulties worldwide. Citibank, Manufacturers Hanover and Chase Manhattan Bank were all on the critical list; the latter, it is rumoured, was rescued by a $3 billion Treasury Department bailout in December 1990 (*Fortune*, 14 January 1991, pp. 90–9). Once invincible Japanese banking giants (DKB, Mitsubishi, Nomura, Fuji, Sanwa and Sumitomo) quaked with shocks in the real estate and stock markets. Their extensive cross-holding created a systematic risk that further amplified their instabilities (*Barron's*, 27 August 1990, pp. 10, 16–7; *New York Times*, 10 March 1991, section 3.)

With such pervasive troubles, it is small wonder that bourgeois economists grasped for a more relevant mode of analysis that would take them beyond the happy valley optimism of static equilibrium analysis, rational investor theories and their macroeconomic counterparts in rational expectations theory and general equilibrium theory. Unfortunately, most neo-classical encounters with Marxism are motivated by a desire to find a 'turning point' or a ray of light. Rarely is there any substantive grasp of Marxist analysis because this would involve a rejection of root neo-classicist precepts, most notably that capitalism itself should not be questioned and investigated. Typically, this is more than most neo-classicists are willing to stomach, their primary reason for fishing outside neo-classical waters being to fabric reassurance that the system will correct itself in the longer term (waves, after all, usually rise after falling).

THE DIALECTIC OF THE VALUE FORM

This chapter presents a Marxist analysis of the historical circumstances leading to the prevailing economic crisis and the travails that specifically afflict the financial services industry. There are, of course, many angles from which a Marxist analysis might be elucidated (Ollman, 1971). Here, I err in favour of Volume I of *Capital: a Critique of Political Economy* (Marx, 1977a) (relative to other works) because it contains the 'general principles' for analysing the evolution of capitalism and has the assured authenticity of being the only volume directly authored by Marx, without the intervention of Engel's editorship.

The importance of finance and banking under capitalism is underscored by the priority Marx (1977a) gives the value form early on in Volume I. He begins with the enormous growth in commodities (production for market not for self-consumption) as the phenomenological and ostensible characteristic of capitalism. More fundamental than this sheer expansion in the variety and quantity of use values, however, is the increasing interdependence of previously semi-isolated communities, who gradually relinquish their autonomy and self-sufficiency through exchange and trade and become articulated within a larger division of labour. The value form is integral to this process in that it refers to the basis on which specialised, interdependent commodity producers establish their terms of trade – the rates of exchange for their products (Dobb, 1973; Meek, 1975; Tinker, 1975). Marx's 'strong' assumption here is that commodities exchange at their values – at rates commensurate with commodity reproduction and therefore the reproduction of producers and their forms of life. The emergence of universal equivalents – tokens, money and financial services – further facilitates the development of trade, specialisation and, thus, growing social interdependence (Carling, 1986).

The above (Hegelian) reading views Volume I as a philosophical or dialectical text rather than a historical record (Hegel, 1969, 1971; Winfield, 1976; Cleaver, 1979). This is reflected in the dialectical construction of the value form and the range of movements it embodies, not just the increase in use values (commodities), but also a reconstruction of the labour processes, a disciplining of working lives and the subjective experiences of commodity producers (through the law of value) and, thus, a continual revolution in the subjective, cultural, juridical, economic and political spheres (Rattansi, 1982; Arthur, 1984). The latter interpretation has been succinctly put by some writers as a 'value theory of labour' (in contrast to a 'labour theory of value') (Elson, 1979; Arthur, 1984).

The value form assumes three dialectical moments in these early passages of the book (Marx, 1977a): first of unity, second of difference and third of unity in difference. Each is already implicit in the previous discussion (Smith, 1990). The growth of the commodity form is a unity phase in that it reflects an increasing commodity exchange between previously separate disparate social systems, a progressive interdependence and a mutual disciplining 'behind the backs' of commodity producers.

The money form is a phase of difference because it expands a community beyond its provincialism, it transforms human subjectivity and it enhances human productivity. Most importantly (in analysing financial services), money introduces a disruptive dualism in that the aims of commodity production and exchange – the exchange of equivalents, of 'value for value' represented by the sequence C > M > C – are supplanted by a sequence of unequal exchange, where the expansion of money capital (rather than the acquisition of commodities of equal value) becomes a new priority. This new sequence is represented as M > C > M'. Hence, in this difference phase, speculation is admitted, logically and historically, as a characteristic of capitalism.

The capital form introduces labour as a commodity as a stage of 'unity in difference'. It is a unity in that it still involves an exchange of equivalents (labour receives the value of its labour power, its reproduction value), whereas it is a difference in that wage labour exploitation permits an enormous expansion in money capital.

Money and its various credit and investment extensions are the present-day commodities produced by the financial services industry. These expressions of the value form expand and accelerate the social division of labour, in both a geographical and an intertemporal sense.

Geographically, the division of labour expands as communities abandon production for self-sufficiency for production for market, with a concomitant dependency on money as a temporary store of value and a medium of exchange (Marx, 1977a, pp. 154–240). This expansion of commodity production, facilitated by developments in the value form, is manifest in such diverse realms as the commodification of housework and female labour to the forced enclosure of lands (for example, of hunter–gather indians in Peru, Nicaragua and Brazil) involving the destruction of primitive, self-sufficient societies and their assimilation as free wage labour.

Financial commodities develop the division of labour in an intertemporal sense because financial instruments – and the institutional arena where they are traded, the capital market – serve to reallocate consumption opportunities over time. In short, the capital market is an institution where savers (those with excess resources) meet borrowers (those with a resource deficiency relative to their investment needs). This is where housebuyers meet employees meet pensioners meet insurance carriers meet car buyers meet credit card holders meet speculators meet foreign governments meet bankers. By stimulating the development of the 'roundaboutness' of production – the capital or producer goods sector – such markets transform the 'real' economy (the division of labour) and, thus, the productivity of labour in an intertemporal sense. These entail both 'objective' and 'subjective' changes.

The dialectics of Marx's value form requires more specificity than that given above if it is to be useful in appraising the present situation. In general, we find in *Capital: a Critique of Political Economy* a mode of analysis that is quite opposed to orthodox economic analysis in several ways. First, the centrality it accords to economic dynamics and the inherent instabilities of capitalism. Second, the pivotal role attributed to the pursuit of surplus value in expanded reproduction that, through the discipline of market competition at the individual firm level, imposes cost saving technologies that continually revolutionise the means of production. This imperative for expansion, dictated through competitive conditions, while inevitably anarchic (Volume II), is rooted in Marx's law of value. Typically, this issue is 'off-limits' to orthodox economics – even to Keynesians – because of the analytic expedient of holding the capital stock constant (Kregel, 1975). Third and relatedly, the importance attributed to dialectical movements in evaluating economic dynamics; these emanate, ultimately, from the kind of class struggle that typifies capitalism as a social system.

These contradictory forces come into play in the following historical review of banking and financial services in the US. This is a history of disruptions to commodity production by the money form – of speculations, scams, financial panics, and bubbles – a continual struggle between acquisitive and speculative forces and the regulatory attempts to curb and socialise them. This is not a pendulum theory of historical movement where the pendulum periodically reaches turning points, but a dialectical sequence that is an eruptive unfolding of speculative crises and reactive regulatory attempts to contains the disruptive movements. The law of value – competition in banking and financial services – animates this unstable dialectic in the form of continual pressure to outflank, undermine and corrupt regulatory regimes. Hence, the corporate migration to low-cost regimes (New Jersey, Delaware, London and the Bahamas), the 'chartermongering' competition by states and nation states to attract new corporate capital and the revolutions in capital market technology, from the anachronistic trading floors of the NYSE and AMEX (American Stock Exchange), to extended trading hours, electronic exchanges and the internalisation and internationalisation of (in-house) capital market markets of large securities firms.

Finally, we will see that this ongoing dialectical struggle between speculation and socialisation is directly implicated in the current economy of the US and the difficulties faced in escaping from it. Accumulation by the banking and financial services sector has not only 'overmortgaged' the economy in a way that precludes traditional expansionary remedies, it has increased the risk of widespread financial default and the possibility of massive transfers in property rights. In the corporate sector, an increased financial risk has been accomplished mainly through 'bonding' and the retirement of equity claims; this has increased the cost of capital and thereby discouraged productive investment. The result has been to impair the growth of the real economy. Most important and less widely recognised, the previous policies of the US to socialise the risk of the financial services sector (insurance programmes for house mortgages, farm loans, bank deposits, Third World loans, student loans, savings and loans deposits and so on) is now the primary factor in a record $300 billion US Government deficit. Unlike previous recessions, this renders the US state powerless in jump-starting the economy with deficit spending. We will examine these matters at the end of the historical review.

THE STATE AFTER REGULATION AND THE 1929 CRASH AND DEPRESSION

The 1929 Crash and subsequent depression induced an all-pervasive change of attitudes among both the public and policy makers regarding the role of the government in relation to market and corporate affairs. As Alfred E. Kahn, ex-chairman of the Council on Wage & Price Stability noted, the shock of the Depression induced a fundamental change, 'a basic reconsideration of the relationship of government to the economy ... a competitive system was excessively prone to waves of over-investment and excess capacity, and thus caused depression'. The pre-Depression view that the economy was inherently self-correcting had proved false and that an unregulated market was too unstable to be trusted.

It was the distrust and fear of the market mechanism itself, both by businessmen and the public at large, that promoted such experiments in industry-by-industry planning and cartelisation as in the National Recovery Administration, the retail price fixing authorised by the Miller–Tydings Act, the quota limits and price fixing permitted by the Bituminous Coal Act, the 'Hot Oil' Act of 1935 that permitted oil states to fix production and shipment quotas and the market share and entry restrictions to the transportation business fostered by the post-Depression policies of the Interstate Commerce Commission. In the first 3 months of Roosevelt's administration, beginning in early March 1933, some 15 major interventionist bills were passed by a special session of Congress and in Roosevelt's first two terms, some 93 separate legislative actions were passed affecting banking, business, agriculture, labour and social welfare.

The scope of 'what was regulated' also expanded following the Depression. Consumer watchdogs have proliferated and developed as in the revised roles of the Food & Drug Administration (FDA) and the Federal Trade Commission (FTC). Originally, these agencies were devised to regulate supply and production abuses such as food adulteration, tainted meat, child labour, unfair competition and price fixing. However, from the New Deal era, they assumed the responsibility of helping consumers make informed consumption decisions: thus, in the financial arena, credit data, the true interest on instalment contracts and proper disclosure in life assurance and insurance have now been assimilated within the regulators' orbit.

These changes were accompanied by comparable changes within the private sphere. Out of the Depression came an expansion in private health insurance in the form of Blue Cross that began as a penny-a-day insurance for teachers. Such developments were an expression of the new psychological need to prepare for future emergencies.

The New Deal era saved the heaviest guns for regulating finance. It is ironic that, despite the popular view that Wall Street's role in the Crash approached that of an institutional mephistopheles, at the time it seemed that Wall Street would get off relatively lightly at first. For some three years after the Crash, the Exchange was left free to regulate almost all such economic matters as commission rates, capital requirements and qualification for membership. Even the Securities Act of 1933 made only modest requirements regarding disclosure. The regulatory crunch did not come until the Senate Committee on Banking and Currency (the Pecora Committee) completed its investigation into the Crash early in 1934.

These investigations revealed that pool operators had manipulated stock prices with the help of corporate executives. It showed how Wall Street had spurred a speculative mania that wracked the economy right up until Roosevelt's inauguration, how promoters had stacked holding companies into levered pyramids that tumbled during the crash and how security prices were rigged in favour of insiders.

The Chase National Bank (now Chase Manhattan Bank) and the National City Bank (now Citibank) were both implicated in the Pecora and parallel investigations, the Chase National Bank because its chairman, Albert H. Wiggin, had engaged in various surreptitious speculative ventures. He had sold the Chase National Bank's shares short and then used a loan from the bank to acquire the shares at the settlement date, for a profit of over $4 million. Charles E. 'Sunshine Charlie' Mitchell of the National City Bank was also found to be speculating and, to create a tax loss, sold securities to his wife and then repurchased them. Such antics were quite common in this era and thus Mitchell was acquitted.

Mitchell and Wiggin were not entirely successful as lightning rods for their banks' misdemeanors and, thus, a considerable amount of criticism was directed at the National City and Chase National Banks. Corporate clients who used these banks to underwrite their new issues were given preferential treatment over other customers by the banks' commercial loan departments. The National City and Chase National Banks were accused of lending money on favourable terms to their own investment affiliates and stuffing their own trust departments with securities issued by their own affiliates. The National

City Bank bought some $10 million of worthless securities issued by its affiliate. The affiliates reciprocated by supporting their parents' stock price when it showed signs of sagging and giving the parents liquidity and profits by buying loans from the latter. The Chase National Bank was discovered to have sold some $25 million in loans to its affiliate; the latter paid for the loans with cash raised by a new stock issue.

At these revelations, there was a great public outcry and, in response, the National City and Chase National Banks were forced to disgorge their affiliates. However, it was too late to avert legislation and several months later, the Banking Act of 1933, known as the Glass–Steagall Act, was passed.

Outrage at the bankers' culpability for the Great Crash was only one of several factors leading up to the Glass–Steagall Act legislation. Financial instability had become a hallmark of the banking industry throughout the 1920s: of the some 30000 banks that existed in the early part of the decade, some 5700 had failed by 1929, leaving around 25000 at the beginning of the Great Depression. A further 10000 closed their doors between 1929 and 1933 and the total bank deposits dropped in that period by 35 per cent from $49.4 million to $32.1 million. Banking crises occurred in 1930 and 1931 and, on the verge of the third in 1933, President Roosevelt declared his famous 'banking holiday' which was followed by a series of reforms designed to restore confidence.

The Glass–Steagall Act was the most far-reaching overhaul of banking legislation to emerge from the Depression. It separated depository banking (taking deposits and loan making by commercial banks, savings and loans and credit unions) from investment banking (underwriting and dealing in securities), prohibited the payment of interest on demand deposits (deposits held for less than 30 days), raised the minimum capital of national banks, substantially extended the monetary management power of the Federal Reserve Board (FRB) by giving it an expanded reserve requirement authority and the power to regulate the rate of interest on time deposits (Regulation Q interest ceiling restrictions) and established, in the teeth of bitter opposition from the American Bankers Association, the Federal Deposit Insurance Corporation (FDIC).

For savings and loans and mutual savings banks, the Federal Home Loan Bank Board was established in 1932 and deposit insurance was introduced in 1934 for savings and loans and mutual savings banks with the incorporation of the Federal Savings and Loan Insurance Corporation (FSLC). As all state deposit insurance plans were defunct by 1930, many bankers predicted that a similar fate awaited the federally based FDIC and FSLC. However, the Depression extirpated the lemons and left a financially robust population of institutions for the FDIC and FSLC to administer.

Commercial banks are the largest depository institutions and the role envisaged for them under the Glass–Steagall Act accorded with the prevailing view of the function of these institutions. Commercial banks began as providers of financial services to business in the form of loans to support short-term business operations. Bank funding did not depend on individual savings deposit accounts but also secured demand deposits from businesses. Consumer loans were very unusual and real estate loans were generally regarded as outside their province.

Other depository institutions were also viewed as performing specialised functions in the financial markets. Thus, savings and loans were formed originally as temporary cooperative building societies, and were subsequently subject to portfolio restrictions that limited them to mortgages. Mutual savings banks, that originated as saving outlets for new immigrants, also came to be heavily invested in mortgages and real estate. Credit unions provided one of the first forms of consumer credit for semi-durables. Although many non-bank depository institutions are state chartered, they became subject to federal regulations as well as through their membership of the FSLC or the National Credit Union Administration (NCUA).

The Glass–Steagall Act split the financial system down the middle. The rationale for hiving off the investment from the depository functions of banking was to reduce the risks of using ordinary consumers' deposits as speculative investments in stock market equities or corporate finance. Commercial banks were responsible for some two-thirds of new stock and bond issues up to that time and the financial capers revealed by the Glass–Steagall investigations prompted Senators Carter Glass and Representative Henry Steagall, along with an angry public, to blame the banks for the Crash. Commercial banks were prohibited from undertaking other forms of investment banking: they were precluded from underwriting issues of corporate securities and purchasing non-guaranteed revenue bonds of the state and local governments.

An elaborate system of federal regulation was established by the 1933 and 1935 Banking Acts and subsequent legislation that is still largely in place today. Branching and merger restrictions are still prominent, as are regulations aimed at limiting the ease of entry to reduce the ravages of competition, including price competition. These entry restrictions, typical of New Deal legislation, put an end to the 'free banking' era. Henceforth, Congress gave the Comptroller of the Currency the power to veto all new national bank charters. The FDIC exercises similar power in that deposit insurance is only awarded to national and state institutions that successfully pass its reviews. As some 96 per cent of all commercial banks and over 90 per cent of the savings and loans have deposit insurance, then the denial of insurance is a *de facto* denial of a charter.

Curbing the risk of bank failure was a centrepiece of the Banking Acts and subsequent legislation. The precautions to minimise risk assumed several forms: commercial banks were prohibited from making certain speculative investments (municipal securities rated below 'investment grade' by Standard & Poor's or Moody's for instance), they were limited by the amount that can be loaned to any one customer, their real estate lending was subject to a ceiling limit and 'credit files' were maintained (and open to federal inspection) that demonstrate that a judicious credit control policy had been pursued.

An extensive system of federal auditing now exists to enforce regulations for all depository institutions. Audits are often 'spot-check' (random) audits and focus on the quality of the internal control procedures, the liquidity position, the capital base adequacy, credit controls, the portfolio risk and even the 'quality of management'. A five-point 'uniform financial institutions rating system' (called CAMEL) was devised by regulators for evaluating bank and non-bank depository institutions.

THE SEC AND THE SECURITIES INDUSTRY

The Securities and Exchange Commission (SEC) did not simply 'move in' to take charge of the securities dealing and investment banking sectors after the Great Crash. The industry vigorously resisted government intervention and only after the opportune discovery of a 'cache of villains' who personified evil, did the New York Stock Exchange accede to SEC regulation. The villains in question were Richard Whitney and 'Sunshine Charlie' Mitchell.

Mitchell was described by Senator Glass as 'more responsible than all the others put together for the excesses that have resulted in this disaster'. It was the outrage surrounding Mitchell's shenanigans that led to the enactment of the Securities Exchange Act of 1934, less than a year after the act of 1933. Unlike its predecessor, the new law had real teeth by putting the exchanges and Wall Street under federal oversight and gave the Federal Reserve the authority to limit margin requirements.

Richard Whitney was exposed in April 1932 by the Senate Committee on Banking and Currency, under the guidance of Senator Ferdinand Pecora. As a previous vice-president of the exchange and holder of various other prestigious positions, Whitney had impeccable qualifications for rousing the lynch mob against Wall Street. In his private capacity as a investment banker, Whitney had made numerous imprudent investments in securities and in order to forestall his firm's loans being recalled (and its share price collapsing) he had deposited additional securities as collateral for the loans. Unfortunately, Whitney did not actually own the additional securities; rather he held them in his capacity of trustee for others.

Whitney claimed that his transgressions were motivated out of a wish to provide other investors in his company with a market for their shares and, thus, he was seeking to maintain the loans so that the share price would not be endangered. The court placed little credence on these honourable and selfless motives and he eventually went to jail for embezzlement.

Thereafter, the exchange capitulated to the strictures of the SEC. The 1933 and 1934 Acts led to a full disclosure for new issues and inside operations and short selling (as per Mr Wiggin) were outlawed. The SEC, with the aid of the bankruptcy laws, has levelled the utility holding company pyramids and the FDIC and FSLC have given greater security to depositors. The Federal Reserve Board was strengthened relative to the Federal Reserve banks (thereby minimising a repetition of Mitchell's personal 'triumph' over the authorities in March 1929). The board was given the authority to fix margins up to 100 per cent if necessary, thereby eliminating the call on market loans. Pool operations, wash sales, the dissemination of tips or patently false information for rigging or manipulating the market were prohibited, commercial banks were divorced from their securities affiliates and some 13 national exchanges became subject to public regulation.

THE REGULATION OF DEPOSITORY INSTITUTIONS SINCE THE 1930s

During the years following the Depression, the restrictions imposed by the Banking Acts of the 1930s were of little consequence for the industry. Depository institutions, including the commercial banks, amassed wealth in a slow and steady fashion under the direction of managers who were little more than caretakers.

In the late 1950s and early 1960s, profit pressures and competition intensified and depository institutions devised a more profitable range of financial products and sought access to geographical markets previously barred to them. Particularly inventive organisational and product strategies had to be engineered to meet the Glass–Steagall Act and other banking regulations.

The new financial products included consumer time certificates in the 1950s, certificates of deposit, credit cards, leasing and repurchase agreements in the 1960s and variable rate loans, remote service units and money market certificates in the 1970s. In order to circumvent interest-rate restrictions, a variety of new instruments were devised: negotiable orders of withdrawal (NOW accounts), telephone transfer accounts, corporate savings accounts and credit-union share drafts. Because of interest-rate ceilings on bank deposits, there are floating-rate notes, rising-rate notes and pooled savings accounts. Non-depository institutions have introduced money market mutual funds. Some of these financial products have wrought traumatic changes in the financial markets: the floating-rate notes alone attracted $120 million in their first year.

One of the most important innovations in the post-Second World War era was the expansion of bank holding companies. These increased from 46 in 1954 to 4500 by 1984 (accounting for approximately 85 per cent of bank deposits). The Bank Holding Company Act of 1956 was intended to curtail interstate banking but had exactly the opposite effect: it stimulated geographical expansion by prompting an increase in the number of bank holding companies (BHCs).

The social upheavals of the 1960s and early 1970s left their impact on depository institution regulations. A variety of legislative measures were introduced to ensure 'full disclosure' in lending agreements (the Truth in Lending Act of 1968, the Fair Credit Reporting Act of 1970, the Real Estate Settlement Procedures Act of 1974 and 1976 and the Fair Credit Billing Act of 1974), the prevention of discrimination in lending (the Fair Housing Act of 1968, the Equal Credit Opportunity Act of 1974 and 1976 and the Community Reinvestment Act of 1977) and privacy legislation (the Right to Financial Privacy Act of 1978).

INTERNATIONAL PRESSURES FOR THE DEREGULATION OF DEPOSITORY INSTITUTIONS

The developments in the 1960s and 1970s provided a vivid replay of the dialectical lessons surrounding the collapse of state chartering as a means of regulation. At that time, the struggle between profit-seeking banking interests and geographically constrained states, seeking to express communal interests through regulatory processes, resulted in the route of state chartering, first with New Jersey's strategems and then with Delaware's deregulatory refinements. Many of the social interests that were defeated in the state chartering conflicts subsequently revived and regrouped in the development of federal regulation and a national monetary system. In short, the struggle moved to a new plane.

The events of the 1960s and 1970s show great similitude with the earlier state chartering struggles, this time involving nation states in a competitive devaluation of their own regulatory standards. The threat of competition from overseas has always provided formidable grounds for exempting US banks from domestic regulatory obstacles. As early as 1919 and the passing of the Edge Act, US banks could be authorised by the Federal Reserve's Board of Governors to form 'Edge Act corporations' (EACs) to engage in international or foreign banking either directly or through the acquisition of institutions based in overseas countries. So eager were the US authorities that US-based EACs be 'free' to meet the foreign challenge, that the EACs were exempted from interstate banking restrictions and were permitted to set up branches in different states in the US.

The willingness of the federal authorities to suspend regulatory provisions in the face of foreign competition (at home or abroad) took on an added significance as US business internationalised in the post-Second World War era, and US banks strove to accommodate their increasingly internationalised clients. US banks opened branches in London, the Bahamas and elsewhere to collect their clients' deposits. Between 1964 and 1969, the dollar deposits of the foreign branches of US banks underwent a substantial increase; in the London branches alone, the deposits increased by 610 per cent during this period.

These deposits are known as Eurodollars: they are deposits with the overseas branches and subsidiaries of US banks. The deposits may be owned by foreign nationals and corporations and in particular the overseas subsidiaries of US corporations. While these deposits fall within the control of US banks, they were not subject to the Glass–Steagall Act's ban on interest payments for deposits held for less than 30 days, the Federal Reserve's Regulation Q limits and US Federal Reserve requirements. Thus, they represented an unregulated source of capital and were used for refunding the maturing obligations of US banks, at a time when there was a liquidity shortage in the US and when Regulation Q interest-rate restrictions prevented US banks from selling new Certificate of Deposits (CDs) at competitive rates. During the 1964–1969 period, the borrowing by US banks from their overseas subsidiaries rose by 675 per cent.

The invasion of overseas markets by US banks was matched by a comparable entry of foreign banks into the US market. Whereas the assets of US banks abroad totalled $400 billion by 1981, the US assets of foreign banks amounted to $300 billion by 1983. Prior to 1978, most foreign banks held state rather than federal charters and, thus, were free of federal examination and supervision – including limitations on interstate banking and securities dealing. The International Banking Act of 1978 attempted to put foreign banks on the same competitive terms as the domestic banks by making them subject to the provisions of the 1956 Bank Holding Companies Act (and the Edge

Act, permitting them to form EACs). The 1978 legislation was not retrogressive and, thus, existing legal entities were grandfathered.

Much of the legislative record since the Glass–Steagall Act has involved amending and adapting its provisions to accommodate contradictions and crises arising from a continuously evolving competitive and international context. The climax of this process of adaptation was the Depository Institutions Deregulation and Monetary Control Act of 1980 (DIDMC) and the Garn–St Germain Depository Control Act of 1982 (DCA).

The 1980 DIDMC Act was a consolidation of several earlier investigations and unsuccessful attempts at legislation (for instance, the Hunt Commission and the FINE Report, the Consumer Checking Account Equity Bill of 1979 and the Deposit Institution Deregulation Bill of 1979). The DIDMC Act revised the legal (and, thus, the economic) status of depository institutions in two ways. First it removed the competitive inequities introduced by previous legislation between the different depository institutions (between the members and non-members of the Federal Reserve System with regard to reserve requirements, for instance) and, second, it extended the range of funding sources and investment outlets open to each type of depository institution (that is, its financial 'mission') in an attempt to improve its economic viability.

THE CURRENT CRISIS

The dialectics of the value form, developed in the first volume of *Capital: a Critique of Political Economy*, provides the groundwork for a more detailed analysis of crises found in the other volumes of the book. Volume II examines the sphere of circulation and the anarchic relations between departments and Volume III extends the analysis to the phenomenological form of capital (categories such as 'profit', 'wages', and 'rent', in contrast to 'surplus value', and 'value'). In no case does Marx volunteer a definitive theory of crises; indeed he specifically cautions against seeking eternal answers, in particular those formulated in monocausal terms (Marx, 1977b, pp. 352–3 and 614–15). The evolving character of capitalism and its capacity to learn from experience, makes replication of history virtually impossible and, thus, a dogmatic theory of crises useless.

What is clear is that, throughout his writing, Marx envisions the banking and finance sector as playing a key role in economic dynamics. The developments in banking and the financial services in the last few years are directly implicated in the current US crisis. Two specific areas are discussed below. First, the enormous restructuring of property claims on real assets –

specifically a vast increase in fixed interest debt claims – that have heightened financial risk and the likelihood of widespread financial defaults. Second, the socialisation of many risks by the US state. The cost of this 'creeping socialism' (*Barron's*, 17 June 1991, p. 10) has been to increase federal borrowing, the federal deficit and, thus, interest rates. As a result, interest rates have remained high, thereby prolonging the depression. A further result is that, with interest payments now approximating to one-third of the overall government budget, there is virtually no likelihood of the state being able to trigger a recovery through further deficit spending.

The Increased Risk of Financial Default

The US $10 trillion debt – including consumer, government and corporate sectors – is now double the country's $5 trillion GNP. This has increased by one-third since the mid-1980s. Between 1980 and 1989, household debt, as a percentage of after-tax income, increased from 80 to 110 per cent, corporate debt climbed from 30 to 40 per cent of the GNP and government debt inflated from 27 to 45 per cent of the GNP. Savings, in contrast, have declined: between 1962 and 1973 they averaged 7.9 per cent of the GNP; between 1985 and 1989, the average dropped to 2.2 per cent of GNP (*US News & World Report*, 6 May 1991, p. 52).

On the face of it, changes in debt merely signify a change in the form of ownership of an asset. In and of itself, this does not appear to affect the use value of the asset and need not therefore present a problem. For instance, corporate debt – relative to corporate equity – is merely a different kind of property relation, promising a (usually) lower return, but greater security for the lender.

The real danger of the debt explosion arises from the contractual character of the debt property claim. Debt instruments 'bond' future income; they unconditionally commit to pay interest, in contrast to equity instruments where dividends are contingent claims – paid only when profits exist. *Ceteris paribus*, increasing the absolute and relative quantity of debt in an economy increases the risk of default, because a minimum commitment to pay now exists where none existed before.

The increased riskiness is illustrated at the corporate level. By 1991, interest payments as a percentage of the cash flow of all corporations were up to 36 per cent; as a percentage of corporate after-tax earnings they were up to 80 per cent (*Barron's*, 10 June 1991, p. 26). This dependency on fixed interest capital reflects an increased leverage and, thus, a higher financial risk to corporations. In an economic downturn, sales and net cash flow decline and firms committed to high fixed-interest payments would be imperilled. Recognising this increased risk of default, Standard & Poor's, the debt rating agency, downgraded 768 long-term corporate debt issues, while upgrading only 189 in 1990.

The real situation is more acute: all things are not equal when the ratio of debt to real GNP is increasing and the real GNP is falling. Moreover, instruments such as junk bonds were sold to investors with the promise of higher returns as well as a greater security of returns. As David Stockman noted, '... there have been somewhere in the range of $35 billion to $50 billion in losses, with more yet to come, as these unsustainable capital structures push up against recession realities in terms of earnings and cash flow and are forced either to file for Chapter 11, or to restructure loans with lenders' (*US News & World Report*, 6 May 1991, p. 62).

The Socialisation of Financial Risk

The US Government deficit is now running at a record $180 billion. In the last quarter of 1996, the federal government borrowed $240 billion – more than all the new credit amassed by homebuyers, real estate developers, non-financial institutions, credit card holders and small businesses.

A major factor behind the federal deficit is that '... the government established safety nets 50 years ago ... all of a sudden, these bills are coming due and the government has to borrow to pay them. So overall, credit isn't being liquidated' (*Barron's*, 10 June 1991, p. 22). These safety nets apply to a range of financial services where federal insurance have provided generous insurance against default. They include S & L deposits, bank deposits, medicare, medicaid, farm loans, student loans and so on.

Defaults are on the rise in several federally insured areas. The April 1991 *Report and Testimony* of the General Accounting Office (GAO) reported that the 'Stafford student loan volume rose from $4.3 billion in fiscal year 1980 to $12.3 billion in fiscal year 1990, an increase of more than 185 percent. Federal default payments to guarantee agencies also increased dramatically, from about $144 million in fiscal year 1980 to $2.28 billion in fiscal year 1990, an increase of over 1,600 percent.' To protect the federally insured deposits of failed thrifts, Comptroller General Charles Bowsher requested a $20 billion increase over the administration's worst estimates (*Daily News*, 12 June 1991, p. 41). The total cost of the bailout was estimated be at least $500 billion, of which some $300 to $400 billion is interest (*Fortune*, 10 September 1990, pp. 82–5; *Guardian Weekly*, 24 June 1990, p. 10). The Commercial Bank Insurance Fund was also virtually exhausted, having paid for the failure of 600 banks over the 3 years ending in April 1991. The Bush administration predicted that the fund would be insolvent by 1992 and proposed to allow the Federal Deposit Insurance Corporation to borrow up to $70 billion. This however would be only a temporary remedy and was condemned by the GAO as a 'pay as you go approach' (April 1991 *Report and Testimony* of the GAO, p. 22).

The discussion in Washington surrounding the 'too-big-to-fail' doctrine provides the most revealing insights into the socialisation of financial services. The 'too-big-to-fail' thesis first emerged in relation to the bailout of the Continental Illinois Corporation in 1984. Instead of simply refunding insured depositors (as had been done with the Penn Square Bank in 1982 and many smaller banks before and since) the regulators took over the operations of the bank because they feared that the failure of the fourth largest US bank would imperil the stability of the whole system. Continental Illinois was a wholesale bank that depended largely on brokered deposits for its funding. Even though only 10 per cent of its deposits came within the $100000 federal insurance limit, many larger depositors were compensated in the $4 billion bailout, prompting widespread public criticism. At the time, the regulators calculated that almost 2300 small banks had nearly $6 billion at risk, 66 banks stood to lose their entire capital and between 50 and 100 per cent of the capital of a remaining 113 was at risk. It was felt that bailing out one big bank was more cost effective than merely refunding depositors.

Since Continental Illinois, the 'too-big-to-fail' doctrine has been applied on several occasions. For instance, the National Bank of Washington was insolvent in 1989, but $450 million in Federal funding kept it afloat until it merged in August 1990 with Riggs National Bank. In the settlement, the regulators made good on all deposits for over $1 billion. It is estimated that a straight pay-out of insured deposits would have cost no more than $400 million. The collapse of the Bank of New England followed closely behind, a fiasco that some financial commentators described as *de facto* nationalisation (*Barron's*, 17 June 1991, p. 10).

There is suspicion in Congress that Federal authorities may have already bailed out a major money-centred bank, Chase Manhattan Bank. Henry Gonzalez, chair of the House Banking Committee, accused the Bush administration of using open market operations to lavish 'subsidies on large bank depositors and permitting brain-dead institutions to compete with sound banks while using public funds for capital ...' (*Barron's*, 17 June 1991, p.10). Evidence suggests that a bailout of a large commercial bank occurred around 26 December 1990, when New York discount window loans totalled $3.5 billion, compared with a weekly system average of $754 million (which included loans to the Bank of New England.) Loans through the discount window jumped again on 23 January 1990, to $2.4 billion, with a $1.2 billion weekly average. Again, on 6 March, New York discount credits peaked above $2 billion on a daily average of $500 million, while repurchase agreements totalled $1.2 billion, compared with near-zero in the preceding months.

The 'too-big-to-fail' doctrine is being played out in other policy arenas in Washington. A major battle occurred between Federal authorities and the American Bankers Association over loans to undercapitalised impaired financial institutions. The banking industry wanted the Federal Reserve to offer unsecured loans when it lends to failing banks. Traditionally, such loans have been collateralised and, even though some 90 per cent of the banks that received extended credit in the first five months of 1991 ultimately failed, the Federal Reserve came out whole by seizing the collateral (usually in the form of government securities). The Federal Reserve opposed the move to make its loans unsecured, claiming the banking industry had a 'too-big-to-fail credit card' (*Barron's*, 17 June 1991, p. 57).

The dialectic moves in mysterious ways. Fears of 'creeping nationalisation' are causing some conservatives to reappraise the wisdom of the 'too-big-to-fail' doctrine. A revised assessment of the Continental Illinois collapse by the Cleveland Federal Reserve Bank now suggests that, if the bank had been allowed to fail, the damage might have been limited to 'only' 6 to 27 banks. The then-FDIC chairperson, William Isaac, wondered 'if we might not be better off today if we had decided to let Continental fail' (*Barron's*, 17 June 1991, p. 10).

The fact that these finely calibrated estimates, produced after the fact by conservative critics, have not yet convinced Federal authorities to abandon the 'too-big-to-fail' doctrine, is beside the point. The debate among conservatives shows that the US state faces a dilemma: that banking is so pervasive and integral to US commodity production that the failure of a large bank 'might' cause a run and economic turmoil. This dilemma reflects the antinomy between commodity production and accumulation introduced by the value form. Ironically perhaps, it fell to the Bush administration to adjudicate this contradiction. They elected not to allow Citicorp, Chase National Bank or other large banking entities to fail and, thus, have undertaken to negate this negation by socialising the banking industry.

New urgencies beset the two administrations under Clinton. The continuing economic slump has forced the Clinton administration to reconsider the until-recently heretical Keynesian solution of demand stimulation. At a three-day summit on the economy, chaired by the then President-elect Clinton, banking sector representatives argued strongly for the removal of 'unnecessary' banking regulations in order to liberate a $68 billion dollar stimulus to the US economy. Even though Congress struggled to finance the

S & L bailout, there was little doubt that Congress would find this offer from the banks too hard to resist.

References

Arthur, C. (1984) *The Dialectics of Labour: Marx and his Relation to Hegel* (New York: Basil Blackwell).
Carling, A. (1986) 'Forms of Value and the Logic of Capital', *Science and Society*, vol. L, no.1, pp. 52–80.
Cleaver, H. (1979) *Reading Capital Politically* (Austin, TX: University of Texas Press).
Dobb, M. (1973) *Theories of Value and Distribution Since Adam Smith: Ideology and Economic Theory* (Cambridge: Cambridge University Press).
Elson, D. (ed.) (1979) *Value: the Representation of Labour in Capitalism* (Atlantic Highlands, NJ: Humanities Press Inc.).
Hegel, G.W.F. (1969) *Science of Logic* (New York: Humanities Press).
Hegel, G.W.F. (1971) *Philosophy of Mind* (Oxford: Oxford University Press).
Kregel, J. (1975) *A Reconstruction of Political Economy*, 2nd edn (London: Macmillan).
Marx, K. (1977a) *Capital: a Critique of Political Economy*, Vol. I (New York: Vintage Books).
Marx, K. (1977b) *Capital: a Critique of Political Economy*, Vol. III (New York: Vintage Books).
Meek, R. (1975) *The Labor Theory of Value* (New York: Monthly Review Press).
Ollman, B. (1971) *Alienation* (Cambridge: Cambridge University Press).
Rattansi, A. (1982) *Marx and the Division of Labour* (London: Macmillan).
Smith, T. (1990) *The Logic of Marx's Capital: Replies to Hegelian Criticisms* (Albany: State University of New York Press).
Tinker, T. (1975) *Paper Prophets: a Social Critique of Accounting* (New York: Praeger).
Winfield, R. (1976) 'The Logic of Marx's Capital', *Telos 27*, Spring.

3 Suburban Subjects: Financial Services and the New Right[1]

CHRISTOPHER GREY

INTRODUCTION

There are many obvious and important ways in which financial services and the New Right are connected in the UK and perhaps elsewhere. The principal theme of the New Right in government has been the transfer of assets and services from public to private ownership. In most, if not all, cases, this involves financial services. Privatisation involves share dealing services. The sale of council houses involves mortgage and insurance services. Opting out of state and company pensions involves private pension services. If private health insurance, school fees plans and consumer credit provision are added, it is plain not just that financial institutions have benefited from New Right policies, but also that individuals have perforce experienced a growing involvement with such institutions.

This chapter will argue that the relationship of financial services and the New Right is not simply an incidental by-product of Conservative Government policies, but that financial services are enmeshed with the elaboration of new forms of government, broadly conceived, and that this has had a profound effect upon social relations irrespective of which party is in power. Traditional conceptions of politics have centred on the distinction of public and private spheres so that debates have tended to focus on the need for more, or less, state control or intervention. Political power was either present – the state acting, controlling and interfering – or absent – individuals and institutions left free of the state. However, recent work on government (Rose, 1989; Miller and Rose, 1990; Burchell *et al.*, 1991; Dean, 1991; Rose and Miller, 1992) has developed Foucault's (1979) concept of governmentality to suggest that government proceeds through a whole variety of different techniques – 'diverse mechanisms of Rule' – which are not understandable in terms of the presence or absence of the state. In particular, and in reference to the New Right, it is argued that '… individuals can be governed through their freedom to choose' (Rose and Miller, 1992, p. 201).

What is at issue here is to grasp how individuals may be constituted as subjects who control themselves through notions of responsibility, autonomy and freedom. This is central to any understanding of what the impact of the New Right has been.

The importance of the New Right in British politics since 1979 has been profound not so much because of the longevity of Tory administrations since that date but because of the transformative effects it has had on political discourse, social relations and subjectivity – effects which continue under the Labour administration. At the most basic level, these transformations may be seen to centre on notions of the individual. The Thatcherite agenda was dominated by the claim that individual initiative was being rescued from the dead hand of the state and the subsequent attempts of Majorism and 'new' Labour to define themselves have sought to emphasise concepts of individual morality, responsibility and common sense. Although such appeals to individualism may be treated simply as political rhetoric, this summation ignores the aim and ability of such rhetoric to be real in its effects. The impact of notions of individualism on public policy means that social relations have been transformed in ways which tend to produce subjects whose sense of self is similarly transformed.

In this chapter, financial services are identified as one of the key sites where New Right political discourse has impacted upon subjectivity and social relations in distinctive ways. The term which is used in this chapter to denote the distinctive form of subjectivity and social relations is 'suburban'. It is argued that the New Right has elevated and validated a suburban subjectivity, that is simultaneously acquisitive and moralistic. The political importance of suburban subjects is not simply, or even at all, that they are likely to vote Tory, although the fact that Westminster Council in London has been accused of using home ownership precisely to secure Tory votes indicates that this linkage has, or had, some accuracy. However, what is more important is that the promotion of suburban subjectivity is indicative of ways of governing that extend beyond those spheres of political control traditionally managed by the state.

Financial services contribute to a process through which individuals are 'responsibilised' and govern themselves by virtue of this responsibilisation. For example, financial services such as pensions and life assurance are predicated upon individuals who plan for the future, who take responsibility for themselves and others and who commit themselves to existing systems of work and ownership. Indeed, the crisis facing the Conservative Party in the early to mid-1990s culminating in their 1997 election defeat could be seen partly in terms of the ways in which suburban subjects believe themselves to have been betrayed by the impact of negative equity, the realisation that opted-out private pensions may have reduced financial security, the spectre of endowment policies failing to repay mortgage debts and, more generally, the consequences of job insecurity on financial and 'life' planning.

The chapter proceeds in four sections. The first section defines the concept of suburban subjectivity and explains its relevance to the New Right. The second section addresses some of the ways in which this form of subjectivity is reproduced through the consumption and regulation of financial services. The issue of regulation and the New Right is developed in the third section, which discusses the place of regulation in liberal and neo-liberal thought. In the fourth section, a brief discussion of the effect of regulation on subjectivity is provided, through the example of endowment mortgages. The concluding section gives consideration to issues of resistance.[2]

THE NEW RIGHT AND SUBJECTIVITY

If the New Right is taken to have instigated a social revolution rather than simply to have presided over a political administration, then it must be seen not just as an articulation which appeals to particular social groups which vouchsafe electoral support, but rather as an element within a reconstitution of social relations and subjectivity, irrespective of the electoral outcomes. This point can be illustrated with reference to home ownership under Thatcherism. Riddell (1985, pp. 155–6) pointed out that the sale of council houses to their occupiers during the first Thatcher administration led to a switch amongst the new owner–occupiers to the Tories in the 1983 election. This policy can be viewed as an electoral strategy and as part of an attempt to contain public sector spending. However, such a policy also has effects upon subjectivity which are individualising, normalising and disciplinary. Individualising: this is mine, I bought it, it is for my exclusive personal use. Normalising: I am a home owner, a respectable citizen, a person of property. Disciplinary: I must work and pay for my home or lose my status as a normal individual if I cannot. Within this it is possible to discern '... two central features of modern subjectivity ... security and self-autonomy ... both of which are outcomes of the exercise of power and their effects on social relations in modern regimes' (Knights and Vurdubakis, 1993, p. 9).

Crudely, in the case of home ownership, security derives from the process of normalisation, as well as from self-autonomy or the process of individualisation. Another way of conceiving this dual process is shown by Baudrillard's (1988) comment on advertising.

> Advertising tells us, at the same time: 'Buy this, for it is like nothing else!' ... but also 'Buy this because everyone else is using it!'. And this is in no

way contradictory. We can imagine that each individual feels unique whilst resembling everyone else: all we need is a scheme of collective and mythological projection – a model (p. 11).

The case of home ownership exemplifies Baudrillard's (1988) insight. The normality of home ownership is simultaneous with the differentiation of, on the one hand, property ownership (exclusion) and, on the other hand, detailed embellishments; personal touches. There co-exists the security of being normal like everyone else and the autonomy of being an individual unlike anyone else, perhaps orchestrated through the myth 'an Englishman's home is his castle'. This has had a particular importance under the New Right because of the contrast between the home owner and the council house tenant. Incidental evidence of the importance of this contrast for subjectivity is found in this account of shop-floor culture where one worker says of another

'He's very simple. He lives in a council house and dips his bread in his fucking beer ... I never let anyone call me simple because I'm a property owner. They say they wouldn't like the responsibility, but it would worry me having a council house.' (Collinson, 1988, p. 189).

Another example is that of the council house owner complaining about her neighbour on the BBC documentary *Cutting Edge* (14 January 1994): 'She shouldn't have her own house. She's not fit to. She never would have before. A council place, yes, but she wouldn't have been allowed a mortgage.'

Home ownership under the New Right became symbolic of responsibility and also of choice, but the effects of ownership and choice on subjectivity are also disciplinary. Without reviewing the substantial literature on consumption and consumerism (see Featherstone, 1991), this aspect of consumption is well described by Baudrillard (1988) '... the abundance of choice, the festival of supply and demand ... can provide the illusion of culture. But let us not be fooled: objects are categories of objects which quite tyrannically induce categories of persons' (pp. 16–17).

Baudrillard (1988) therefore recognised the profound effect of 'consumer society' as a series of relationships through which subjectivity is produced and reproduced. Hence, the New Right's 'rhetoric' of freedom, individualism and the denial of class ceases to be rhetorical given such truth effects. These truth effects are not confined to the targets of policy, but also structure the terms of notionally opposed discourses, for example the Labour Party's recognition of the appeal and acceptability of home ownership. More generally, Blair's 'New Labour' indicates the sense in which the truth effects of the New Right discourse have decentred (although not destroyed) competing truths.

However, the effects of the New Right have not simply been to produce or validate the consuming subject. A more subtle process has occurred which links material acquisitiveness with a literally reactionary morality: the morality of unimaginative common sense, of small-minded, restrictive and restricting self-righteousness and the morality of the Grantham shopkeeper, the *Daily Mail* and the 'classless' (read petit bourgeois) John Major.

This conception of the simultaneously acquisitive and moralistic subject may be called *suburban*, in line with Krieger's (1986) definition of suburbanism as

> ... the xenophobia of the private housing estate, the pragmatic conservatism engendered by the inevitability of mortgage payments the 'narcissism of minor differences' expressed in gardens and clothes and automobiles [which] became the touchstone of her [i.e. Thatcher's] political morality. Suburbanism is the experience and reality behind the catchphrase 'Victorian Values' – it is hard to imagine a successful campaign orchestrated around the theme 'suburban values' – and suburbanism is the spiritual source of Thatcher's innumerable paeans to enterprise and initiative. The 'new Victorians' of shopping malls and package tours, of modernised pubs and video-cassettes, have come of age. Thatcher's ascendency marked the suburbanisation of the Conservative Party. Toryism was transformed as the party's ethos shifted from the playing fields of Eton to the housing estates of Grantham (p. 63).

To this impressionistic account of the suburban subject (which explicitly refers to financial services in the form of the mortgage) and its relation to the New Right may be added an associated impression of a vulgar and vicious decency giving rise to the 'Whitehouseian' notion of family, nation and morality. This impression may partially be discerned in the demands of Mary Whitehouse's 1965 *Clean Up TV* manifesto.

> We ... believe in a Christian way of life ... for our children and for our country. We deplore ... attempts to belittle or destroy it ... we object to the propaganda of disbelief, doubt and dirt that the BBC projects into ... homes. Crime, violence, illegitimacy and venereal disease are steadily increasing, yet the BBC ... pander[s] to the lowest in human nature and accompany this with a stream of suggestive and erotic plays which present promiscuity, infidelity and drinking as normal and inevitable. We demand programmes ... which encourage and sustain faith in God and bring Him back to the heart of our family and national life.

In this sense

[Thatcher] has always spoken quite authentically on behalf of those people who felt they were left behind by permissiveness ... challenged by the sexual revolution, who never wanted a libertarian society (Hall, quoted in Whitehead, 1985, p. 216).

Moreover, John Major's conception of 'back to basics', in the early 1990s, was an attempt, albeit one which foundered on political ineptitude and scandals, to connect with precisely the same reactionary moralism. In more conventional terms, the suburban subject can also be linked with the concept of the new middle class as demonstrating one of the social locations of the New Right. Carter (1985) noted that

... the concentration of the Conservative Party on the need to reward skills and responsibility, to attack 'irresponsible' trade unionism, to reduce taxes and increase social inequality, echoes the desire of many of the new middle class to maintain their power and petty privileges over other sections of labour (p. 205).

However, despite the linkage of a 'new middle class', suburbanism and Thatcherism, there is a sense in which the suburban subject is not defined by reference to class so that '... a new yearning not for embourgeoisement (what class am I really?) but for suburbanisation (how can I acquire the things that make life worth living?) transformed the arena of national politics' (Krieger, 1986, p. 63).

The suburban subject may therefore be conceived of as one who has been produced through exercises of power which emphasise acquisitiveness and respectability as the significant definitions of the individual. The New Right makes an appeal to such people, but also constitutes them through the provision of legitimating discourses and through the effect of policy initiatives. In the next section the specific relation of suburban subjectivity and financial services is discussed.

FINANCIAL SERVICES AND SUBURBAN SUBJECTIVITY

The linkage between financial services and suburban subjectivity is accurately captured by Bernard's (1987) humorous account of the sort of person he is *not*. It will serve as an introduction to the issues raised in this section.

You've seen those old posters advertising insurance. Well, I'm the man in one. I'm with my wife, a sweet, harmless, devoted little thing and we're striding forth purposefully into the future under a symbolic umbrella. We're safe because we're prudent and responsible. We've got the obligatory two children with us, a boy of fourteen and a girl of twelve – decently spaced out – and they're beaming, he under his school cap and she in her gymslip. Behind us there's our little mock-Tudor house. I think we live either in Chislehurst or Haselmere. Apart from my loving family I love my lawn mower and my Ford Escort, which I lie under most Sunday mornings. I may have a glass of whisky and soda when I get back from the office, but I don't chew the cud with the lads down the local. I may have fifty pence on the Grand National, but both my feet are firmly on the ground. But best of all, I am not the slightest bit frightened of opening buff envelopes. In fact I'm not frightened of anything except possibly Mrs Thatcher losing the next election or there not being enough rain for the herbaceous border (Bernard, 1987, p. 20).

In this account, Bernard links consumption, subjectivity, morality and politics and further links these, implicitly or explicitly, to financial services. We can readily hypothesise that Bernard's 'suburban' subject has a mortgage, a pension, life assurance, a school fees plan and private health insurance.

The most obvious of these financial services in the context of suburban subjectivity is, perhaps, the mortgage and, associatedly, the endowment assurances which are used for repaying such loans. Nor should these be seen entirely as mechanisms of acquiring the centrepiece of the suburban dream – a semi-detached desirable residence. The acquisition of the mortgage itself reinforces important features of subjectivity in that it signifies the status of a responsible borrower and the larger the mortgage the greater the status, since it indicates the recipient's income and creditworthiness in the eyes of the lender, even when this causes considerable financial hardship to the home owner. The practices of mortgage lenders enhance this effect. The ritualistic interview may be regarded as a rite de passage into the adulthood of debt. This was most obviously true during the mortgage famines of the 1970s, when to secure the approval of a building society assistant manager represented a substantive goal. In the 1990s, one of the problems for mortgage lenders has been the extent to which 'generous' lending in the 1980s has led to extensive repossessions in the face of increased unemployment and declining house prices. Whilst mortgage lenders need new business, they also seek to operate greater control over the amount of money lent to borrowers relative to the house value and the applicants' income and status. Thus, the relatively high availability of mortgage funds has not undermined the extent to which potential borrowers are subject to scrutiny and to judgement in the course of financial institutions' lending decisions.

Notwithstanding the need for caution in lending, the mortgage glut of the 1990s has produced new messages to woo potential borrowers, with different institutions presenting a range of 'glamorous' images to sell their services. Thus building societies produce, for example, grainy monochrome images of foreign lands in order to sell mortgages to first time buyers in Bolton. The fact that these images are not intrinsically more appropriate to one mortgage lender rather than another should alert us to the sense in which, although particular lenders advertise in order to attract business to them, what is being advertised is rather more than that. The ideas of having a mortgage and having a home are partly constituted as significant goals by the cumulative effect of the seductions attempted by the mortgage lenders as 'individual' organisations. The attempt to attract mortgage business (and other financial business) has also led to the development of the invidious (because inauthentic) practices known as 'customer care', intended to create the situation in which customers can feel valued and important.

To the extent that these various initiatives are successfully implemented, the following situation may be seen to obtain: the customer is the object of the competing, albeit fundamentally similar, messages of advertising. She/he is constantly being invited to choose this or that institution. Having made a choice between institutions she/he is treated with politeness and courtesy. This effect is enhanced by the fact that the customer passes the tests which determine creditworthiness. These developments therefore offer the chance of assuming the identity of the 'valued customer', weighing up different options in a sober and judicious manner. In acquiring a home and a mortgage, the customer also potentially acquires or articulates a subjectivity which enhances a sense of individual worth in the suburban mould, through the normalising and disciplinary effects of home ownership and mortgage payments.

It is also possible to see the linkages of the suburban subject and financial services in a range of cases which are unrelated to home ownership. The high street banks have developed a number of (more or less successful) personal accounts which reproduce the conditions of such subjectivities through the application of 'lifestyle'-targeted brand marketing. Similarly with pensions and the concept of savings in general. For whilst debt is symbolically significant for the suburbanite (assuming it to be owed as a mortgage rather than to a bookmaker) so too is saving. Indeed the former is frequently represented as the latter (as in: 'saving the rent' and 'putting my money into bricks and mortar'). The saver is responsible, solvent, rational and worldly.

A television advertisement run in the late 1980s by a pensions firm (the TSB Trust Company) presented a 'vox pop' culminating with a young white man, in the smart casual wear beloved by provincial nightclub owners, favouring viewers with his opinions on the matter: 'Anyone who doesn't plan for the future ... {facial expression of amazement that such creatures could exist} ... is going to come unstuck!'

More than a suspicion was present that the demise of the imprudent and the feckless would prompt self-righteous self-congratulation on the part of this exemplar of suburban subjectivity.

The representations made by the producers of financial services are useful material in illustrating how the meanings of such services are related to suburban subjectivity. A more recent example, this time the early 1990s television campaign of the National & Provincial Building Society, underscores the issues of prudence and responsibility. Here, an image of a foetal scan is accompanied by the father's voice: '... and suddenly, you realise the responsibility and I said to myself "I'm going to take care of you, see you're alright"'.

At the same time, the words 'Life Assurance' appear on the screen. The unmistakeable meaning is that the father has a moral responsibility to his unborn child which can be discharged, at least in part, through life assurance. Such exercises in manipulation are important to the extent that they produce real effects in terms of the responsibilisation of subjectivity.

It is responsibility and prudence as important elements in subjectivity that help to explain the nature of scandal, which has frequently been given as one of the conventional explanations of financial services regulation (for example, Clarke, 1986). If the sensible, responsible person acquires a life assurance policy, a pensions plan or a savings account (and part of the issue is just 'having' a pension and so on), then she/he is elevated above the 'other', above the imprudent, the feckless, the pensioner who has to knit gloves rather than hang-glide in the Alps.[3] It is, then, rather devastating if someone runs off with those savings. The idea that a prudent and judicious choice has been exercised is somewhat undermined if the outcome is a luxury yacht for a Northern businessman[4] and, at best, aggrieved interviews on a local radio station for investors.

This leads to the significance of financial services regulation, which names as unacceptable and punishes those practices which would undermine important elements of normality as exemplified by suburban subjectivity. In so doing, it resonates with other themes within contemporary social relations. For example, regulation re-emphasises the conventional concepts of honesty and of integrity and in two ways.

Firstly, regulation delineates the acceptable and the unacceptable. That is, it reinforces property rights in general and arranges property rights in their particularity. It also embodies notions of 'telling the truth' (product disclosure, for example) and of solvency (capital adequacy requirements, for example). Moreover, these measures put a disciplinary onus upon subjects to make informed choices, a point which will be taken up subsequently.

Secondly, regulation of the financial services, including life assurance, produces and reproduces particular representations of 'the other' – in this context generally the 'cowboy' or the 'rogue' (Grey and Knights, 1990). This stereotype is analogous to that of the rapist who pounces on an unknown victim in the street or the pervert who sexually abuses children in the playground. The latter are more obviously potent metaphors of exclusion, but they are analogous in that they confirm both the status of the excluded 'other' as despised and the included as absolved. Thus, it is possible to understand and deplore rape and the sexual abuse of children as being excluded from ordinary/family life and being instead anomalies which do not require the included to reflect upon their own practices.

In the case of the 'cowboy', he is stereotyped as an individual or small organisation who acts dishonestly in a way which large, established, reputable practitioners never would or could.[5] This allows practitioners to see regulation as something forced upon them by the activities of these marginal elements and reinforces the solidity of established firms and the established world. Since most consumers are clients of the large established firms (hence their largeness), this definition of the rogue as a target of regulation means that regulation reinforces the security of the suburban saver in their own prudence and respectability. The 1986 Financial Services Act's 'fit and proper persons test' for life assurance salespeople precisely sums up the naming of the other and its exclusion.

So far, financial services have been discussed as they directly impinge upon the world of the suburban subject. However, moving from personal financial services to the financial markets of the City of London reveals some different issues. From a suburban perspective the City is viewed rather ambivalently. On the one hand it is an element within the nexus of acquisitive relationships, but, on the other hand, it diverges from the suburban morality of the work ethic. Thus, whilst the City makes individuals wealthy, the processes by which it does so are puzzlingly abstract to those who conceive of work in terms of the wage relation, career structure and nine-to-five grind. Thus, when, for example, a commodity broker gets into trouble, the suburbanite does not simply fear for the structure of society but simultaneously has aspects of that structure reinforced. For this reason the scandal in the 1990s in the Lloyds insurance market is a very different phenomenon from that of the mis-selling of personal pensions, not just because more people are affected by the latter than the former, nor because the Lloyds 'Names' form a rich, privileged and, arguably, greedy élite. The pensions scandal strikes at the heart of attempts to constitute responsibilised subjects, whilst the Lloyds scandal is overlaid by the view that Lloyds members must take personal responsibility for the losses they suffered. The apparent failure of regulation in the pensions case clearly reveals the role of the state in providing the conditions for suburbanism. The regulation of financial services must therefore be seen as a key site where New Right discourse and suburban subjectivity encounter each other and it is to this that attention is now turned.

REGULATION AND THE NEW RIGHT

In this section, financial services regulation is discussed with reference to the New Right discourse. In particular, it will be argued that the development of extensive financial services regulation does not contradict, but rather reinforces and is entailed by New Right political theory. Financial services regulation refers here to the Financial Services Act, the Building Societies Act and the Social Security Act of 1986.[6] In different ways, these Acts reproduce a number of important meanings within the New Right discourse and help to render these meanings real. It can also be claimed, as previously mentioned, that financial services regulation is of particular importance because it has been implicated within a wide range of New Right policies including the privatisations of industry and welfare. In general terms, the acts under discussion represent elements within the production of a truth, that is that markets can be made to 'work' given the creation of appropriate conditions.

Whilst this statement would seem to contradict liberal conceptions of the market, there is in fact a regulationism immanent within liberal theory. Free market theories obscure their regulationism because they constrict the notion of regulation. Regulation is not distinct from deregulation, it merely delimits the form of state involvement in the market. But free market theories are obscurantist in that they maintain a rigid separation between institutional law (what governments do) and economic law. Thus, a market is unregulated in that it is only regulated by economic law. However, once it is understood that economic law is not 'naturally given', but rather determined by our collective construction of it, then it becomes clear that the unregulated market is ordered by the application of this historically specific construction. This may also be expressed in terms of the role of the state in creating those conditions which allow market exchange to occur, for example through the provision of the legal structures which allow the creation and enforcement of commercial contracts.[7]

The regulationism immanent in free market theories also arises from the concepts of human nature deployed within such theories. For example, Smith (1904) had it that the self-interest of human nature is what leads to market exchanges which have the unintended effect of increasing general prosperity (that is, the 'invisible hand' argument). This self-interest means that certain (essential) goods and services, such as law, defence and infrastructure, will not be provided by free markets. This is because it is not in any individual's *self*-interest to provide them. Hence Smith (1904) argued that 'The third duty of the sovereign is the erection and maintenance of those public works and institutions which are useful but not capable of bringing a profit to individuals' (p. 214).

Whilst one consequence of the assumption of self-interest is that certain necessary goods will not be supplied since they are unprofitable, another consequence is that there is the possibility of people cheating each other for individual gain. However, such cheating will undermine the functioning of markets and must therefore be effectively prohibited, which means prohibited by law. Thus the human nature assumptions of self-interest, rationality and utility maximisation cannot be dropped without undermining the theory of market activity, but they also imply and require regulatory arrangements. It is not just that this is logically entailed within the theory but also that the assumed human nature does have a corresponding reality in the subjectivity which the market order tends to produce.

This leads to another general point about regulation, which concerns rights in liberal and neo-liberal political theory. The individualised conception of human nature is associated with the notion of individual rights. In essence, the whole of the free market/government regulation debate or distinction is about who has rights to do what to whom. Free market theories have long had problems with rights theory. The main reason for this is that they need to hold simultaneously a notion of inviolable rights (if there is to be self-determination in supply and demand, only limited government and property holdings) and of negotiable rights (if there is to be bargaining, even limited government and property exchange). This is seen clearly in the work of the neo-liberal, Nozick (1974) who is explicitly concerned with rights as such. Nozick (1974) had to switch rights conceptions midway in *Anarchy, State and Utopia* to derive and limit the state and have a meaningful concept of market (Mack, 1981). Nozick (1974), like all Liberals, must defend the notion of a minimal state. This means that he must defend the idea of the state from anarchism and the idea of minimalism from socialism. In terms of rights theory, this becomes contradictory since, against anarchism, the state can acquire rights over citizens, whilst citizens' rights must be inviolable if socialism is to be avoided.

The traditional way in which Liberals have sought to overcome this contradiction is classically illustrated by Mill's (1972) separation of self-regarding and other-regarding actions.[8] Thus, the state may seek to interfere with citizens only to the extent of modifying those other-regarding actions which adversely affect others. Since, as Mill (1972) says 'trade is a social act' (p. 163) and, therefore, other-regarding, this means that trade which has adverse effects is susceptible to regulation by the state. The question then becomes one of a judgement of what constitutes an adverse effect.

In liberal and neo-liberal political theory, then, the state is not separate from the market for three reasons.

1. The state creates the preconditions of market exchange.
2. The Liberal theory of the market requires a human nature assumption which, in turn, requires the state to provide unprofitable goods and suggests that individuals are likely to commit rights violations.
3. The state may or must regulate the market insofar as it leads to such violations.

The distinctive contribution of Liberal theory consists not of the denial of the legitimacy of state regulation but of the specification of what constitutes appropriate regulatory conditions for the market to work and to work without violating rights. The Financial Services Act and Building Societies Act set out in detail just what those conditions are and seek to be persuasive of the benefits of market exchange. Thus, the Building Societies Bill was commended to parliament because it would '... bring healthy competition into housing and finance' (Hansard 89 c592).

Edelman (1988) indicated the importance of language as a political resource. The juxtaposition of the terms 'healthy' and 'competition' is particularly suggestive in this context. This metaphor is common within New Right discourse and couples the (presumably generally) unproblematic notion of health as 'a good thing', with competition. Yet any attempts to justify the connection would be highly problematic – problematic to the precise extent of neo-liberalism itself. The metaphor of healthy competition therefore tends to short circuit contestable issues and, thereby, tends to produce 'truth'.

In addition, when questioned about the protection of borrowers in the primary and secondary mortgage markets, the proposer replied that, on the one hand '... with increased competition within the Building Society movement and between building societies and banks, those building societies which seem to impose unacceptable conditions ... are not likely to get ... business' (Hansard 89 c598).

Whilst on the other hand, 'It would be for the borrowers to ensure that the terms of the second mortgage were suitable. That applies whether it is offered by a building society or by any other lender' (Hansard 89 c601).

The debate on the Bill thus contained an articulation of some central concepts in New Right discourse. Firstly, that competition is healthy, provides choice and increases the quality of products. Secondly, that the consumer (that is, the consuming subject) is rational and both the best judge of his/her own interests and responsible for these judgements.

Precisely the same themes emerge in the Social Security Act – that a market in personal pensions leads to choice and to quality. Whilst choice can be seen as representing the self-autonomy of the modern subject, it is coupled with the problems of security. These two themes are nicely linked in the parliamentary debate so that

> Hand in hand with choice must go effective investor protection. The Bill [i.e. Social Security Bill] taken with the Financial Services Bill [i.e. the precursor of the FSA] currently before the house will enable us to achieve a proper measure of investor protection (Hansard v.90 c821).

The Financial Services Act was avowedly legislation for the protection of the investor. This is suggestive of two themes within Liberal and New Right discourse. Firstly, there is a notion that human nature is such that people will try to cheat others. That is, the market is likely to contain a trend towards such behaviour. Secondly, 'investor protection' is indicative of the neutrality of the state in that it is concerned with protecting citizens and not profits.

On the first theme, the idea of the inevitability of 'immorality' (that is, the whole weight of Liberal theorisations of human nature and also perhaps Christian concepts of 'original sin') is contained within the two words 'investor protection'. The same notion is to be found throughout the minutiae of the Financial Services Act regulations – for example 'best advice' or 'good advice' only make sense as regulation if it is accepted that commission-based or inadequately researched advice would otherwise be given. Similarly, 'product disclosure' indicates that, in the absence of legal coercion, sellers would tend to deprive buyers of potentially important information.

The second theme – the neutrality of the state – again lies amongst the central tenets of the liberal tradition. Whilst undermined both by theoretical (in particular Marxist) arguments and the experience of redistributivism, investor protection can nevertheless be read as a reaffirmation of the idea of state neutrality. In terms of New Right discourse, investor protection can be seen as expressing State neutrality in the sense of protecting individual rights from rapacious capitalism. However, it can also be related to the themes of law and order, given the links between scandal and regulation. In addition, the more formal regulation of the City may be interpreted as signalling the divergence between the Thatcherite discourse and traditional élites alluded to earlier under the rubric of suburbanism and the 'new Toryism'.

Thus, far from being contradictory, the New Right's extensive regulation of markets in personal financial services acts so as to reproduce the truth claims of Liberal and New Right discourse. The aim of the regulation is to secure the conditions for the successful operation of these markets. This requires regulation because 'human nature' is such that, without regulation, sellers will cheat buyers, thus violating their rights. Such regulation cannot be provided by the market in that it is not profitable. Thus, the state, supposedly acting for the general good, provides the conditions under which the market can work. Put in this way, the argument appears to be a traditional Marxist one about the role of the state in a capitalist society. The difference, however, is ontological. For whilst regulation could be read as *really* bolstering the capitalist relations of production, this would entail an ontological claim which is not made here. Personal financial services flourished as a commercial activity without regulation and regulation has been costly for firms, without providing any clear benefits for them. Thus, to treat the truth claims of regulation as being the false cover for a deeper reality would beg more questions than it would answer. Rather than seek to identify such a reality in order to falsify the truth claims of the New Right, it may be possible to make visible the effects of such truth claims whilst remaining sceptical as to whether they are true or false in a transcendental sense. This will entail, in particular, a discussion of the effects of truth claims on subjectivity.

REGULATING SUBJECTIVITY

As mentioned earlier financial services policy is implicated within wider New Right political strategies. In particular, the Financial Services Act can be related to the idea of 'popular capitalism' and the Social Security Act to the project of eroding the welfare state. As such, these acts are also implicated in the production and reproduction of the human subject. One problem with the idea of a New Right hegemony (Hall, 1983) was that it failed to recognise that popular capitalism and the autonomous individual are not – or not simply – rhetorical devices which produce false consciousness but are real in their effects. These effects are embodied in the social practices and subjectivities associated with neo-liberal 'power–knowledge' regimes (Foucault, 1980).

Similarly, the fact that the New Right tends to avoid reference to class, as mentioned earlier, should be seen in tandem with the project to undermine class as a social practice. Again, the terms employed are suggestive. 'Popular capitalism' implies precisely the dissolution or erosion of traditional conceptions of class (perhaps it also carries the suggestion that capitalism is a popular system). The term 'personal pension' is particularly suggestive of the simultaneously autonomous and secure subject – free both of the state and the threat of poverty in old age. In addition, the encouragement of an increased personal pensions market also contributes to the erosion of the meaning of the category 'class'. In terms of Marxist theory, it might be possible to explain this by saying that the individualisation of the 'personal' pension undermines the subjectivity required for a class-for-itself, whilst the connection with ownership involved in a personal 'pension' undermines the social practice of class-in-itself.

The Financial Services Act, Building Societies Act and Social Security Act are all elements within the construction of such a subjectivity and social relations. Their symbolisms invite us to envisage a world of small investors, pension policy holders and mortgage borrowers who satisfy their wants within a competitive and secure market. The effects of this discursively produced world impact upon the subject in two main ways. Firstly, in the sense of direct, lived experience for those who are small investors through privatisation, unit trusts and pensions, who use the extended facilities of building societies and who purchase personal pensions. These people are participants within a reality which is ordered in terms of New Right concepts. Secondly and more widely, all members of society are exposed to this world as potential direct participants or as observers. It is this relationship between the truth claims of the New Right and contemporary subjectivity which are now discussed. This discussion moves away from the terms of the legislation towards its impact upon social practices. In order to illustrate how subjectivity and the financial services are linked in social practices, the example of endowment mortgages will be used. However, a similar analysis could be applied to other financial services.

Earlier, the ritualistic nature of the mortgage interview was identified. Through regulation new rituals attend the purchase of endowment mortgages, endowment assurances being investments in terms of the Financial Services Act. Before an endowment can be recommended, the adviser must satisfy 'know your customer' requirements – through the completion of a questionnaire or 'fact find'. On this basis, she/he can then dispense advice – frequently with the aid of a computer which bestows an aura of scientific objectivity upon the advice given.

These practices suggest that a very personalised service is being offered – the adviser diligently 'measuring' the client, considering all his or her personal idiosyncrasies and then, using the latest technology, finding the single, perfect, congruent, best product to suit the discerning customer. Like the mortgage interview, this practice has corresponding effects in terms of subjectivity. For, surely, the customer is a unique and valued case – or else, why all the fuss? However, there is also the edge of anxiety: questions are being asked and the customer is being measured up, with the possibility that he or she is not up to much. It is as if a tailor-made suit is being prepared: flattering to have personal attention and a personalised suit, but revealing of the expanding waistline, pigeon chest, ample buttocks and too short legs. In the case of the endowment assurance, this anxiety is produced through questioning, yet is more substantively manifested by events thereafter. For the dispensation of advice is only the prelude to applying for the recommended product. This involves questions of whether the applicant is 'a good life'. Or is the applicant sickly, diseased or dangerous? Has the applicant got AIDS, had an HIV test, or had any sexually transmitted disease?

In the early 1990s the issue of HIV, AIDS and life assurance received attention in terms of its relationship to homophobic prejudice. What has not been recognised is the effect of these questions upon those applicants who pass quickly over them ticking the 'no' box with complete honesty. For them, their status as normal is clearly reaffirmed. For them, not just the respectability of home ownership but also the knowledge of not being diseased, a drug addict or a homosexual. In short, they are confirmed as normal and as respectable.[9]

And finally, the letter of acceptance from the life company, arrives. Acceptance indicating more, clearly, than the acceptance of business. Thus, the whole process of acquiring an endowment mortgage has important effects on subjectivity. The most superficial of analyses indicates that home ownership tends to tie individuals into the established order, to make them respectable. The insight that new home owners have been more likely to vote for the Tories than previously is equally superficial. Instead, the process of becoming a home owner should be seen as contributing in a myriad of subtle ways to the construction of subjectivities in the 'suburban' mould.[10] This process involves the affirmation or reaffirmation of key elements within subjectivity: the status of being creditworthy, the status of individual attention, the status of a 'tailored' product and the status of being accredited and accepted as normal, as a good life. Certainly, the process is simultaneously productive of anxiety. Yet this only goes to underline the power effect of the process, since to pass the anxiety-provoking tests of normality confirms the normal in the legitimacy of the exclusion of others.

CONCLUSION

This chapter has argued that financial services are an important site in which New Right political discourse and contemporary modes of subjectivity encounter each other. The simultaneously acquisitive and moralistic suburban subject has been depicted as a responsibilised subject, self-governing through individual choices. Financial services are one of the terrains in which such subjectivity may be formed and expressed. The chapter has tended to focus upon the examples of mortgages and life assurance, but it has been indicated that bank accounts, savings accounts, health insurance and private pensions are also relevant. These financial services allow the possibility of individuals who are able to take responsibility for themselves and thereby discipline themselves, whilst also enjoying the security of normality, respectability and financial well-being. One of the key aspects of the New Right in this regard has been the provision of regulations which underpin the viability of this form of subjectivity. It has been shown that such regulation in no way contradicts free market principles, but reinforces them.

However, in positing the construction of suburban subjectivity, it might be objected that this analysis leaves no scope for resistance or political critique. Whilst such an objection would require a more lengthy and complex reply than can be made here, an outline response may be suggested. Firstly, the construction of subjectivity must always be a provisional and contingent matter. There is no monopoly in subjectivity or discourse which would close off other possible subjectivities. Certainly the consumption of financial services does not lead deterministically to the production of suburban subjects. The New Right, for all that it may have decentred other discourses, has not destroyed them. Indeed, were this the case it would be impossible to write the present chapter. On the other hand, certain forms of resistance can paradoxically have the effect of reinforcing existing trends. For example, in the case of financial services, the predominant form of resistance to the practices of financial institutions has been in terms of consumer rights (for example, rights of compensation and rights to good service). Such resistance has the effect of reaffirming subjects as *consumers* and does nothing to claim or reclaim subjectivity from its acquisitive moment.

A second possibility for resistance would consist of a refusal to consume financial services. Such a strategy would be difficult to sustain in that so many everyday activities require that such services are consumed, for example it is increasingly rare for workers to be paid in cash, thus bank accounts become compulsory. In any case, this form of resistance is problematic in that its primary point of reference is the thing which it seeks to subvert. Thus, non-consumption is always defined by consumption. Nevertheless, it might be said that, for example, a widespread refusal to purchase health insurance could be politically important in defending the provision of public medical services. Moreover, it may well be that the contradictions which financial services continue to give rise to will undermine the production and reproduction of suburban subjectivity. For example, if private pensions give rise to widespread financial hardship or endowment policies fail to pay off mortgages or if substantial negative equity in housing persists indefinitely, then the effects on subjectivity may be profound. It does not follow, however, that these effects will be more desirable than what they replace.

A more promising, albeit more subtle and contradictory form of resistance, lies not in the refusal to consume, but in a refusal of the meanings which are embedded within the consumption of financial services. For example, it is possible to own a house without understanding such ownership as conferring moral and existential status upon the owner. The danger of such resistance would be that it could tend towards a romanticised and individualised distance from consumption and ownership which would have no effect upon political change. For that reason, it will not be enough to refuse the meanings of consumption privately. Instead it will be necessary to articulate publicly a discourse of refusal which exposes the constructed, limited and limiting nature of the meanings surrounding consumption. This chapter has aspired to contribute to such a discourse of refusal.

Notes

1. This chapter originates in my PhD thesis ('Governing Life Assurance, Governing Lives: Discourse, Discipline and Subjectivity', UMIST, 1992) and I gratefully acknowledge the very significant contribution made by my supervisor, Brian Bloomfield, and my internal examiner, David Knights, to the development of the ideas expressed here. In the same context, I would like to acknowledge my appreciation of Peter Miller's contribution as external examiner of the thesis.
2. In order to focus on financial services, a discussion of the theoretical approach which implicitly informs this chapter has been avoided. That approach is Foucauldian (see Dreyfus and Rabinow (1982) for an overview). In general, the thinking on subjectivity and social relations has polarised between the Foucauldian approach and the Marxist and, in particular, Althusserian approach (Beechey and Donald, 1985). In many respects, the analysis of financial services provided in this chapter could be compatible with either of these traditions.
3. The latter – the young active pensioner – was a theme successfully promoted in the television advertisement campaign of the Prudential insurance company for a number of years from the late 1980s.
4. This is a reference to the Barlow Clowes scandal in the UK where elderly clients had been persuaded to transfer their life savings into supposedly gilt-edged bonds but were actually funding a highly speculative venture that ultimately led

to the bankruptcy of the company and the imprisonment of Peter Clowes, the architect of the fraud.

5. Grey and Knights (1990) argued that the practices of so-called cowboys were in fact an outcome of the actions of 'respectable' players in the insurance market. Scandals such as those involving Norwich Union's appointed representatives have borne out this analysis and the pensions scandal of the early 1990s even more so (see Chapter 1).

6. In the case of the Social Security Act, the concern is only with those sections relating to personal pension provision.

7. This idea is akin to Durkheim's notion of the non-contractual bases of contract.

8. Self-regarding actions affect only the actor involved. Other-regarding actions affect other actors as well. The distinction is, of course, sociologically problematic. On the one hand, actions can (always?) be said to have some effect on others. On the other hand it can (never?) be said that an individual's actions are the outcome of an autonomous agency. This is the central problem of liberal social and political theory.

9. Recent changes in insurance companies' questioning about HIV testing illustrate how 'normality' is a moving target. For whilst until recently, the disclosure of an HIV test even if negative, would lead to further questions and possibly refusal, such a disclosure has now become acceptable. Why? Because it has now been located within the arena of normality – an expression of responsibility and concern about health rather than an indicator of homosexuality or drug abuse.

10. The analysis which sees Tory voters as produced by their instrumental concerns as home owners (or shareholders and so on) merely replicates the commonsensical and problematic notion of 'economic man' whose behaviour is guided by rational economic calculus. It is precisely these sorts of assumptions which must be dropped in order to provide a space for critical analysis. The acceptance of the human nature assumptions of liberalism and neo-liberalism is an indication of the centrality of those discourses (cf. 'New Labour'). The electoral difficulties faced by the Tories in 1997 show very clearly how there is no automatic linkage between suburban subjectivity and voting. Indeed these difficulties could be seen as an unintended consequence of the earlier success of the New Right in contributing to the construction of the suburban subject and the reconstruction of political discourse.

References

Baudrillard J. (1988) *Selected Writings* (ed. M. Poster) (Cambridge: Polity Press).

Beechey, V. and Donald, J. (eds) (1985) *Subjectivity and Social Relations* (Milton Keynes: Open University Press).

Bernard, J. (1987) *Low Life* (London: Pan).

Burchell, G., Miller, P. and Gordon, C. (eds) (1991) *The Foucault Effect. Studies in Governmentality* (Hemel Hempstead: Harvester Wheatsheaf).

Carter, B. (1985) *Capitalism, Class Conflict and the New Middle Class* (London: Routledge).

Clarke, M. (1986) *Regulating the City* (Milton Keynes: Open University Press).

Collinson, D. (1988) 'Engineering Humour. Masculinity, Joking and Conflict in Shopfloor Relations', *Organization Studies*, vol. 9, no. 2, pp. 181–200.

Dean, M. (1991), *The Constitution of Poverty. Towards a Genealogy of Liberal Governance* (London: Routledge).

Dreyfus, H. and Rabinow, P. (1982) *Michel Foucault: Beyond Structuralism and Hermeneutics* (Brighton: Harvester Press).

Edelman, M. (1988) *Constructing the Political Spectacle* (Chicago: University of Chicago Press).

Featherstone, M. (1991) *Consumer Culture and Postmodernism* (London: Sage).

Foucault, M. (1979) 'On Governmentality', *Ideology and Consciousness*, vol. 6, pp. 5–22.

Foucault, M. (1980) *Power/Knowledge* (ed. C. Gordon) (Brighton: Harvester).

Grey, C. and Knights, D. (1990) 'Investor Protection and the "Cowboy" Stereotype: a Critical View', *Managerial Finance*, vol. 16, no. 5, p. 13.

Hall, S. (1983) 'The Great Moving Right Show', in S. Hall and M. Jacques (eds), *The Politics of Thatcherism* (London: Lawrence and Wishart), pp. 1–31.

Knights, D. and Vurdubakis, T. (1993) 'Calculations of Risk: Towards an Understanding of Insurance as a Moral and Political Technology', *Accounting, Organizations and Society*, vol. 18, nos 7/8, pp. 729–64.

Krieger, J.(1986) *Reagan, Thatcher and the Politics of Decline* (Cambridge: Polity Press).

Mack, E. (1981) 'Nozick on Unproductivity: the Unintended Consequences', in J. Paul (ed.), *Reading Nozick: Essays on Anarchy, State and Utopia* (Oxford: Blackwell), pp. 169–90.

Mill, J.S. (1972) *On Liberty* (London: Dent).

Miller, P. and Rose, R. (1990) 'Governing Economic Life', *Economy and Society*, vol. 19, no. 1, pp. 1–31.

Nozick, R. (1974) *Anarchy, State and Utopia* (Oxford: Blackwell).

Riddell, P. (1985) *The Thatcher Government* (Oxford: Martin Robertson).

Rose, N. (1989) *Governing the Soul. The Shaping of the Private Self* (London: Routledge).

Rose, N. and Miller, P. (1992) 'Political Power Beyond the State: Problematics of Government', *British Journal of Sociology*, vol. 43, no. 2, pp. 173–205.

Smith, A. (1904) *The Wealth of Nations* (London: Methuen).

Whitehead, P. (1985) *The Writing on the Wall* (London: Michael Joseph).

4 The Acrobat of Desire: Consumer Credit and its Linkages to Modern Consumerism

MICHAEL SHAOUL

INTRODUCTION

The title of this chapter is taken from a novel by Angela Carter.[1] In this book it is the name given to a troupe of mysterious acrobats that appear at a travelling circus. The acrobats perform an act during which they seemingly display the power to disassemble, multiply and juggle their limbs in a grotesquely erotic spectacle. As any reader of this book will discover, although undoubtedly beguiling, they are not without menace.

The connection between this fictional episode and a chapter that purports to discuss the expansion of consumer credit may therefore demand some justification. Primarily this comes from the linkage between the growth of credit and the changing patterns of desire in our society. It is a contention in the writing of this paper that in order to bring some understanding to the undoubted growth in consumer credit that has occurred in the last 20 years one must unite the investigation with a consideration of the increasingly commodified nature of relations in our society. In other words we must unravel the process by which our understanding of desire is increasingly mediated by the limited metaphor of commodity ownership. As Strathern (1990) recently claimed, 'Consumer culture, it would seem, springs from the perpetual emanations of desire held to radiate from each individual person. This well spring is like the bottomless pit of need that Western individuals are held to suffer ... In meeting need and desire. the individual person expresses the essential self' (p. 19).

It follows from this argument that the generation of a coherent explanation of the phenomenon that is consumer credit will first necessitate a discussion of consumerism. Central to this argument is an understanding of consumption that does not originate from the economistic notion of utility, but goes beyond to recognise that consumption is a social, communicative process in which meanings and aspirations are linked to the goods purchased and, indeed, the very act of consuming.

This approach distinguishes the discussion contained in this chapter from the majority of publications that examine consumer credit. There is a marked tendency in many studies for the nature of credit itself to be to be taken for granted. Ford (1988), for example, claimed that 'Today credit use is expected. unexceptional, and increasingly acceptable' (p. 191).

The validity of this commonly held view is rarely questioned in studies of consumer credit. Attention is instead directed towards the effects that credit growth has either had or is expected to have in the near future. The following is a typical example of this approach: 'It is not the phenomenon of credit, as such, that gives cause for concern ... In the present context, though, what is worrying is not so much the rapid rate of growth of consumer credit but rather the plethora of easily available credit' (Kahn and Longmead, 1988, p. 32).

To many authors the 'problem' of expanding consumer credit is one of economics (Lacey, 1981; *European Motor Business*, 1988). Credit is seen to be a threat to 'inflation' or the 'balance of payments':[2]

> 'Our dreadful balance of payments deficit which has built up over the last three years is a direct result of a weak policy of credit control. Availability is more important than cost, very often, to the consumer and as a result, internal demand for goods increased dramatically even though the cost of credit rose also (Clayton, 1974, p. 33).'

Other studies of credit growth have stressed more 'social' concerns. The problem of overindebtedness and the resulting misery for a substantial number of people is currently extremely topical in the UK media and there have recently been a number of studies published (Borrie, 1986; Ford, 1988, 1990; Jubilee Centre, 1988; National Consumer Council, 1990) which rightly raise worrying questions about the prudence of the level of lending extended by the recently deregulated financial institutions over the last decade.

It is undeniable that the considerable number of individuals and families that have found themselves unable to service the debt forwarded to them in the deregulated environment of recent times is a genuine topic worthy of investigation (and more pertinently some attempt at remedy). However such represents a study of debt, which, while a vital and significant side effect of credit expansion, does not encapsulate the wide scope of this topic.

The focus on the issue of debt leads to a narrowing of the focus of investigation which bypasses many of the more sociologically intriguing facets of credit growth. Significantly, the conditions of possibility behind the rapid growth of consumer credit are left unexplained other than by a 'change in attitude' (National Consumer Council, 1990) by consumers or 'manipulation' by grantors (O'Connor, 1984).

It should, however, be recognised that as well as there being more credit in the UK economy now than at any previous time, the whole nature of the products, the institutions and indeed the consumers involved in the production and consumption of consumer credit have changed vastly in recent years.

The primary aim in writing this chapter has been to focus on the neglected question of why credit use should be more evident now than ever before. In order to address this problem it must be recognised that credit cannot be discussed separately from the phenomenon of consumerism. The first section of this chapter is therefore directed towards a critique of the existing interpretations of consumerism and the construction of a viable alternative framework for the rise of consumerism in our society.

In particular the tendency of marginalist discourses to reduce the rich and mysterious facet of desire to the economistically 'calculable' concept of demand will be challenged, as will the tendency of many critics to simply dismiss the legitimacy of the growth of consumerism by relying upon a 'false asceticism that employs a vulgar materialist concept of need to attack the so-called materialism or consumerism of advanced capitalist countries' (Cohen, 1977, p. 172).

In their place will be substituted an alternative perspective that portrays the growth of consumerism as the outcome of a complex intersection of a series of connected events that occurred from the seventeenth century onwards.

Finally consumer credit itself will be examined. Its position as the 'acrobat' of desire will be outlined for credit will be seen to be both an inevitable companion and subtle transformer of this phenomenon. Recent innovations in the promotion of consumer credit will be considered and this discussion will be used to provide an explanation of the appeal of consumer credit to members of our society. A complex relationship between credit and consumerism will emerge and it will be argued that, although the extensive use of consumer credit would be impossible in a society in which the commodification of desire as 'consumer culture' was not deeply embedded, credit is a distinctive entity in its own right and a powerful influence upon the very phenomena that served to encourage its growth.

VALUED POSSESSIONS

Perhaps the most important point that can be made about consumerism is that there is nothing *natural* about consumption in modern societies, but that instead it is a social phenomenon, an artefact of our society. This may appear to be a simple claim to make, but it is one which renders many attempts to understand consumption incomplete. For instance consider the following: 'Consumers know how much they get in their paypackets and quickly adjust spending according to changes. Unless taxed or saved, extra earnings means extra spending' (*Financial Times*, 23 July 1988, p. 4).

At first glance this may seem to be uncontentious enough; indeed the experience in the UK of the effects of the post-1987 election 'Lawson boom' certainly seemed to fit in admirably with that statement. The problem arises when one starts to wonder *why* this should occur.

Traditional economic theory skips this crucial issue and relies on the notion of utility, which assumes that an individual will purchase a good if she/he values it more than the money it will cost: 'In a market economy, the only factor which determines whether a product has "value", that is, a positive price, is whether people are prepared to pay for it' (Chrystal, 1990, p. 12).

The process by which the consumer will assess the value of the good is not considered, instead, 'For the marginalists, the only issue of any relevance is the fact that a good has entered the realm of the economic because an individual wants it, or wants more of it, and expresses that want' (Xenos, 1989, p. 70).

The recent rapid expansion of credit can thus be explained by an increasing willingness of individuals to pay the extra cost of interest compared to previous times. While this may suffice for the construction of econometric models of consumer demand, it is of little use for helping one understand the processes from whence this 'demand' originates.

Nor is it mere detail that is missing from this conception; the founding principle of this framework is that of the sovereign nature of *individual* action:

'It is up to individuals to plan their own consumption path in relation to their income stream over time ... It is up to individuals to establish their priorities and no-one has the right to say those priorities are wrong. Of course individuals have to live with their decisions, but that is just as true in crossing the road as in saving and borrowing (Chrystal, 1990, pp. 13–14).'

This is, however, a thoroughly erroneous starting position, for the wish to consume should not be located solely within the individual. Douglas and Isherwood (1978) are surely right to complain that

'it seems extraordinary, but it is an outcome of the way that traditional utility theory has been used, that the consuming unit acts as if its decisions to spend on this or that were made in isolation and independently from those of all other consumers ... the case of the solitary consumer is a weak counter to the argument that consumption activity is the joint production, with fellow consumers, of a universe of values' (pp. 43 and 67).

As will be described in this chapter, an understanding of consumption cannot be limited to the goods and services themselves but must also be extended to a consideration of the *values* that are associated with them. Furthermore, these values should be understood to be created intangibly in the social context the individual consumer contributes to, but cannot control.

CONSCIOUSLY CONSUMING

In an attempt to look beyond the constricted vistas held by marginalists and provide an explanation of the origins of demand, 'critical' theorists have directed their attention towards the producers of goods and services realising that 'Affluent societies have very high levels of capital stock accumulation and a productive capacity which can only be sustained and made profitable if demand for goods and services runs at a level high enough to justify mass production' (Mason, 1981, p. 114).

The crux of this argument is that, since the purchasers of the goods and services palpably do not need to own/use them and that at any given time there is a vast surplus of goods on offer relative to the spending power of most people, great efforts must be made by producers to create the demand of consumers for their own products primarily by the use of advertising (Packard, 1957).[3]

Consumer credit is seen to play a crucial part in this process, its very presence signifying the overconsumption indigenous to modern society (Lipietz, 1985), allowing far more goods to be purchased than would otherwise be the case: 'The whole system of product competition and product cycles presupposed regular increases in the demand for and supply of business and consumer credit' (O'Connor, 1984, p. 100).

An example of this approach is provided by Haug (1986), whose book *A Critique of Commodity Aesthetics* attempts to debunk what the author interprets to be the success of capitalist concerns in controlling the West German public.

One of his most detailed exposés concerns the market for men's underwear. In the late 1960s West German clothing manufacturers wished to expand this market; however, there was a problem in that their research showed that German men only changed their underwear about once a week. Obviously, it sales were to be increased, this behaviour had to be changed, so an intensive advertising campaign was launched which sought to 'educate' men that it was desirable to change their underwear more often, preferably daily.[4] At the same time, new brands of underwear that were far more 'styled' than previous designs were actively promoted, normally using alluring insinuations of increased sexual success: 'What is being thrust on the public is a whole complex of sexual perception, appearance and experience. Since capital producing underpants is aiming for a niche in a profitable market, underpants are necessarily in the spotlight' (Haug, 1986, p. 83).

As a result of the campaigns, according to Haug (1986), German men did start to change their underwear more often and also to purchase the new designs, a notable success for the will of the manufacturers to boost their profits, through the manipulation of the needs of consumers.

'Once again, people share the same fate as commodities. Each one is supposed to behave like a cheap and powerless carbon-copy of a brand-named commodity manufacturer; and each must market themselves in a brand article ... Considering more closely the context of the commodity's promise of use-value alongside the consumer's needs, one discovers one of the rules of the game, the basic quid-pro-quo of commodity aesthetics, which shows how, when an object is focused by commodity aesthetics, the consumer's need can disappear into obscurity' (Haug, 1986, pp. 84–5).

On the surface, Haug (1986) presented a telling case, showing the ease with which the minds of consumers can be controlled by the skilful use of commodity aesthetics, a strategy that it would seem, can be repeated as many times as manufacturers wished.

There are, however, some serious flaws in this line of argument, for one still has to ask why the underwear manufacturers were successful in changing the behaviour of so many Germans.

To Haug and other Marxist critics of consumerism, the ability of manufacturers to shape the 'wants' of consumers appears to be unbounded, echoing the 'radical' view of power propounded by Lukes (1974):

'Indeed is not the supreme exercise of power to get another or others to have the desires you want them to have – that is to secure their compliance by controlling their thoughts and desires? ... To assume that the absence of grievance equals genuine consensus is simply to rule out the possibility of false or manipulated consensus by definitional fiat' (pp. 23 and 24).

Such a conception of power, however, is problematic, primarily because of the problem of differentiating between 'real' and 'false' interests. This poses a problem of identification that is, in practice, impossible. More problematically, as Knights and Willmott (1989) indicated, '[If] power is an inherent and intractable part of social existence, then to speak of the "real" interests of subjects as if these could be identified outside of the power–knowledge relations is a contradiction of terms' (p. 5).

In this case Haug (1986) is making assumptions about the 'real' need to buy underwear, that is in fact based upon his *own* as opposed to universal beliefs. These arise primarily from what appears to be a rigidly minimalist interpretation of what clothing and, in particular, underwear *should* be used for, namely its function as a shield for the body from the elements.

Clothing, however, in virtually all cultures has been used as a communicator of values and meanings. This 'use' of attire is in no way new[5] or, more importantly, less *legitimate* than the use of clothing for, for example, warmth. The argument that Haug (1986) proposed, fails because 'the very distinction between "use" and the "sign" functions does not make much sense in view of the fact that it is precisely the signifying capacity which constitutes the main attraction, indeed the true "utility function" of marketable goods' (Bauman, 1988a, p. 58).

Moreover, Haug (1986) treated the 'power' of producers to instigate demand for their products, as a commodity to be used as and when required, to which consumers apparently have *no option other than to acquiesce*.[6] It is not clear how the numerous failures of new products, such as Sinclair's notorious electronic car, the 'C5', despite very large amounts of promotion and advertising, can be accounted for by this conception of commodity power.

Haug (1986) failed to perceive of power to be a relational multidirectional phenomenon. As Foucault (1984) described it, 'Power is not something that is acquired, seized or shared, something that one holds on to or allows to slip away; power is exercised from innumerable points, in the interplay of nonegalitarian and mobile relations' (p. 92).

The use of this 'radical' framework of power has resulted in the tendency in Marxist critiques of consumerism for too much emphasis upon the ability of industrial concerns to sell their produce to *passive* consumers. Haug's (1986) argument is thus left relying on the ability of advertising and marketing to produce some sort of 'false' need for products in the minds of consumers (Leiss, 1978, 1983; Campbell, 1987). It is significant that this manipulative framework cannot account for the production of wants within the population in the absence of the promotional activity of manufacturers.

In his novel *Life is Elsewhere* (set in Stalinist post-war Bohemia), Kundera (1987) too tackled the demand for underwear in an entirely different society: 'During this epoch we have been describing, elegance was considered a political crime in Jaromil's homeland. The clothes worn at that time were awful ..: Elegance of underwear, especially, was considered in that dour epoch almost as a luxury deserving of severe punishment!' (p. 239).

As a result of this attitude, the authorities (in addition to far more blatant attempts to manipulate public opinion than Haug's (1986) German underwear manufacturers) endeavoured to proscribe the wearing of colourful underwear by only producing dull grey 'drawers'.

This however, did not prove to be popular to much of the population who rejected the 'drawers' and started to wear more colourful shorts, intended to be sportswear, instead.

'That epoch thus witnessed the peculiar spectacle of men all over Bohemia climbing into the beds of their wives and sweethearts garbed like soccer players ... but from the point of view of sartorial elegance this was not so bad: the 'trainers' had a certain sporty rakishness and came in gay colours – blue, green, red, yellow' (Kundera, 1987, p. 239).

In this episode, Kundera (1987) described how the central figure in the novel, Jaromil, meets a woman he finds exceptionally attractive at a party and realises that the attraction is mutual. As the other guests leave and he is on the point of fulfilling his desire, to his horror, Jaromil remembers that while whenever he visited his girlfriend he would wear 'trainers': 'This time, however, he had no inkling of what the night would bring and he was wearing a horrible pair of drawers, wide, shabby, dirty grey' (Kundera, 1987, p. 240).

He finds the thought of exposing his inelegance to her quite unbearable and so hurriedly, without any explanation, makes his leave:

'Jaromil soon found himself back in his room. Before his eyes he saw the image of a beautiful rejected woman. Driven by an impulse of self-punishment, he examined himself in the mirror. He took off his trousers in order to see himself in his ugly, shabby underwear. Consumed with loathing, he continued to gaze for a long time at his ridiculous homeliness' (Kundera, 1987, p. 242).

There is more to this story than a humorous description of the gauche attempts at romance made by a rather vain youth, for it demonstrates many important aspects of consumption. Firstly, the 'inadequacy' of the state-produced underwear was decided, promoted and widely accepted by a large sector of the *public*, the latter resisting vigorous attempts by the state authorities to restrict clothing to a drab, utilitarian minimum.

Secondly, once this belief becomes widely held, it becomes fruitless to point out that the 'wide, shabby, dirty grey' drawers are all that the youth *need* wear, because this is ignoring why he does not *want* to wear them. From the point of view of Jaromil (and many others), to wear 'drawers' is to identify with the state, 'homeliness',[7] conventionality and the body as a machine. To wear 'trainers', however, is to communicate something entirely different; a sense of choice, sophistication, 'rakishness'.

It should thus be seen that *both types* of underwear are communicators of values[8] and that these values, once believed in, are entirely 'real'. As Millot (1988) wrote, 'Signs and symbols are important not so much *on behalf* of what they represent but because they are themselves *real*; they are produced, they are consumed no matter what they signify' (p. 680, original emphasis).

Thirdly and perhaps most importantly, it shows that this encoding of goods and services with signs is not invariably benign. If one's identity is constructed and projected with reference to the ownership of commodities, then the failure to possess those which impute a positive connotation, both to oneself and to others, can be extremely hard to cope with. As Kopytoff (1986) wrote, 'In any society, the individual is often caught between the cultural structure of commoditization and his own personal attempts to bring a value order to the universe of things' (p. 76).

For Jaromil, it is not enough that the girl may have been attracted by his wit, powers of conversation or status as a young-and-coming poet. Without the 'ring of confidence', provided by his 'trainers', he dare not risk replying to her advances. Moreover, his fears of ridicule could have proved to be well founded, his facade of sophistication providing scant protection against the accusation of the 'homeliness' emanating from his 'drawers'.

THE PRODUCTION OF MODERN CONSUMERISM

While, as has already been mentioned in this chapter, consumption has always been a social and communicative process, in current societies it plays a role that is of an entirely different scale to that of years ago.

'In present day society, consumer conduct (consumer freedom geared to the consumer market) moves steadily into the position of, simultaneously, the cognitive and moral focus of life, integrative bond of society, and the focus of systemic management' (Bauman, 1988b, p. 807).

In this section an attempt will be made to describe the factors that have led to this situation, before turning towards a more specific examination of consumer credit.

Campbell (1987) offered the significant insight that the location of emotion within the individual is a phenomenon arising out of modernity. Previous to this words such as 'merry' or 'fear' only made sense when used to describe a general situation (Campbell, 1987, p. 72). This was closely connected to the generally held belief in the absence of individually controllable feelings, as opposed to 'spiritual' forces acting on a suprahuman plane.

The rise of puritanism, with its emphasis on the *direct* relationship between the individual and the Creator, played a crucial part in encouraging this shift (Campbell, 1987, p. 75). Once emotion became stationed within the individual, the entire relationship between individuals, each other and the environment was radically altered. A new sense of separateness arose as people 'realised' their emotions as personal attributes. Henceforth, the route towards personal satisfaction through individual action was crucially opened.

Campbell (1987) further described how this process led to the rise of the 'romantic ethic' and the subsequent development of the syndrome of 'modern autonomous imaginative hedonism', which dominates the behaviour of individuals in our society. This refers to the phenomenon of the constant generation of images of well-being connected to commodities. To Campbell (1987), the pleasure that can be obtained from these 'day-dreams', in which the ownership of commodities plays a central role in providing gratification, is the motive that lies behind modern consumerism.

The fact that the reality of ownership often fails to live up to the expectations merely leads to the 'disacquiring' of the commodity, leaving the day-dreams of the consumer free to attach themselves to alternative products rather than disillusionment with the dream. This is because it is the period of 'longing', before the commodity is owned, from which the consumer derives so much enjoyment.

According to Campbell (1987), this not only explains the phenomenon of fashion, with the increasingly short lifetimes of styles, but also is borne out by the advertising strategies often employed:

'That the imaginative enjoyment of products and services is a crucial part of contemporary consumerism is revealed by the important place occupied in our culture by representations of products rather than the products themselves ... the dream nature of the images suggests that this is the case, as is the fact that the people regularly enjoy looking at products which they cannot – nor are ever likely to be able to – afford' (p. 92).

There is much to commend in Campbell's (1987) analysis; his illuminating focus upon the importance of imagination is of considerable help in understanding modern consumerism and, as will be shown, credit use in particular. However, there are some shortcomings to be associated with it.

His argument is considerably weakened by an exaggerated presentation of the *individualised* nature of dream construction: 'It should also be obvious that this process owes little or nothing to the activity of other consumers, and that neither imitation nor emulation are required to ensure that the momentum is maintained' (Campbell, 1987, p. 90).

This is a wholly unrealistic exposition of what can only be conceived of as a deeply *social* process. It is virtually impossible to conceive of day-dreams centred around commodity ownership that do not constantly refer to what the significance of this ownership has for the relationship between the consumer and friends, peers, neighbours and so on. As a result he tends to understate the social, communicative effects of and influences upon consumption levels and styles.

A more serious failing of his thesis, however, is the neglect of any discussion of other factors behind the growth of individualised behaviour and its connection with the desire to consume, other than that which arose from the flowering of the 'romantic ethic' in the last two centuries.

The works of D'Amico (1978) and Bauman (1983, 1988a, b), are of considerable help in enabling one to understand the development of this desire. Both authors draw off the work of Foucault to demonstrate that the growth of industrialised production, from the seventeenth century onwards, was accompanied by a deepseated pedagogic preoccupation with the human body, shown by the authorities of this period. The combination of these two events was crucial for propelling the desire to consume commodities to the central position that it occupies today and it is important to understand that their simultaneous occurrence was in no way coincidental.

Bauman (1982, 1983) depicted pre-modern societies as being predominantly made up of small tight-knit communities. The very size and intimacy of these communities rendered any deviant behaviour highly visible, while the low level of tolerance of anything perceived to be strange ensured that punishment was typically severe and often brutal. As such, an extremely high level of control over the population was available to the authorities of this time.

The collapse of the feudal society, combined with a rapid demographic expansion, at the onset of modernity led to the rapid disappearance of such communities. Instead, large concentrations of populations appeared in towns and, more problematically, roving bands of unroofed individuals without any form of communal control became prevalent, leading to a crisis of order in society.

The response to this problem centred around the invention of the new types of institutions described by Foucault (1977, 1980): the prisons, workhouses, clinics, asylums and hospitals, which sought to replicate the conditions of control that had occurred in pre-modern communities.[9] All of the above institutions were characterised by what Foucault termed 'disciplinary power' – enormous efforts were made to codify the inmates' behaviour down to the smallest detail, via the imposition of intrusive, unyielding rules. These were combined by the new 'sciences' of surveillance which sought to make any transgression instantly visible.

The first factories should be understood to be an important part of this process. Within them, the mass of unskilled labour was coerced into cooperation through the use of detailed and stringent rules coupled with the skilled use of the new techniques of surveillance. The aim of such regimes was to gain control over the actions of individuals, down to a most intimate detail, as an end in itself, rather than as a deliberate attempt to produce economically efficient workers.

Bauman's (1983) thesis was that 'the emergence of the industrial system followed a political logic, rather than the logic of technology' (p. 37) and that 'It might be true that pure economic greed induced the masters of early factories to install the stern and merciless regime for which these factories were famous. But such a regime was to be expected whatever the personal motives of the factory owners (p. 54).

That is to say that the first factory regimes were not only concerned with the profitable production of commodities, but were also specifically designed to produce a disciplined workforce, that would remain controlled both within and *outside* the workplace. The fact that this process produced comparatively docile subjects, who were far more productive as workers, was used by entrepreneurs to great advantage, but it is important to realise that their wish for profits was not the origin of these techniques.

The effect of these disciplinary techniques over time was to place the locus of control within the subject, as individuals internalised the preoccupation with their own bodies drilled into them at work and in wider society. This control was, however, not entirely negative in nature. The insertion of the body into the public domain brought with it the possibility (and indeed the duty) of attending to its deficiencies, or even self-improvement, through one's own activities.

'"Being human", instead of remaining a natural condition enjoyed by all though in many different forms, became now a skill to be learned, an end to a tortuous effort, which everyone had the duty to undertake, but few only were able to accomplish unassisted ... Disciplinary power, as we remember, was first and foremost about bodily control. It was the human body which for the first time in history was made, on such a massive scale, an object of drill and regimentation' (Bauman, 1983, pp. 37 and 40).

At the same time as much of the workers' autonomy was being so ruthlessly expunged, an escape route was being offered; the possession of the commodities whose production their subordination had made possible. The control over working conditions, brutally denied in the factories of the industrial revolution, was over time supplanted by the ability to construct a life, with the aid of commodities, outside the workplace. As D'Amico (1978) wrote,

> 'The purely negative control exercised by society which contain and localize desire, but therefore grant its autonomy, is replaced by a massive occupation of the body at all levels. This is the meaning of Marx's statement that what is produced is not only the commodity but the need to be satisfied, not only the object but the subject who desires it' (p. 122).

The consumer market, unlike so many structures in society, was open to all, at least to some extent. Furthermore, while one's own actions could be seen to increase the ability to participate through the appropriation of wages, one apparently had the choice over how to enter and which direction to follow in this maze of commodity ownership. It is these aspects above all others that ensured the willing participation of the populace in the expansion of consumerism to the present situation in which it is the dominant influence upon the securing of our identities as full members of society (Wernick, 1983).

The actions of manufacturers and retailers should not of course be excluded from this process. The massive increase in the availability of different types of goods and services, since the dawn of industrialisation and the rigorous marketing of them, have been crucial factors in this development.

It should further be noted that these commodities have combined both 'use' and 'sign' functions; it is futile to deny that over this period many products have been developed and made widely available and that they have considerably improved people's material well-being. This is of immense importance, as without tangible reward the will to consume would rapidly diminish. The constant real increase in material standards (ignoring brief setbacks due to wars and depressions) has been vital for ensuring the continuing development of consumerism.

That commodities are important signifiers of values becomes obvious when the vigorous marketing efforts of producers and retailers that have accompanied the growth of consumption are considered. Increasingly these have concentrated on presenting the commodity to be sold within a broad social setting, pregnant with social messages – images of rich successful car drivers, happy families eating new foods, beautiful lovers wearing the marketed clothing.

However, as was discussed in the critique of Haug's (1986) work, this should not be interpreted as proof that individuals' wants can be manipulated at will, but can be seen to be examples of the skilled use of the powerful values that have been invested into commodity ownership before the very birth of mass consumerism. This is not to deny that the marketing efforts have no influence upon consumers' actions, but to suggest that they are only successful because they use and at the same time dramatically reinforce an existing willingness to employ goods as signifiers: 'The consumer society does not set up its own fixed models of behaviour to replace traditional ones but rather constructs through marketing and advertising successive waves of association between persons, products and images of well being' (Leiss *et al.*, 1986, p. 239).

In the final section of this chapter an attempt will be made to bring in a discussion of the role that the recent rapid increase of consumer credit is playing in influencing both the level and nature of modern consumerism. In doing so, three specific facets of consumer credit will be explored: its role as a facilitator of consumption, its position on the border between money and commodities and, finally, the bond it encourages between consumers and grantors.

OUR FLEXIBLE FRIEND

The most obvious role that credit plays is as a facilitator; it allows people to buy goods and services that, at a given time, they would not otherwise be able to purchase. This may appear to be a simple statement to make, but it has significant ramifications for the development of consumerism in the context of what has been written above.

As Bauman (1988b) wrote, in our society, 'Reality, as the consumer experiences it, is a pursuit of pleasure. Freedom is about the choice between greater and lesser satisfactions, and rationality is about choosing the former over the latter' (p. 808).

The ready availability of consumer credit is nothing if not the extension of consumer choice – it enables not only additional products to be bought, but also better (that is, more expensive) alternatives to be considered. As such credit is increasingly identified as a source of freedom from the bondage of the need to earn and save before purchase becomes possible.

Whereas in the relatively recent past this was a source of disapproval, the use of credit being commonly associated with a profligate attitude to spending, increasingly the opposite is the case. Just as the growth of that which Bauman (1988b) identified as 'consumer freedom' suggests would occur, the use of credit is now commonly promoted as being entirely rational: 'BORROW UP TO £7500 TO SPEND ON WHATEVER YOU LIKE – A Marks & Spencer Personal Loan is the sensible way to spread the cost of larger purchases.' (original emphasis) (Marks & Spencer's Personal Loan leaflet, September 1990).

While credit may appear emancipatory, there remains the question as to why the stringent restrictions, imposed by the interest charges (in this case 23 per cent APR), over future spending plans are apparently little deterrence. The most persuasive explanation is that while the initial sum provided by the loan is both large and instantaneously available, the interest payments are relatively small and tail off into the distant future. In this way credit can be perceived as allowing a sizeable and *identifiable* purchase, while the diminishing of future spending power prevents ownership of products that are (when the loan is taken out), in comparison, both marginal and nebulous in nature.

The case with which credit can be obtained is also of crucial significance for encouraging the process of 'imaginary hedonism' described by Campbell (1987). In removing the dampening nature of an individual's earning capacity and savings levels, it dramatically increases the range of products that one can *realistically* imagine owning. Thus, the process of day-dreaming takes on a new and far more powerful meaning: no longer just empty fantasy, but something far more tangible – the planning of future choices that can actually be executed.

This aspect of credit usage is increasingly used in the advertising strategies of grantors.[10] For instance Feldwick (1990) described how Security Pacific dramatically increased both the turnover and profitability of their 'executive and professional loan', by placing carefully worded adverts in classic car magazines. The following is an excerpt from one: 'Your dream car could well be a Daimler, Triumph, Morgan, Bentley, Lotus or Jensen instead. The real point is this: the more special the car, the tougher you'll find it to meet the cost. And that's where Security Pacific can be a little, or a lot, of help' (Feldwick, 1990, p. 265).

The beauty of this strategy is that it is the desire to own a classic car that sells the loan and that this desire is reinforced by the whole of the magazine that the advert appears in, as well as the advert itself. However, the advert goes one stage further; it seriously weakens one of the primary barriers to the purchase – the excuse that the car cannot be 'afforded' at present. The enthusiast is thus placed under increasing pressure to satiate the desire to own a 'classic car', as to choose not to do so when Security Pacific are making it so 'easy', is a serious challenge to one's identity as an enthusiast.

This tactic is in no way restricted to the more esoteric types of goods and services as the following excerpt from a clearing bank's loan application form shows:

> 'Why is it that when the time comes to refit the kitchen or bathroom, replace the lounge suite or buy a car you invariably find yourself short of money? What do you do – put your ideas to one side and spend the next few months feeling deflated; or do you take out a Midland Personal Loan and enjoy the benefits of your purchase. And then pay the money back in easy stages' (Midland Bank Personal Loan leaflet, May 1990).

The text is packaged in a glossy booklet whose cover shows a painting of a couple embracing, while over their head a rainbow arches, within which one can make out a convertible car, furniture, an engagement ring and other goodies.

The message contained in the picture and the accompanying text is clear: a full and happy life can be constructed with the aid of commodities and a personal loan is a great help in this process. On the other hand, the failure to purchase the right products at the right time inevitably leads to one feeling 'deflated', unhappy and incomplete. No other alternatives are accommodated for in this uncompromising view: the possibility of shrugging one's shoulders and using the same old bath, cooker or car is not on offer without the accompanying price of anomie, for *the time has come* and replacements must be sought.

Both these campaigns draw off and at the same time reinforce the value that Strathern (1989) so accurately termed 'prescriptive consumerism': 'Prescriptive consumerism dictates that there is no choice but to always exercise choice ... Satisfaction is not in this rhetoric the absence of desire, but the meeting of desire. To imagine an absence of desire would be an affront to the means that exist to satisfy it' (pp. 10 and 9).

While the ready availability of consumer credit offers the prospect of more choice over one's actions, an increase in 'freedom', these choices are being forced more and more to lie within the limited arena of commodity ownership. The increase in credit thus allows fulfilment on one level, while simultaneously raising the cost of future satisfaction.

Since there is no evidence to suggest that as income levels rise consumers consume up to a certain point and then become satiated, it seems reasonable to suppose that over time the increased level of spending permitted by credit expansion will steadily come to be seen as the bare minimum that is deemed to be acceptable.

Furthermore, since consumption is a social process, this effect will not be restricted to those people who are indebted, but will steadily filter through to influence all our expectations and values to some extent. This is to state that the very existence of consumer credit creates effects upon the process of consumption, even *when it is not used.*

The increase in the importance of consumption should not however, only be linked to what is consumed, but should also be seen to encompass the very actions of choosing and purchasing. With regards to the process of choice, great efforts are made by manufacturers to make products that are recognisable as 'quality' items and to ensure that they are perceived as such by the combination of market research – to find out what consumers 'want' from a product – and marketing – to communicate that their products possess the desired feature: 'Choice has become the privileged vantage from which to measure all action. The producer manufactures according to the consumer's choices, and the consumer purchases according to the choices the manufacturer lays out' (Strathern, 1989, p. 7).

There is more to this though than a need for 'better' products in terms of 'use' values, for concomitant with choice is the possibility of failure. What can be observed is an almost manic obsession with obtaining the *best* products available and an equal need to communicate this success to other people, thus confirming one's place in the hierarchy of consumption.

Manufacturers and retailers have done their utmost to encourage the growth of this phenomenon. Enormous trouble and expense is invested in the creation and maintenance of famous brands whose very names embody the promise of 'quality'. It is interesting to note the success of the relatively recent phenomenon of 'brand imperialism', in which familiar names are attached to additional products, for instance 'Mars' (from chocolate bars to milk and ice-cream) or 'Persil' (from clothes detergent to washing-up liquid).

While in the past, retailers would commonly rely on pushy, hard-sell strategies to impress upon their customers the value of such products, increasingly the emphasis is turning towards a pastoral, counselling approach, in which the shop assistant is there to help the customer come to the 'right' decision.

An example of this is provided by the following quote, made by the managing director of a major car dealership. It describes recent changes made to the methods of selling second-hand cars:

'We have gone away completely from the old fashioned style of the 'sheepskin jacket'. They (the salesforce) are all neatly uniformed, the uniform is different from the new car sales, they have green blazers, they have different badges, ties, shirts, because they are something *special* and people are actually buying something *special* from us as well, it's not just second class' (research interview).

Under the new ethos, the whole emphasis is placed upon making customers feel that they 'matter' as people; the activity of shopping becomes a source of reassurance. Rather than relying upon the position of adversarial dominance to pressurise customers into buying a car, the salesperson takes on the persona of a well-informed friend, advising and comforting the customer until the point is reached when a 'sensible' choice can be made.

'The first thing to do for a car salesman is not to sell a car, not even to mention a car, it is to walk him (the customer) round the dealership and sell *himself* and then the dealership ... By walking him (the customer) around the dealership you say – 'let me take you to the service bay where we would look after your car for you. You can see here the latest testing equipment we have invested substantially into, to make sure that your car is running perfectly.'

And you go on, what it's called is *price conditioning*. So you're building up the price of everything, so you're taking out a lot of steam of the negotiation argument, because *he has perceived all this value*.

In fact when you actually come down to it he might almost be psychologically built up to think: 'this is marvellous but it's probably ageing to cost a bit'. You still come in with a sensible price – albeit not the cheapest or rock-bottom you'll get – and he really becomes, he thinks it's all rather nice' (research interview).

Consumer credit has an important role to play in the engendering of the increasingly close relationship between consumers, on the one hand and manufacturers and retailers on the other. The very act of accepting an application can be envisaged as the granting of the right of entry into a restricted world, for it defines the consumer as having passed the test of creditworthiness that others will fail.

Great efforts are made, particularly by retail creditors, to make their storecard holders feel that they are valued members of a privileged club. Special evenings are set aside when their local branch will remain open 'exclusively' for card holders, while their monthly bills come accompanied with glossy mini-magazines offering goods that can only be bought by account holders.

At present most of this linkage is on a generic level, with standardised letters, containing widely available offers, sent to all creditworthy customers. As such, the effectiveness of this strategy is limited, although some companies (most notably Marks & Spencer) have had surprisingly successful results (Miller, 1988). In the near future the move will be towards a far more individualised form of contact, as grantors begin to use the major advantage of credit as opposed to cash purchases: the opportunity to obtain information of an unprecedented level of detail and depth about the consumption habits of the users of the facility.

The primary source of this information is the application form, which provides information as to the sex, age, marital status, geographical location, earning capacity and occupation of the applicant. This knowledge does not only allow the grantor to assess the creditworthiness of the applicant, but also, by cross-reference to the many thousands of other applications, is used to construct of what 'type' of individual the applicant appears to best represent.

As Curtis (1988) asserted, 'There is a clear and rapid trend towards collection, storage, and use of massive quantities of specific individual information for the purpose of discriminating among segments of the public on the basis of differences in their motivations and likely political and economic behaviour' (p. 103).

In the case of rolling-credit facilities (credit cards, storecards and budget accounts) the application data, however, is only the starting point. Each time the facility is used more information about the spending habits of the consumer can be learned. This is of particular significance to retail creditors as it offers the prospect of 'knowing' their customers down to the detail of a village shopkeeper, an aim propounded by a retail credit director when interviewed:

'You accept that you are not going to make massive profits out of it, but you are going to find out a great deal about your customers, and that is something which, frankly, in this country, and really worldwide – including the States – is still in its infancy. People talk glibly about all this marketing information and how they are going to use it. All the customer performance data, it is all there, many people are storing it – very few people know what to do with it' (research interview).

At the present time such information is used, if at all, to help target selective marketing campaigns, which help save resources by eliminating consumers who are thought unlikely to be interested in the product being offered. However, he envisaged a point in the near future when the mass of available information would allow the *tailoring* of products to small niche markets identified amongst the clientele. Such products would then be offered as having been specifically designed for these customers, accompanied by 'personalised' letters written on the basis of information gathered from the original application and subsequent monitoring of the account.

Thus, one travels full circle; one's past choices determine one's future opportunities in a manner that has never occurred before – under such a system one becomes defined as *be what one buys*, not as a result of the haphazard communicative nature of consumption, but by the cold, 'accurate' eye of the expert system.

CONCLUSION

The growth of consumer credit should be understood to be both a result of modern consumerism and simultaneously a major influence upon its future development. As has already been discussed, consumerism has steadily been moving towards the centre of the stage on which the drama of everyday life is enacted. It is not simply that more objects are bought than previously or that the communicative nature of goods is a recent phenomenon; the significant change has been the continuous rechannelling of meanings into commodities and the actual process of consumption.

In recent years in Western societies, we have been entering an era in which the dominant arena of communication is mediated by the metaphor of the consumer. It is as if elements of our relationships with others that had long been taken for granted in positions of mutual self-respect, such as simple politeness and decency, are now *only* to be available through the market-place: a shop assistant who would coldly brush past you in the street now greets you with the sickly smile demanded of the 'customer care' programme, while one can be treated with disdain as a mere patient, one's status as a *consumer of healthcare*, the current administration promises, will result in a far higher standard of service.

This is because it is increasingly the case that the consumer is becoming elevated above the position of the mere mortal, not so much a case of 'I shop therefore I am' as 'I shop therefore I am *more*'.

Proponents of consumer market imperialism exalt the benefits of this trend, on the basis of an increase in the choice for individuals: 'One of the major benefits of a market economy which has capital markets as well as goods markets is that the choices available to individuals (and firms) are expanded. More choice is almost always going to dominate less choice in individuals' preferences' (Chrystal, 1990, p. 13).

However, what such weakly supported rhetoric fails to make clear is the limited nature of such 'choice' and the hidden social costs that inevitably accompany it. The increase in consumer credit for instance not only permits people to buy products that would otherwise not be affordable, it also arguably increases the pressure upon people to do so, as has been outlined in the previous section.

Thus, it is vital to understand that credit should not only be understood as an economic phenomenon that allows people to consume more goods and services than would otherwise be the case, but instead to be recognised as both a marker, or 'icon' (Leiss, 1983) of the growing significance of consumption and simultaneously a vital influence upon the future development of this process.

Notes

1. *The Infernal Desire Machines of Doctor Hoffman* (1971) (London: Penguin). This book, as well as being immensely enjoyable in its own right, offers a penetrating insight into the possibilities of desire. For a discussion of this work see Schmidt (1989).

2. Tomlinson (1985) investigated the manner in which various macro-economic discourses of 'crisis' have arisen in post-war Britain. He found that macro-economic issues would steadily be built up as important by a combination of academic economists, economic advisers and journalists without any critical attention being directed towards the origin of concern. For instance, the actual importance of low inflation was taken for granted in the dispute between Keynesians and Monetarists in the late 1970s. The increasing attention shown towards credit growth as an economic factor in recent years is an interesting example of this tendency.

3. Packard (1957), whose work is best known for his 'uncovering' of the use of subliminal messages by advertisers, is heavily influenced by a strong belief in the efficacy of behavioural psychology and other 'sciences of the soul':

   here are some of these additional kinds of specialist in human behaviour whose insights the admen have been tapping: voice pitch analysts; psychographic segmenters; psycholinguists; neurophysiologists; subliminal communicators; psychobiologists; hypnotechnicians; operant conditioners; psychometric specialists; and message compression technologists (p. 10).

4. An example of the advertising used was a photomontage of pigs' heads superimposed over the bodies of men who, it was made clear in the accompanying text, had not as yet 'seen the light' and started changing their underpants more regularly. As such the campaign delivered a clear and unambiguous message.

5. One can find examples as far back as the story of Joseph in Genesis:

   Now Israel loved Joseph more than all his children, because he was the son of his old age; and he made him a coat of many colours. And when his brethren saw that their father loved him more than all his brethren, they hated him and could not speak peaceably to him (Chapter 37, 3–4).

6. Myers (1986) showed several examples of adverts whose very imagery have stimulated resistance, in the form of superimposed graffiti. For instance a picture of a domineering male in a jeans advert had the words 'I am a Macho Bore' spray painted on top of it.
7. In the case of Jaromil, 'drawers' also had strong connections with his suffocatingly parental mother who strongly disapproved of the wearing of 'trainers'.
8. There presumably were those who would want to wear 'drawers' (though Kundera (1987) does not mention any) precisely because of their minimalist nature, fulfilling their wish to minimise the 'surplus value' in them. However, in practice, the following point made by Miller (1989) (substituting 'apparatchiks' for 'academics', of course) is a telling one:

> For all the verbal attacks on modern goods, the more effective critique of practised asceticism is rarely encountered; that is to say, the private practice of many academic critics, amongst whom there are very few Gandhis and Tolstoys, may well contradict the substance of their argument (p. 188).

9. Bauman (1983, p. 34) differed crucially from Foucault in that he recognised that the use of 'disciplinary power' in such institutions did not constitute an invention by the authorities of the seventeenth century, but rather an attempt to *re-create* the immensely powerful communal controls of the pre-modern communities.
10. The most extreme example of this is the introduction of heavily subsidised interest rates (sometimes actually down to 0%) by car manufacturers, in an attempt to increase sales volume. A full discussion of this strategy can be found in Shaoul (1990).

References

Appadurai, A. (ed.) (1986) *The Social Life of Things* (Cambridge: Cambridge University Press).

Bauman, Z. (1982) *Memories of Class* (London: Routledge and Kegan Paul).

Bauman, Z. (1983) Industrialism, Consumerism and Power', *Theory, Culture and Society*, vol. 1, no. 3, pp. 32–43.

Bauman, Z. (1988a) *Freedom* (Milton Keynes: Open University Press).

Bauman, Z. (1988b) 'Sociology and Postmodernity', *Sociological Review*, vol. 31, no. 4, pp. 790–813.

Borrie, Sir G. (1986) 'The Credit Society: its Benefits and Burdens', *Journal of Business Law*, May, pp. 181–95.

Campbell, C. (1987) *The Romantic Ethic and the Spirit of Modern Consumerism* (Oxford: Blackwell).

Chrystal, K.A. (1990) *Consumer Debt: Whose Responsibility?* (London: The Social Affairs Unit).

Clayton P. (1974) 'Credit Control', *Credit*, vol. 15, no. 2, pp. 32–6.

Cohen, A. (1977) 'Book Review of *The Theory of Need in Marx* by A. Heller (1976)' *Telos*, vol. 33, pp. 170–84.

Curtis, T. (1988) 'The Information Society: a Computer Generated Caste System?', in V. Mosco and J. Wasko (eds), *The Political Economy of Information* (University of Wisconsin).

D'Amico, R. (1978) 'Desire and the Commodity Form', *Telos*, vol. 35, pp. 88–122.

Douglas, M. and Isherwood, B. (1978) *The World of Goods* (London: Allen Lane).

European Motor Business (1988) *The UK Car Market Since 1972*, no. 13, May, pp. 77–93 (Economist Intelligence Unit), London.

Feldwick, P. (ed.) (1990) *Advertising Works 5* (London: Cassell).

Ford, J. (1988) *The Indebted Society: Credit and default in the 1980s* (London: Routledge).

Ford, J. (1990) 'Credit and Default Amongst Young Adults: an Agenda of Issues', *Journal of Consumer Policy*, vol. 13, pp. 133–54.

Foucault, M. (1977) *Discipline and Punish* (London: Allen Lane).

Foucault, M. (1980) *Power/Knowledge: Selected Interviews and Other Writings 1972–1977*, C. Gordon (ed.) (Brighton: Harvester).

Foucault, M. (1984) *The History of Sexuality* (London: Penguin Books).

Haug, W. (1986) *Critique of Commodity Aesthetics* (London: Polity Press).

Jubilee Centre (1988) *Families in Debt: the Nature Causes and Effects of Debt Problems and Policy Proposals for their Alleviation.*

Kahn, B. and Longmead, J. (1988) 'Economic and Social Implications of the Growing Volume of Consumer Credit', *Management Accounting* (ICMA) 66(12), December, pp. 30–3.

Knights, D. and Willmott, H. (1989) 'Power and Subjectivity at Work: from Degradation to Subjugation in Social Relations', *Sociology*, vol. 23, no. 4, pp. 1–24.

Kopytoff, I. (1986) 'The Cultural Biography of Things: Commoditization as Progress', in A. Appadurai (ed.), *The Social Life of Things* (Cambridge: Cambridge University Press).

Kundera, M. (1987) *Life is Elsewhere* (London: Penguin).

Lacey, M. (1981) 'A Review of the UK Car Market', *Credit*, vol. 22(4), December, pp. 88–97.

Leiss, W. (1978) 'Needs, Exchanges and the Fetishism of Objects', *Canadian Journal of Political and Social Theory*, vol. 2, no. 3, pp. 27–48.

Leiss, W. (1983) 'The Icons of the Marketplace', *Theory, Culture and Society*, vol. 1, no. 3, pp. 10–21.

Leiss, W., Kline, S. and Jually, S. (1986) *Social Communication in Advertising* (London: Methuen).

Lipietz, A. (1985) *The Enchanted World: Inflation, Credit and the World Crisis* (London: Verso).

Lukes, S. (1974) *Power: a Radical View* (London: Macmillan).

Mason, R. (1981) *Conspicuous consumption* (Aldershot: Gower).

Miller, D. (1989) *Material Culture and Mass Consumption* (Oxford: Basil Blackwell).

Miller, R. (1988) 'Shoppers say M & S Plastic is Fantastic', *Money Observer*, February, pp. 4–7.

Millot, B. (1988) 'Symbol, Desire and Power', *Theory, Culture and Society*, vol. 5, pp. 675–94.

Mosco, V. and Wasco, J. (eds) (1988) *The Political Economy of Information* (University of Wisconsin).

Myers, K. (1986) *Understains*, (London: Comedia).

National Consumer Council (1990) *Credit and Debt* (London: HMSO).

O'Connor, J. (1984) *Accumulation Crisis* (New York: Basil Blackwell).

Packard, V. (1957) *The Hidden Persuaders* (London: Longman).

Schmidt, R. (1989) 'The Journey of the Subject in Angela Carter's Fiction', *Textual Practice*, vol. 3, no. 1, pp. 56–75.

Shaoul, M. (1990) *Driving on Debt: the Use of Credit in the UK New Car Market* (Manchester: FSRC Working Paper, Manchester School of Management, UMIST)

Strathern, M. (1989) *Enterprising Kinship: Consumer Choice and the New Reproductive Technology*, paper presented at 'The Values of the Enterprise Culture Conference' University of Lancaster.

Strathern, M. (1990) *Partners and Consumers: Making Relations Visible*, presented at 'The Gift and its Transformations', National Humanities Center, University of North Carolina.

Tomlinson, J. (1985) *British Macroeconomics Policy Since 1940* (Beckenham: Croom Helm).

Veblen, T. (1970) *The Theory of the Leisure Class* (London: Unwin).

Wernick, A. (1983) 'Advertising and Ideology: an Interpretive Framework', *Theory, Culture and Society*, vol. 2, no. 1, pp. 16–35.

Xenos, N. (1989) *Scarcity and Modernity* (London: Routledge).

5 Bringing the Consumer In: Sales Networks in Retail Banking in New Zealand

TERRY AUSTRIN

Sociological literature has generally treated the career hierarchies which constitute banking as a site to construct general discourses of class and class consciousness (Lockwood, 1958, 1990; Crompton and Jones, 1984) or, more recently, as a site from which to make statements about general trends in deskilling and gender (Smith and Wield, 1988; Crompton, 1989; Smith, 1990; O'Reilly, 1992). A different approach deployed by Eccles and Crane (1987) focused upon the organisational practices of firms operating in the financial services market. In Eccles and Crane's (1987) account the emphasis is upon the continuous construction, deconstruction and management of the 'firm internal' and 'client external' networks of relations. Their specific example is that of investment banking operating in an uncertain environment. In this chapter I will develop a similar argument to that of Eccles and Crane (1987), concerning the construction of internal and external networks in retail banking.

I will argue that one consequence of the deregulation of financial markets has been the moves made by financial institutions to organise their local markets in new and novel ways. This reorganisation, which is still proceeding in experimental form, involves a shift from branch banking, composed of stand alone units in a bureaucratic hierarchy for the monitoring of lending, to area retail sales networks based upon employees selling a rapidly expanding range of financial products. As in Eccles and Crane's (1987) account, the work practices in these sales networks come to be concerned more with constructing personal networks and doing deals and less with carrying out routine bureaucratic transactions.

Drawing on case material from New Zealand, I will argue that this redrawing of the balance of the hierarchies of lending and local personal networks is fundamental to understanding how the control systems, which are in the process of being generalised throughout retail banking, actually work. The crucial element in these control systems is the place of the customer. My account of this inclusion of the customer into control systems differs from those offered by both Fuller and Smith (1991) and DuGay and Salaman (1992). In their accounts, both sets of authors stressed that the inclusion of customers into the management circuit operates to perfect already existing hierarchical forms of managerial control. The customer comes to represent the 'anonymous surveillance of the panopticon' (Fuller and Smith, 1991, p. 11). By contrast, I argue that far from anonymous surveillance, what is critical in the new system is the personalisation of networks of customers.

DEREGULATION

The deregulation of the finance industry in New Zealand was brought about by a series of legal changes begun in 1984. These changes removed the legally enforced segmentation of the domestic financial market and therefore allowed exchange activities to take place in a more open market. The 'new banks policy' does not limit the number of banks that can be registered in this open market and nor is there any limit on the entry of banks from other countries, whether they be branch operations or subsidiaries of foreign banks. Further, there are no requirements, other than a specification of some form of financial service, as to the type of business registered banks must engage in. The new framework also provides little basis on which to distinguish between 'bank' and 'non-bank' financial institutions. The only real difference is that registered banks retain the right to use the word 'bank' in their names. In all other respects, the non-bank institutions are able to compete with registered banks.

This radical version of financial deregulation has had the intended effect of transforming the boundaries and operation of the finance sector. Where the boundaries of financial institutions were once fixed by law they have become permeable and therefore open to commercialisation from below (Lie, 1992). As a result, the financial market-place is now constituted through new organisations and new practices. The new organisations have not generally been established as new entrant companies but rather arise from the removal of the legislated divisions between international commercial banks, regional savings or trustee banks and building societies (Harper, 1986). Under the new banks policy, savings banks and buildings societies applied for and gained full banking licences. In turn, international banks, some already operating and others, new entrants to the New Zealand market, expanded their retail banking operations by buying out these new local banks. These acquisitions internationalised the operation of retail banking but at the same time also led to attempts to further embed retail banking in local economies.

In the New Zealand case, these developments have involved the almost complete reorganisation of the industry by Australian and British banks. In 1988, the Australia and New Zealand Bank purchased the former state-owned Post Office Savings Bank. In 1989, the Commonwealth Bank of Australia purchased the Auckland Savings Bank. In 1990, the State Bank of South Australia purchased the former United Building Society. In 1992, after considerable resistance from small shareholders, the National Australia Bank purchased the formerly state-owned Bank of New Zealand. The British influence is maintained by the Countrywide Bank which is owned by the Bank of Scotland. In 1991, the Bank of Scotland bought out the United Building Society and merged its network with the Countrywide Bank network. In 1992, the National Bank, a subsidiary of the British financial services firm, Lloyds, bought out the former state-owned Rural Bank. It is expected that further mergers and buy-outs will occur and that the current number of 22 registered banks operating in New Zealand, a society of 3.5 million, will therefore be dramatically reduced in the near future. What is clear already is that the separate category of financial institution known as the building society has all but been eliminated and that, as Child and Loveridge (1990) noted, there is a tendency for 'the historically rooted differences between banks now appear to be overshadowed by the homogenising consequence of removing barriers to competition within the financial sector as a whole' (p. 160).

The collapsing of the boundaries of the organisations involved in this restructuring process has been accompanied by an equally significant amount of restructuring of the work organisation of branch networks. This restructuring of the work organisation has not been secured automatically but rather has resulted from a series of very difficult managerial changes, workforce cutbacks and trials involving the use of information technology. The experiments in employee organisation which have taken place have varied according to the strategies pursued by different banks and the solutions arrived at so far have resulted from the negotiated struggles inside those banks. In all cases, however, the intended solutions involve moves towards radically reorganising and specialising service delivery and sales.

These moves towards specialisation involve attempts to construct a flexible interface with consumers. These attempts open up the boundaries of financial service firms in two different ways. Firstly, the further extension of automated networks of electronic funds transfer in the form of automatic tellers, extensive point of sale installations and home banking. These developments in networking draw the consumer into self-servicing and are a general feature of retail banking. Secondly, the boundaries of financial service firms are opened up by drawing the consumer into sales and service networks established by individual employees. In this respect employees construct their own networks of clients. This chapter focuses on an experiment in this form of organisational boundary change. I will call this an experiment in decentralised employee networking.

The experiment reviewed was carried out by a bank which I will call Enterprise Bank. What is involved in the decentralised employee networking, which this bank has attempted to establish, is much more extensive than the introduction of specialised insurance sales personnel into existing bank branches (Knights and Morgan, 1990; Morgan and Knights, 1991). The strategy adopted by the bank has been one of completely restructuring all the work practices in and the organisational form of their retail networks. Following Powell (1987, 1991) I will call the result of this strategy a hybrid. In this case the hybrid that has been produced is a combination of decentralised sales networking features and the centralised, hierarchical bureaucratic form with which banking is traditionally associated.

In the following six sections of this chapter I will discuss how this hybrid is in the process of being put together and how it operates. In the first section, I will discuss the form of organisation of the new retail network. In the second section, I will locate the centrality in the new retail network of the new sales position of the personal banker. In the third section, I will discuss networking and the way in which the customer is brought into the management circuit of the bank. In the fourth section, I will explain how a loose hierarchy of interlocking teams attempts to secure employee performance. In the two concluding sections, I will discuss the contrasts between the hierarchical and networking forms of organisation. These last two sections will focus upon the shift in the nature of control involved in banking before and after deregulation.

The research for the chapter was carried out in two stages. Between 1988 and 1990, almost 100 interviews were undertaken with bank employees in retail outlets in a number of established and new entrant banks. The employees held positions ranging from managers through to tellers. These interviews were supplemented by further interviews with senior managers, human resource managers and marketing managers. In addition, interviews with salespersons and managers were also undertaken in the insurance industry and a further set of interviews, together with extensive participant observation, were carried out with trade union officers of the finance unions representing both industries. The aim of these interviews was to explore the different agendas that the banks and insurance companies adopted with respect to flexibility in work design (Austrin, 1991).

In 1992, a further series of interviews was undertaken with managers (by this time known as coaches) and bank clerks (now known as personal bankers). These interviews were focused upon Enterprise Bank. In addition, interviews with organisers from the finance union organising these employees were also undertaken. These additional interviews were carried out in order to monitor the changes that had taken place over the time period following the first part of the research project. I was concerned with following the actors in their attempts to reconstitute branch banking in the form of retail sales networks. In particular, I was concerned with recording the views of the new personal bankers. In other studies generalisations concerning these new employees have been made (Smith, 1990, p. 116) but they have not actually featured as the subject of the research.

ENTERPRISE BANK

Within the financial services sector there are minimal differences between the products offered across competitors. As a consequence, the potential for strategic advantage is only likely to occur through the differentiation of banks in terms of customer service. Enterprise Bank, like other financial service firms, came, therefore, to focus upon strategies to assemble new markets for the bank's products in insurance and superannuation. These strategies involved, firstly, expanding the number and types of products that the bank sold and, secondly, transforming the work organisation in an attempt to allow sales employees to create their own personal networks of clients. In this case, then, innovations in the work organisation were to be used to secure customer loyalty.

The first consequence of the implementation of these strategies involved the elimination of the traditional, hierarchical form of work organisation. The key personnel in this hierarchical system were middle management based in decentralised branches and clerks. This middle management group of male branch managers was skilled in monitoring lending functions. As middle managers, positioned in a career hierarchy of different sized branches, they were rated according to the number of clerks they had in their branches. As a result, as managers, they had had an interest in bidding up and 'hoarding' the number of clerks in their respective branches. Their success in this bidding programme was the degree to which they could run their branches in a more or less indulgent way.

Male clerks remember this type of hierarchy as always having spare staff. They also remember that the internal social relations of work in such hierarchies were constructed through maximising the degree of social distance between the branch managers and themselves. In such a hierarchy, for example, it was normal practice for the person on the lowest grade of work to take tea into the manager in his office on a tray every morning. It was also normal practice for the manager to keep his door closed and to rarely enter the main banking or customer area. The social relations of work were therefore constituted out of a balance of indulgent paternalism and required deference. In this context, to acquire a branch management position could involve a male clerk in a 30-year wait. For female clerks such thoughts were not even entertained.

The work for the clerks, both male and female, was structured according to the alternation of slack and fast periods within the day or week. They were expected to be flexible in a range of tasks which coupled together their information processing work and their customer work. However, the hierarchical emphasis on task fragmentation meant that customers could often be seen as a source of irritation since they interfered with the clerks' processing work by calling them to the counter. Further, the work conducted with the customer took the form of perfunctory transactions (Goffman, 1981) and could not therefore be described as a source of involvement.

This hierarchical form of gendered work organisation was not, therefore, conducive to informal relations between managers and clerks. Nor could it tolerate clerks' criticism of work practices. In addition, this form of hierarchical work organisation was designed in such a way as to not incorporate customers as either performers of routine work tasks, such as those carried through by automatic tellers today or as sources of information on employee or managerial performance. Most significantly this hierarchical form was not geared to retail selling practices.

In place of this type of hierarchy, Enterprise Bank has established a new system of customised services and sales which involves all employees in their retail networks. This new system has not only restructured the positions of the specialised layer of middle management but, at the same time, it has extended the control system through which this level of managers was monitored down to all employees. This control system, in part, relied upon personal reputation gained in the networks of clients. Enacted by branch managers it was expressed through an individuating mystique of quality and autonomy (Stinchcombe, 1990).

This reconstruction of control means that the social distance between the branch manager, now called a coach and the employee, now called a personal banker, has been collapsed. The personal banker is now allowed to criticise management openly. Further, the formality of the employee–customer interface has also been collapsed and the personal banker's work has come to be focused upon customers who become their individual clients. Bank work in the new retail outlets has, therefore, shifted from a task orientation involving elementary and fragmented customer service, to customer orientation involving management of the customer's needs over a series of transactions with the bank. The personal bankers have become client managers and responsibility has been dispersed down to them.

Enterprise Bank has constructed 40 separate area retail networks with approximately six retail outlets, six coaches, 35 personal bankers and a similar number of tellers in each. The new retail outlets are uniform in size and have play areas for the customers' children. They are staffed by a single coach, personal bankers and tellers. The coach positions are filled by women and men in their twenties. These positions have had larger business loans removed from their areas of discretion but, as the senior credit officials in the outlets, the coaches still deal, like those under them, with small business and residential housing mortgages. In the words of a coach, her job has become similar to that of 'a car salesperson rather than an office manager'.

The new coaches are required to keep down the number of employees in the retail outlet (Smith, 1990). They can no longer, therefore, accumulate or hoard staff to cover for difficulties. The result is a system of very tight staffing which requires flexibility from all the employees. Unfortunately, such flexibility is more often than not a feature of what should be rather than what actually is the case. For example, one major tension point in the system is that product knowledge and computer skills are not always generally acquired by all and as a result not all staff and in particular the coaches are actually flexible. Given tight staffing this inflexibility can create acute problems of work flow and the servicing of customers. Further, it can generate considerable resentment between employees in the retail outlets.

To resolve tensions of this type the coaches are required to do one-on-one counselling and coaching of their personal bankers:

> I have fits and starts of sitting down with each sales person once a week and talking about their sales, talking about their weekly results, talking about overall where they are heading, where they are at with their outcalling, where they are at with their product knowledge, what leads they have got coming up and how can I help them, what they have got planned (outlet coach).

These counselling sessions were, in theory, supposed to take place every week but, again, owing to pressures on both the personal bankers and the coaches, they did not always take place.

In addition to the overall responsibility for sales, which can vary very widely from week to week, the coaches are required to run the retail outlets as cost centres with budgets for salaries, which are an area of potential negotiation over staff loadings, data processing which is out of their control, fee collection, overhead costings for hire of fixtures like plants and the cleaning contract. These combined functions of sales and budget holding mean that the coaches are no longer positioned within a hierarchy of general lending and, given the uniform size of outlets, this means that their career progression within the bank is dramatically reduced.

In this new organisation of work, then, the reduction of hierarchy or, put another way, the contraction of the internal labour market, is accompanied by pressure to maximise the points at which personal lending and sales can take place in retail outlets. The retail outlets have therefore become totally differentiated in terms of their sales function. In smaller service centres the position of coach is dispensed with and senior personal bankers run them.

PERSONAL BANKERS

The new network organisational form of Enterprise Bank corresponds to general developments involving the use of budgets and the construction of internal markets in firms (Eccles and White, 1986). In the case of Enterprise Bank the aim was to promote and emphasise face-to-face exchanges between buyers and sellers as the central customer transaction. This means that the success of the new networking practices is entirely dependent upon the performance of sales employees who do not, as in traditional banking, simply follow prescribed rules but rather interpret and use them in creative ways. They are employees who have to develop their own ways of doing deals (Eccles and Crane, 1988) with customers.

What is required of these employees at this new customer interface is clear from the views expressed by a sales manager of the bank:

> The emphasis from the bank's point of view is on aggressive selling to the extent that the people who are appointed we run through 'psych' tests before they get the job. They must fall within the top 25% of the adult population in terms of numeric reasoning, the top 25% of the adult population in verbal reasoning and they must be above average in their liking and ability in a sales job and some 30% of their job by description is to be outside the bank physically calling on people, visiting people in their place of work and residence (sales manager).

In the new style of work, then, it is the personality and negotiating sales skills of the employee and not the formal routines of bureaucratic work which are important.

These selling skills should not be underestimated for Enterprise Bank is a full service bank selling products across a wide range of areas. In Enterprise Bank the sales employees are expected to be familiar with and sell the following types of accounts and products: the standard checking and savings accounts; sole trader accounts, which are standard small business accounts requiring sole signature for authorisation; and offshore accounts which allow customers to keep their money in foreign currency. These offshore accounts do not function as tax havens but do earn interest and they do allow customers to determine at which point they will bring their money into the country. Other accounts sold include retirement income or high interest pension plan accounts and revolving credit or overdraft accounts.

The personal bankers also sell personal loans, mortgages and car loans. In addition, they can sell a range of investment products including monthly bonds, travel bonds, unit trusts, insurance bonds and life insurance. On top of these there are all the 'internationals', products such as telegraphic transfers, drafts, travellers cheques and cash. As yet there are no requirements that the personal bankers should have, as insurance agents have in Britain, special qualifications covering the provision of investment advice or the selling of life insurance. In New Zealand's deregulated financial services market there is no equivalent of the British Financial Services Act (Knights and Morgan, 1990).

Enterprise Bank refers to the position of a personal banker as multiskilled. The position requires an extended repertoire of talk from the employee and is much more than an enquiry clerk which O'Reilly (1992) noted of a similar position in British bank. The design of the new position is built around the organisation of a paired conversation (Sacks *et al.*, 1978) with the topic being the customer's full banking needs. This design incorporates a strong element of interpretation of rules and the content of the interaction. In this sense it requires the employee to orchestrate the encounter (Goffman, 1959, 1961; Dingwall, 1980) with the customer. This was formally recognised in the 'competency profile' for the position.

This profile of psychological attributes that a personal banker must be potentially able to employ, was assembled in a joint management and union exercise in 1989. It argued that the positioning involved in the new set of tasks demands a high degree of interpersonal sensitivity, an achievement orientation and perseverance. Also identified were two other categories termed 'overcoming the odds' and 'making an impact'. Coupled with these was the category of 'persuasiveness'. The behavioural practices in this competency profile included the requirements to smile, use the customer's name frequently, engage in slightly broken (good) eye contact and make comments to convey the message 'I care'. Those occupying the new position were also expected to compliment the customers personally and engage in follow-up work with them. In the matter of interpersonal sensitivity, they were trained to understand, interpret and respond to the customer's concerns, motives and feelings. Most importantly, they were instructed to hold their 'opinions in check' whilst they listened for underlying meanings and they should not lose emotional control when faced with difficulties.

The personal bankers in the new outlets have trained themselves directly from computer packages in product knowledge and procedures and have sat internal bank examinations which have assessed their competency levels. Within the branch they are responsible for selling products and organising the sales of other personal bankers. This form of organisation is achieved by each personal banker having responsibility for a product of which they oversee the sales. In effect the personal bankers have positions as product managers in which they are required to organise their own promotion schemes and see that others fulfil their sales targets. They also exercise lending functions up to a maximum point.

The key to the new position lies in a policy of the customisation of files carried out by the personal bankers themselves. This move to customisation is the basis on which the employees build their own networks. A personal banker explained:

> I keep my own files. We have what I term our own customers. The emphasis is on relationships and we build relationships with our own customers. I will build up (from bank records) a profile of my customers. The only information I can get from them is general information such as date of birth, where they live, their occupation and the accounts that they have, the rest of the information about perhaps products that I have approached them about, mail out campaigns that they may have been interested in, all that information is recorded by me personally ... initially I picked up customers in a haphazard way, the concept was that you came in to see me every time you want something done.

Out of this process the personal banker builds their own client base and then begins to service it by 'out-calls'. These involve either a home or a work visit. At present all personal bankers are required to make two 'out-calls' a week but this is projected to be raised. The out-calls serve the dual function of selling and 'prospecting' customers.

The employees' personal networks are ultimately dependent upon the complete elimination of back office clerical work from the scene of the customer transaction. This work has been removed to centralised support centres which are linked to the outlets by daily courier runs. The work in the support centres is organised along the lines of repetitive tasks and, increasingly, part-time employment. This polarisation of work and skills allows the personal banker to carry out all the transactions a customer might require. In effect, it means that aspects of the personal service, provided by the old branch manager role, have been generalised and devolved to the personal banker. As a result all transactions can now be potentially customised.

The personal banker is the key to the new retail outlets. The success of the new system, however, depends on getting these personal bankers to sell. This is the prime function of the coaches but rather than overtly organise and supervise the personal bankers, they are required to listen to them to glean better ways of working. To this end, the personal bankers are included on area task forces and consulted on projects. This recognition of the personal bankers allows information to flow upwards but they are also required to cooperate to help out others. Thus, experienced and successful personal bankers could be borrowed by another retail outlet to show others ways of working successfully with clients.

Hochschild (1983) labelled the type of work that these personal bankers carry out as 'emotional labour'. In the context of banking, the deployment of such a model marks a transition from the containment of emotions in a formal transaction model of exaggerated hierarchical deference, to one of informal, personal friendliness, coupled with politeness. This new commercial civility is, like the deference relation before it, a part of the work itself. However, where the former was developed as character over time in the extremely long internal hierarchical career of the male banker, the latter is developed in the horizontal networks developed with external customers.

NETWORKING

The personal bankers take up their positioning not, as in the old system, fixed by a hierarchy but as a moving point in a network or new configuration of ties. This network is tied together both horizontally and vertically as a sales network but exists, as explained, in order to promote the construction of client networks. The function of the personal bankers and the rationale of the system lies in the construction of these personal networks which they service. The personal bankers, then, have membership in two networks and both are required for their positioning. The first network, that of the bank, is given. The second, they have to create themselves. As the bank argues, being an employee today requires constructing one's own job. It does not, as in the old system, involve the bank offering a career of positions. The personal bankers, then, position themselves in networks rather than being positioned in a hierarchy.

This emphasis on positioning is important when it is considered that if personal bankers choose to leave the bank then it is possible that they could take some of their clients with them. As the banks' representative they have deployed their social skills and local knowledge to construct networks but, in doing so, the networks are tied to them, not the bank. Their organisational experience with clients has therefore taken on the form of property. The bank, then, has an interest in keeping successful employees. More to the point, unlike in the old banking system, Enterprise Bank no longer wants to move its employees around. In the new system the dual positioning of the employees, in the banks and in their own networks, is crucial.

Enterprise Bank, then, has moved beyond the boundaries of a fixed hierarchy of positions in order to generalise the mobilisation of local networks to all employees. Their employees are chosen for the knowledge of the local areas and clients with whom they will work and they are locked into their own sales networks. At the same time their performance is conditional upon these networks.

In effect, work for the personal bankers in Enterprise Bank has shifted from a set of bureaucratic routines, in which responsibility was still displaced upwards by the employee, towards a network form in which responsibility is to be ultimately taken by the employee. This driving down of the responsibility to manage to employees was generally welcomed by the personal bankers and is the key to the consent given by them to the new system. This is not to argue that the problems associated with sales networks in Enterprise Bank have been eliminated. But those personal bankers who have made the shift from the hierarchical form to the new network system do not indulge in nostalgic talk of hierarchical careers working for the one organisation.

At the core of the personal bankers' networks is a new 'game' between worker and customer in which the worker works for the customer while being employed by the bank. This form of indirect control allows the personal bankers to exercise their judgement in work and, further, to pit their judgement and knowledge on equal terms against the coaches of the new retail outlets. The removal of an overt bureaucratic form of administration is therefore crucial to the new position. The result is a system which makes visible not only the personal bankers but also the coaches and the area managers.

In the new networking system the coaches have lost the advantage of a bureaucratic line of authority and with it has also gone the automatic deference granted to the positions formerly occupied by branch managers. The new system, then, opens up the old hierarchical form of top-down monitoring to the mutual surveillance of each other. Coaches and personal bankers are therefore more vulnerable to each other and have a great need to 'get on' and survive with each other. In situations in which coaches do not have access to relief staff this requirement is crucial.

In addition to this form of mutual surveillance, further forms of surveillance involve the customer. In the case of customers it should be noted that they are brought into the organisation as both a source of work for the personal bankers and as a source of information on the way in which this work is performed. On the other hand, customer visits now also take the employee outside of the boundary of work to perform functions in the customers' own settings. This extension of customer relations means that work relations can shade over into friendship. In this configuration, the personal bankers look to both the bank and the customer in a series of diverse encounters which they must skilfully manage. Surveillance should therefore be seen as being run both inside and outside of the boundary of work.

A focus on the customer is fundamental to the new organisation. Each sales network of Enterprise bank carries out a six-monthly survey of 500 customers. Each outlet within the network has six-monthly focus group meetings of eight customers representing a broad cross-section of the outlet's customers. These take place in the outlet. In addition to these practices of customer feedback each outlet is also subject to a 'secret shopper' carrying out investigations on customer service every six months.

These developments in the forms of consumer appraisal are representative of the fact that the locus of control in Enterprise Bank has shifted from a direct and continual hierarchical supervision of work tasks by management to a looser networked form. In effect, control has been dispersed or multiplied and one form has been externalised beyond the boundary of the bank and located in the employees' own personal networks. This means that recognition of performance is now partly in the hands of the customer who is encouraged by employees to make it known to the bank when a satisfactory or unsatisfactory service has been supplied. This change is fundamental to the new system. In the words of one of the personal bankers, 'I do think about work more, I am thinking about the customers a lot more than I used to and management less'.

This addition of the customer to the already extensive amount of monitoring means that the network is not driven from above. On the contrary, in order for it to work it must be driven from below. A personal banker explains how this works. Firstly, they have a greater say in the organisation of work:

> It used to be the case that you come to work, you do what you are told to do and then you go home again. Now if you don't like something then you can say that I don't like this and we have more say so in the lay out of the branch, what sort of posters we have up and how we treat the staff and the customers and so on. We have a lot more say so.

Secondly, they are made to feel more accountable for their performance to the bank:

> They give us more decision making and we are more in touch with the actual selling and we get a lot more feedback than we ever used to on how many of this we have sold and how many of that and what our profit ratios are ... as a team. In a way you can see how your efforts make a difference but it is definitely a more pressured environment.

Thirdly, they are more accountable to the customer:

> In a sort of perverse way I feel a loyalty to some of my customers and I will go out of my way to make things run smoothly for them. I will quite often give them my home phone number and say feel free to ring me on a weekend ... I do that because I put myself in the customers' shoes and also because that is a choice of mine ... you see the bank hasn't said to me you will do this for the customer in your own private life ... if they had said to me I want you to do this in your private time I would have said no way but I feel a loyalty to my customers and there are things that I will do and because the customer trusts you, you don't want to let them down.

These forms of recognition which provide employee voice, company information and allow autonomy in dealing with clients allow the establishment of trust between employee and customer.

This form of trust can, however, only be established if the employee can work for the customer:

> It makes it more interesting to tailor it to the customer. I am allowed to do that. There are rules, there are things I just can't do and I will apply the rules as often as I can. But if it looks like the customer is going to go out of the door or we are not going to get the business then yes the rules are there to be bent.

This bending of rules is practised because transactions are now viewed as sales and therefore a 'shading of a rate' or a dropping of a commission payment on drafts still earns a return that might otherwise have been lost. To build client bases in the new work environment requires more than a smile; it requires knowing how to extend such favours and commitments to the customer. As Pinch and Clark (1986) noted, 'sales are interactional accomplishments'. Products are sold through talk.

The networking nature of the new position can, therefore, be seen to give rise to the development of reciprocal obligations between the employee and customer. As employees the personal bankers position themselves as experts in consumer transactions. In doing so they are able to escape the overt forms of deference that their predecessors, the bank clerks, who were trapped in fragmented tasks, were forced to display to the customer. Further, and again in contrast to the bank clerks, the personal bankers have to learn how to receive and use 'gifts' and information from the customer.

In conclusion, then, networking for personal bankers means that their relative honour and worth become variables which they can influence and work on. It is for this reason that appraisal by customers on a good job is actually sought by the personal bankers. The personal bankers, therefore, come to invest in the new multiple control system because it gives them some space to secure their identities. It should be added that having this space is for them far more preferable than having evidence on their performance reduced to a specific measurement grounded in sales.

HIERARCHIES OF TEAMS

The outlets in which the personal bankers work do not conform to a simple hierarchy of functional positions but rather are constituted through flexible but hierarchical teams. At the base of this hierarchy are two-person teams of tellers and personal bankers. The tellers' opportunities to involve themselves in sales are in principle not restricted but in practice are, as Enterprise Bank discovered, extremely limited. The tellers, therefore, refer sales to the personal banker. The two positions are combined together as 'buddy systems' of cooperation in which a teller and personal banker work together on sales.

On a second level above these two-person teams, there are sales teams of personal bankers:

> We have sales team meetings of the personal bankers with management on a weekly basis. The meeting is for the personal bankers not for the manager. We talk to him about what we are doing and we talk to each other. We have broken the sales teams down into retail bankers, tellers and retail support so we have split the whole branch into two different teams and we meet fortnightly with those teams to talk about perhaps inter-departmental issues which is everything from staff personalities, people who are not getting on to problems that are arising in jobs … The manager is not involved in those meetings (personal banker).

These teams of personal bankers are located within the retail outlets.

On a third level of teams, the coaches of the retail outlets are linked together into area teams composed of sales networks of a number of retail outlets. These network teams are overseen by area managers who meet with the outlet coaches on a monthly basis. The function of the area managers is to coach the coaches, enforce credit policies and fabricate the area sales network into a cohesive entity with which employees can identify. This includes setting up social functions and sports teams based on the network.

More significantly, the area managers compare the performance of the different coaches through weekly operational meetings which they hold with them. The agendas at these meetings are given by the weekly reports produced on each outlet's asset quality, loans, deposits volumes, fee collection and overtime payments. This comparison allows the area managers to encourage outlets to compete against each other. This is important since, in turn, area managers are measured on their performance against the area managers of the other networks in the region. These area managers also meet as a 'third level' regional team.

The area networks are in turn measured on their performance against each other. Those areas performing less well can then be singled out for special attention by the banks' retail financial services consultants teams. These teams, composed of personal bankers pulled out of the retail outlets for specified periods of time, are charged with working out why areas are not performing or why a particular product is not selling. To do this they move around branches teaching employees how to sales 'rap' (the term used by the bank) and offer sales seminars to which they pull in managers, retail bankers and teller representatives to discuss the barriers to selling. These consultant teams, like the coaches in the retail outlets, are expected to facilitate rather than instruct. They deal only in positive sentiments.

For example, the atmosphere in the seminars run by the consultants teams is informal, as those attending are allowed to wear jeans and t-shirts:

> Every course you go on you get the standard 'what are we here for, who are we and what are we going to achieve' and there are little thought provoking quotes all over the place like 'you make a difference' or 'from a tiny spark can burst a mighty flame' ... They always start off with 'well primarily we are here to have fun' and they always have a box of chocolates and if you get a question right or you make a good answer then you get a chocolate, which you get to choose. This creates a friendly fun sort of atmosphere (personal banker).

The seminars work through small groups which discuss and draw up lists of the barriers to selling. These lists predictably include lack of confidence and fear of rejection on the part of the personal bankers but they also isolate more structural problems such as too many sales campaigns, customer resistance to endless sales propositions and, most importantly, inadequate staffing and the pressures of time. The latter two are the sticking points which come up in all the sales courses but the consultants, who like to focus on the psychological issues, have no brief to even attempt to open up questions of remedy for such matters.

These different strategies of teams, internal network competition and seminars, which facilitate discussion between personal bankers and coaches across the networks, are supplemented by monthly meetings of outlet coaches which are concerned with cooperation across the network. These may include guest speakers, or personal bankers might be invited to 'brainstorm' on campaign ideas. The area managers also produce monthly newsletters. In addition, area managers base themselves in the different retail outlets for two-month periods. This allows the area managers direct monitoring of the different coaches' leadership style and staff morale. Free of their own central office, the area managers position and reposition themselves with their teams. For outlet coaches this arrangement is difficult because of the ambiguity generated by the presence of an additional manager. Given this ambiguity, ground rules have to be negotiated between the coaches and the area managers.

Formally, the role of the area managers in the outlets is to facilitate the achievement of agreed upon sales goals. The area managers, then, are the coaches to the outlet coaches. In practice this involves the area manager encouraging the good performers in the outlets but also 'stepping in' in cases of employee performance problems. The pay-off for the bank is that this additional monitoring is balanced by the fact that the outlets' staff also get to know and work with the area manager. In an area manager's words, she is 'no longer seen as authoritarian'.

DISCUSSION

There is a growing literature concerned with explaining and theorising about new forms of organisation and control over the labour process in service industries. This literature has either been informed by Foucault's (1979, 1982) analysis of power and subjectivity (Knights and Sturdy, 1990; Knights and Morgan, 1990, 1991; Morgan and Knights, 1991; Fuller and Smith, 1991; DuGay and Salaman, 1992; Kerfoot and Knights, 1992) or, alternatively, has sought to establish the significance of new control practices through reference to developments in work such as emotional labour (Hochschild, 1983) or corporate culture (Ray, 1986). I have sought to develop this work in a slightly different direction to incorporate the empirical findings from Enterprise Bank.

Following Eccles and Crane's (1988) account of networking in investment banking, I have argued that the development of sales networks in Enterprise Bank means that work at the level of retail banking is now constituted through negotiations and collaborations which occur as much with customers as with other employees. As a result, employees are led to seek alliances with customers just as the customers have new sets of claims upon employees. In these alliances the idea of customer evaluation is not envisaged as a threat to employees but rather as another way of reminding the bank that work which might otherwise have remained invisible is recognised. The employee therefore has a stake in customer evaluation.

Thus, in the shift from a bureaucratic form of processing transactions to a more network type of selling, the employees willingly incorporate the customer as both an effective controller of and voice speaking for them. In the absence of any effective group solidarity or power, their network and their customers become an important resource that they can use in their favour. Their network is the potential basis of their autonomy. More specifically their autonomy arises from the intersection of hierarchy with the requirement that employees construct their own local networks of customers.

The key contrast between a hierarchy and a network is located in the forms of control used to stabilise institutions. This is particularly important in Enterprise Bank. Disputes over control in the new network arrangement now occur not over the rigidity of hierarchical rules and their enforcement by management but over their ambiguity. Two versions of this ambiguity can be identified. Firstly, in a soft sell version, indirect control is exercised through the reputations and success that employees build over time through doing deals with and for customers. This is the version of which the personal banker quoted above has spoken. The ambiguity of this type of control lies in the degree to which it is both independent from management and at the same time is dependent upon the employee choice over how far they will allow their work to invade their private life. There are no rules on this matter.

In the case quoted above, for example, it was precisely this boundary between work and private life which was breached. But if asked about it personal bankers will argue that they wish to keep the two separate, that going the 'extra mile' and always carrying business cards to make a possible sale is asking too much. At the same time, it is precisely this collapsing or blurring of boundaries between customers and friends that makes the job attractive. The attraction is that of embedding the employees' identity in extended and variable forms of social organisation. The concern is that the instability of the rules could be used against them to threaten their own choices.

This ambivalence over collapsing the boundary between work and private life, and, therefore, personalising customer relations, is important for explaining resistance to the second, more hard sell version of control of their jobs. This second version would be directly located in the numbers of sales achieved and therefore make employees solely responsible for their earnings and place them in direct competition with each other. Ultimately, it could shift payment of sales staff onto a commission basis. The result of this move would lead not only to insecurity in earnings but also to an inevitable collapse of the distinction between work and private life. This move is feared by employees and would be resisted by them.

However, even if it could be implemented a commission system of the type used in life insurance (Knights and Morgan, 1990) or real estate would also throw up its own problems. In a deregulated environment, agents selling financial products that could be easily cloned would not only be extremely vulnerable with respect to earnings but it is also very likely that, as in life insurance and real estate, it would result in a high turnover of staff. The irony for the bank would be that employee exit of this type would either collapse personal network arrangements or, more significantly, the employee could move them to another firm.

This structural tension at the core of the network system was put very well by a senior manager:

> The insurance companies would love our networks. We would love our people to have their ability to sell.There is a race on and we will win and win easily. We will move in the direction of commission payments but not all the way ... a compensation and benefits package is being looked at where you have performance measurement and recognition and your salary at risk.We agree your package is worth x you have to make the performance to get it. The trick is how you measure performance.

In the hierarchical system the organisation of work meant that information on measuring performance was not really available. The 'trick' of measuring performance was not therefore governed by explicit criteria governing individual output. The new system, however, calls for explicit criteria in all transactions. In doing so it collects information and constructs different ways to monitor work but the problem of getting employees to sell and the evaluation of performance remains.

For Enterprise Bank, this dilemma in the new system is not the employees' concern of how the boundary between work and private life should be structured but, very simply, how to raise sales in a deregulated and very competitive market. Their new system was brought in as a 'soft sell' but increasingly senior managers point to the 'hard sell' as the solution. For the reasons given above this is unlikely to involve moving the personal bankers' contractual status towards more direct market controls and establishing commission payment as an incentive. Alternatively and more likely, the bank can retain a mix of salaried employment and bonus and further extend the idea that employees organise their own networks and sales. Given that all employees' sales are 'PC based' and traceable to their specific transactions, this would, in theory, be a simple procedure.

For example, it is possible now for Enterprise Bank to work out the 'product champions' and who is selling what and employees feel that their individual sales averages are probably being worked out in this way. The employees are also aware that individual contracts are being offered by some managers. What is significant, however, is that, despite multiple forms of surveillance and knowledge, senior management still feel unable to move to a system which completely 'exploits' the information. Senior managers talked openly about this problem when discussing the necessary shift from banking to sales:

> It is a job. It is a commercial activity. Nothing more, nothing less. I've been trying to tell people that we are retailers. In this part of the world Countdown sell groceries, we sell financial services. We are no better and no worse than they are. Now can we please stop thinking of banking chambers and ethereal nonsense and start talking about retailing (sales manager).

In practice, however, such talk of retailing usually meant addressing the outlet coaches' major problem of how to get their staff to sell. It was clear that they felt that neither hierarchical forms of surveillance and information technology nor sales seminars and employee networks had finally solved this problem for them.

The shift to sales networks and decentralised forms of client management has therefore operated to set up new debates on appropriate workloads and how sales staff should be rewarded. This issue cannot be resolved through the construction of multiple monitoring points. These have operated, as intended, to increase rather than decrease the employees autonomy within paid employment but this autonomy is not accompanied by set understandings on effort or the sales recorded. Despite the extensive use of information retrieval on work performance, output criteria and even the arrangement of tasks, performance criteria still remain ambiguous and subject to informal bargaining. This bargaining occurs at every point over which the monitoring is established. This includes the appraisal systems which are increasingly being used as systems of self-reporting and discipline (Austrin, 1994).

CONCLUSION

The result of the deregulation of the finance sector has been the construction of new organisational forms geared to networking sales and the management of clients. In the case of Enterprise Bank this new form removed hierarchically structured careers and at the same time dispersed elements of decision making to the client interface. Moves towards deskilling employees through further hierarchical subordination, fragmentation of tasks and detailed monitoring of individual performance would not have allowed this process of decision making and nor would it have resolved the problem of the organisation of the flow of work with customers. Attempts to carry this type of strategy through in financial services have met with resistance from both middle management and employees (Smith, 1990; Austrin, 1991).

It is in this context that the shift away from a total reliance on hierarchical forms should be seen as significant. In the case of Enterprise Bank, further hierarchical subordination would have meant subverting the sorts of deals that sales work is based upon and, further, restricting the work of employees to a point at which resistance to rather than involvement in work would have been the most likely response. I have argued, however, that a model of deskilling through the construction of extended hierarchies is neither necessary nor a recipe for maximising visibility. In my argument the development of employee autonomy has been shown to be dependent upon the use of a range of methods of visibility such as technical monitoring through the computer, the use of budgets and targets and managerial and customer appraisals. These different methods complement each other to the point of removing the necessity for direct supervision. In the case of management by customers the system of employee networking involves the social construction of the market and the stabilisation of client ties. These client ties offset any rule by anonymous customers operating in an unknown market.

This design of work in Enterprise Bank should not be seen, however, as part of an evolutionary moment in which control is more tightly secured by management. Control in Enterprise Bank is simply a matter of business strategy. In this case the business strategy involved the generalisation of networking practices to a retail network of sales outlets. The strategy has features drawn from traditional sales practices in insurance and other sales occupations. These features have been extensively documented by Knights and Morgan (1990, 1991; Morgan and Knights, 1991). These authors also stress the way in which control in selling occupations does not lie in monitoring the adherence to operational rules. In their examples they show how control over insurance salespersons relies upon outcomes which are constructed as targets. By contrast, I have stressed how control in Enterprise Bank lies in the construction of personal networks. At the same time I have argued that the bank also seeks to supplement this control by introducing salary risk schemes which will link up performance, targets and salaries more systematically. Such schemes will also, of course, promote individual performance appraisals as central to the new work organisation.

I have characterised Enterprise Bank as a hybrid form combining decentralised networking with customers and a centralised bureaucracy. In this hybrid form of sales networks and bureaucracy, management cannot directly intervene in either the production of the employee networks or sales output. At the same time it retains its own modified but nevertheless hierarchical elements of employment as opposed to making employees solely responsible for their output through self-employment. For the employees, the advantage of this balancing of controls lies in a much more open system of autonomy, recognition and rights. The new organisational form does not, however, remove issues of ambiguity or insecurity from work but, on the contrary, increases them.

How far this latter condition of insecurity can be pushed is management's problem. The dilemma for management is that to move back towards a standard employment contract and a hierarchy of fragmented tasks or to move the other way and attempt to implement a straight market relation through a contract of self-employment would be to destroy the network advantages of employees' personalised client bases. The power relations of the new system are such that management is dependent upon the personal bankers' abilities to manage from below. This dependence is a product of pursuing an upskilling strategy in a deregulated, highly volatile and competitive financial services market.

This strategy of upskilling and investing in an important section of sales staff in the bank has, therefore, produced a hybrid form of organisation which has remodelled internal and external environments and, in doing so, changed the futures of those who work in it and those who were removed from it. This hybrid has dissolved the boundaries of the interface between employee and customer, established by the previous hierarchical form of the bank and has called into question traditional banking working practices.

However it too is also called into question for this hybrid is an experiment in organisation which is on hold.

Deregulation, then, can be seen to be another way of saying that new actors and new practices now constitute the financial services industry. The example of Enterprise Bank has revealed what some of these new actors are doing, how they are networked with others and the problems that they have thrown up in the process.

ACKNOWLEDGEMENTS

Barbara Pringle made it possible for me to carry out the research for this chapter. Without her and the time given up by personal bankers and managers, who remain anonymous, this chapter would not have been put together. I would also like to acknowledge and thank Geoff Fougere for his very valuable comments on drafts of this chapter and David Knights for his very helpful editorial comment. Tracey Robinson pulled it together in the end.

References

Austrin, T. (1991) 'Flexibility, Surveillance and Hype in New Zealand Financial Retailing', *Work, Employment and Society*, vol. 5, no. 2, pp. 201–21.

Austrin, T. (1994) 'Positioning Resistance and Resisting Position: Human Resource Management and the Politics of Appraisal and Grievance Hearings', in J. Jermier, W. Nord and D Knights (eds), *Resistance and Power in Organisations* (London: Routledge), pp. 199–218.

Child, J. and Loveridge, R. (1990) *Information Technology in European Services: Towards a Microelectronic Future* (Oxford: Basil Blackwell).

Crompton, R. (1989) 'Women in Banking: Continuity and Change since the Second World War *Work, Employment and Society*, vol. 3, no. 2, pp. 141–56.

Crompton, R. and Jones, G. (1984) *White Collar Proletariat: Deskilling and Gender in Clerical Work* (London: Macmillan).

Dingwall, R. (1980) 'Orchestrated Encounters: An Essay in the Comparative Analysis of Speech Exchange Systems', *Sociology of Health and Illness*, vol. 2, no. 2, pp. 151–73.

DuGay, P. and Salaman G. (1992) 'The Culture of the Customer' *Journal of Management Studies*, vol. 29, no. 5, pp. 615–35.

Eccles, R. G. and Crane, D. (1987) 'Managing Through Networks in Investment Banking', *California Management Review*, vol. 30, no. 1, pp. 176–95.

Eccles, R. G. and Crane, D. (1988*) Doing Deals: Investment Banks at Work*, (Boston: Harvard Business School Press).

Eccles, R. G. and White, H. (1986) 'Firm and Market Interfaces Profit Centre Control', in S. Lindenberg (ed.), *Approaches to Social Theory* (New York: Russell Sage), pp. 203–22.

Foucault , M. (1979) *Discipline and Punish* (Harmondsworth: Penguin).

Foucault, M. (1982) 'The Subject and Power', Afterword in L. Dreyfus and P. Rabinow, *Michel Foucault: Beyond Structuralism and Hermeneutics* (Chicago: University of Chicago Press), pp. 208–6.

Fuller, L. and Smith, V. (1991) 'Consumer's Reports: Management by Customers in a Changing Economy', *Work, Employment & Society*, vol. 5, no. 1, pp. 1–16.

Goffman, E. (1959) *The Presentation of Self in Everyday Life* (New York: Doubleday).

Goffman, E. (1961) *Encounters: Two Studies in the Sociology of Interaction* (Indianapolis: Bobbs Merrill).

Goffman, E. (1981) *Forms of Talk* (Philadelphia: University of Pennsylvania Press).

Harper, D. A. (1986) *The Financial Services Industry: Effects of Regulatory Reform*, New Zealand Institute of Economic Research, Research Paper 35.

Hochschild, A. R. (1983) *The Managed Heart: The Commercialisation of Human Feeling* (London: University of California Press).

Kerfoot, D. and Knights, D. (1992) 'Planning for Personnel? Human Resource Management Reconsidered', *Journal of Management Studies*, vol. 29, no. 5, pp. 651–68.

Knights, D. and Morgan, G. (1990) 'Management Control in Sales Forces: a Case Study From the Labour Process of Life Insurance, *Work, Employment and Society*, vol. 4, no. 3, pp. 369–89.

Knights, D. and Morgan, G. (1991) 'Selling Oneself: Subjectivity and the Labour Process in Selling Life Insurance', in C. Smith, D. Knights and H. Willmott (eds), *White Collar Work: the Non Manual Labour Process* (London: Macmillan), pp. 217–40.

Knights, D. and Sturdy, A. (1990) 'New Technology and the Self Disciplined Worker in Insurance', in M. McNeil, I. Varcoe and S. Yearly (eds), *Deciphering Science and Technology* (London: Macmillan), pp. 126–54.

Lie, J. (1992) 'The Concept of Mode of Exchange', *American Sociological Review*, vol. 57, pp. 508–23.

Lockwood, D. (1958) *The Blackcoated Worker: a Study in Class Consciousness* (London: Unwin).

Lockwood, D. (1990) *The Blackcoated Worker: a Study in Class Consciousness*, 2nd edn (Oxford: Clarendon Press).

Morgan, G. and Knights, D. (1991) 'Gendering Jobs: Corporate Strategy, Managerial Control and the Dynamics of Job Segregation', *Work, Employment and Society*, vol. 5, no. 2, pp. 181–200.

O'Reilly, J. (1992) 'Where Do You Draw The Line? Functional Flexibility, Training and Skill in Britain and France', *Work, Employment and Society*, vol. 6, no. 3, pp. 369–96.

Pinch, T. and Clark, C. (1986) 'Patter Merchanting and the Strategic (Re)Production and Local Management of Economic Reasoning in the Sales Routines of Market Pitchers', *Sociology*, vol. 20, no. 2, pp. 169–91.

Powell, W. W. (1987) 'Hybrid Organisational Arrangements: New Forms of Transitional Development', *California Management Review*, vol. 30, no. 1, pp. 67–87.

Powell, W. W. (1991) 'Neither Market nor Hierarchy: Network Forms of Organisation', in G. Thompson, J. Frances, R. Levacic and J. Mitchell (eds), *Markets, Hierarchies and Networks: The Coordination of Social Life* (London: Sage), pp. 265–76.

Ray, C. (1986) 'Corporate Culture: the Last Frontier of Control', *Journal of Management Studies*, vol. 23, no. 3, pp. 287–97.

Sacks, H., Schegloff, E. and Jefferson, G. (1978) 'A Simplest Systematics for the Organisation of Turn Taking for Conversation', in J. Schenkein (ed.), *Studies in the Organisation of Conversational Interaction* (New York: Academic Press), pp. 7–56.

Smith, S. and Wield, D. (1988) 'New Technology and Bank Work: Banking on IT as an Organisational Technology', in, L. Harris (ed.), *New Perspectives on the Financial System* (London: Croom Helm), pp. 27–302.

Smith, V. (1990) *Managing in the Corporate Interest* (Berkeley: University of California Press).

Stinchcombe, A. L. (1990) *Information and Organisations* (Berkeley: University of California Press).

6 Financial Services in Transition: an Examination of Market and Regulatory Forces in Denmark and the UK

JON SUNDBO

INTRODUCTION

This chapter examines strategic developments within financial services companies and the resulting changes in the relationship between these firms and their customers. The types of companies focused upon in the chapter are general insurance companies, life insurance companies, retail banks and associated institutions (for example, credit card companies). This is the market for personal or retail financial services.

Detailed empirical data is drawn from two studies carried out in Denmark. One study is a comprehensive project (the SELFI project; cf. SELFI, 1988; Sundbo, 1991b) which has investigated the development of self-service as a production and delivery system and other attempts to create product and delivery systems in the financial sector. The second study involves research on the innovation process in Danish financial corporations (Sundbo, 1990, 1991a, 1992, 1996, 1997) where data collection and interviews have been performed in 19 financial firms, primarily banks and insurance companies. Despite this focus on Denmark, the trends described have an international flavour. The analysis will, therefore, be supplemented by broad-ranging data from Europe as a whole and, more particularly, from research carried out in the UK (Knights and Willmott, 1993; Knights et al., 1993).

The research seeks to show how consumers of financial services are beginning to change from a situation of almost 'blind' loyalty and comparative inertia to one where a calculative ethic influences customers as they seek out a competitively advantageous service that is perceived as 'value for money'.[1] This change is itself further stimulated by economic deregulation and its competitive effects. What is questioned in the paper, however, is the extent to which these changes in consumption and the competitive environment are bringing distinct advantages to consumers. Although in the UK in particular product and price transparency is increasing, it is not clear that consumer inertia has declined sufficiently to secure competitive benefits. Let us summarise the changes as follows.

1. Until recently, the relationship between each customer and the provider of financial services has been characterised by loyalty, inertia and stability. The pressures for this to change are considerable and widespread.
2. Deregulation of the financial sector has become widespread throughout Europe and this further destabilises the behaviour of suppliers, distributors and consumers.
3. Companies feel a necessity to generate new strategies as a response to the changes. They are becoming more conscious of the costs and more aggressive in marketing new products and concerned with charging the customer for all their services.
4. Brand loyalty or consumer inertia is put under some pressure as competitive opportunities appear in the market-place. Consumers are encouraged to become market agents in the neo-classical economic sense: they search for information and buy the 'best' and 'cheapest' product wherever it is sold. This means abandoning the traditional one supplier pattern of consumption in financial markets.
5. Though the advantages of neo-classical competition should provide the stimulus to more efficient production and distribution as well as benefits to the consumers, the situation remains incredibly mixed because of variable responses on all sides.
6 Further stimulus may have to come from the public regulation system. New regulations designed to protect consumers have been instigated in the UK and are percolating into other European economies through the European Community (EC). However, these are not guaranteed to advance the potential benefits of competition in these markets.

The chapter is organised as follows. The second section describes some of the changes with reference primarily to the Danish situation whereupon in the third section the strategic responses of financial service companies are examined. In the fourth section there is a focus upon consumers and their reactions to the changes and in the final section there is a discussion of regulatory interventions and their impact on firm–consumer relations.

CHANGING MARKET CONDITIONS

In the 1980s the market conditions for financial service firms weakened, at least temporarily. Competition increased although simultaneously new opportunities to expand the market emerged. Both these factors forced financial firms to change their behaviour in order to secure or retain a competitive advantage. In this section, the changes in the market which represented a challenge to financial service firms are described. First, there was the general economic recession which forced companies to constrain their costs in order to maintain profitability. Second, there were new opportunities created by deregulation and competitive pressures.

The Economic Recession

The economic recession of the 1980s hit the financial sector in a way that earlier recessions had not. The first segment which stagnated in Denmark was the market for general insurance (for example, fire, accident and motor) at the beginning of the 1980s (SELFI, 1988; Price Waterhouse, 1989). This was caused largely by market saturation and intensified competition leading to an international price war. General insurance is a mature industry and there is little scope for product innovation or the discovery of new markets. By contrast, the banking industry in Denmark, as elsewhere, was not at first directly hit by the economic recession. Nonetheless, in an analysis of the French banking industry, Pastre (1985) characterised the banking industry as an institution of crisis management. Because of the recession, savings were often placed in banks instead of being invested in active production. On the other hand, there was a new demand for venture capital for new entrepreneurial business. The private saving quota increased in Denmark in the late 1980s. The greatest problem for the banks was the reduction in inflation, according to Pastre (1985), because it limited the total amount of money in the financial system and restricted the demand for financing consumption through loans. The level of inflation varies as and between different countries, but has been generally lower in the Western world in the 1980s and 1990s compared with the 1960s and 1970s.

However, the banks were hit indirectly by the recession. One effect of the recession in Denmark was the stagnation of the construction industry and, thus, stagnation in the market segment for mortgaging. With an increased number of foreclosure auctions, this generated bank and, in particular, building society losses. In the early 1990s almost every financial firm in Denmark had a deficit on the accounts. The general recession also diminished private customers' consumption of financial services except in the field of pensions. In many countries, particularly in Denmark, the recession and government economic policy also restrained wage increases. In Denmark wage earners have sought pension agreements or improvements in place of wage rises. Pensions business has therefore been a major source of growth in

Denmark as well as in other countries, in particular the UK (see Chapter 1), for financial firms. In addition, the pension funds have increased the demand for securities and contributed to an enlargement and growth of this market segment in the 1980s and 1990s.

Altogether, the economic recession has not reduced the absolute size of the total financial market, although the growth has not been so great as it was in the 1960s and early 1970s. However, the recession has produced great changes and turbulence within the market. The financial market is no longer a steady growing market with cemented segments. The wholesale market, security trade and financial business services has increased heavily and so has the market for pensions. However, the retail market (for example, bank services to private customers and general insurance) has been stagnating.

Decreased Profitability and Increased Costs

General insurance began to lose money on its primary business at the beginning of the 1980s (for Denmark see SELFI (1988) and Price Waterhouse (1989) and internationally see SEMA-METRA (1986)). Only as a result of the return on the investment of premiums paid in advance has it been possible for the insurance companies not to have deficits. The banking industry was doing well until 1980 when a decline in the profitability set in (Pastre, 1985). This has particularly hit small and medium-sized banks where the profit in some institutions became negative in the late 1980s. In Denmark, the total group of small and medium-sized banks (each with under 4 per cent of the total turnover in the sector) had a negative profit. The forecasts for the future all predict that the profitability problems will be greatest among the small and medium-sized banks (SELFI, 1988; Arthur Andersen and Co. 1989).

The poorer economic results are only partly caused by a reduced income. Some sources of income have improved and others have worsened as was demonstrated earlier. Much of the decline in profits is a function of the increased costs in the financial sector. In all the service sectors, productivity has been low by comparison with the manufacturing industry (de Bandt, 1989). However, in the financial sector, labour productivity has been extremely low. This is not because of the absence of technological development and rationalisations. The financial sector has been a leader in introducing electronic data processing and informatics as production instruments. However, until recently when the policy has been put into reverse, the savings on technology have facilitated branch and staff expansion particularly among banks (Pastre, 1985; SELFI, 1988). Thus, financial firms, in particular the banks, have suffered increased costs both for technology investments and for salaries. This can be acceptable and not a threat to profits when the market is buoyant; in a recession, however, these costs begin to take on a greater significance.

Recent regulatory changes most particularly in the UK as a result of the Financial Services Act have imposed further cost burdens in terms of administration, publicity, compliance, training and financial compensation to consumers affected by rogue or insolvent distributors. More generally, compliance with the harmonisation of regulations within the Single European Market have generated considerable costs for all EC financial services organisations. Moreover, competition within the Single European Market should result in a general reduction of prices as companies seek to compete with a standard set by the more efficient providers and countries. This in turn will create a pressure to reduce costs precisely at a time when, due to reconstruction, business expenses are rising. In discussions of the EC, costs are seen as a major problem as well as their reduction being a possible effect of the single market (*The Cost of Non-Europe in Financial Services,* 1988). Even the OECD (1987) has emphasised the high costs in the banking industry due to overstaffing.

Although wages and salaries constitute the major costs in financial services (Pastre, 1985), there are other expenses. For example, the large branch networks impose considerable costs. An indication of that is the difference in the answers in two forecast surveys made by Arthur Andersen and Co. in 1986 and 1988 (Arthur Andersen and Co., 1986, 1989). In the last survey, there was a more modified expectation of the future technology investments than in the first. Introducing new technology not only means capital expenditure for the hardware and software but also increased costs for training employees in its use and making good the general disturbance on the work process.

New Opportunities

As in the service sector generally, there are in the financial services many opportunities for product innovation and for expanding the total market (for example, Gershuny and Miles, 1983; Fifield, 1989). For example, in the life insurance industry the development of unit-linked products had a major growth impact as these could more easily be sold for their potential as investment or capital accumulation plans rather that as mere life insurance (Knights, 1988; Knights and Willmott, 1993). New financial instruments are continuously being developed to serve a growing sophisticated consumer and to secure a strategic advantage in increasingly competitive markets. Credit cards, debit cards, personal equity plans and low cost and low start mortgage endowments are just a few of the innovations in product development that have occurred over the last two decades.

The Danish projects (SELFI, 1988; Sundbo, 1991a, 1992, 1996) conducted interviews with representatives from financial service firms who provided examples of several market areas where product innovations have been or could be accomplished. However, the new opportunities are not always easy to exploit, not least because their existence may not be obvious. Changes in the market are occurring so quickly that it is not easy for companies to keep pace. There are also obstacles stemming from the conservative and paternalistic tradition and culture internal to financial services companies (Kerfoot and Knights, 1993). They have a limited experience of product innovation and entrepreneurship (cf. Pinchot, 1985). Thus, while the general dynamic for financial services is one of change and new opportunities, the conservative and previously complacent nature of the industry creates several problems in terms of responding to the new environment. Survival in increasingly competitive markets may require companies to become less risk aversive so as to exploit the opportunities for new profitable developments rather than to continue merely with defensive cost reduction strategies (Sundbo, 1992).

FIRM RESPONSES: THE POTENTIAL OF STRATEGIC MANAGEMENT

Financial firms have been forced to react to the changed market situation by exploring new markets, distribution channels and advancing corporate and business strategies that are appropriate.

A part of these strategies is to seek to distribute financial services in ways similar to that of manufacturers. This means standardising products where price or discounts, not extra services, is the competition factor. Generally, in the service literature it has been assumed that services are very unique kinds of products connected with free extra services or 'peripheral services' (Gronroos, 1983, 1990; Norman, 1991). There is, however, a limited literature discussing how services can be produced and sold like manufacturing products (see Levitt, 1972; Sundbo, 1991b, 1994). However, the strategies cannot follow the 'commodity line' precisely. Companies must try to maintain traditional distribution systems and extend the degree of targeting through market segmentation (see Chapter 8) and by developing a commitment on the part of customers to one-stop shopping. We now turn to an examination of the new strategies within Danish retail banks and insurance companies.

Adapting to a Strategic Role

The financial sector has enjoyed a long period of stable growth until comparatively recently partly because of consumer inertia and limited competition. This stability has been undermined of late as a result of economic deregulation and an intensification of competition, both domestic and international, which has threatened the boundaries within and between the different businesses (for example, banks, insurance companies and credit institutions). While previously the financial sector could be compared to the Roman patron–client relationship or be characterised as paternalistic with clients as well as staff, there is now far more concern to extend commercial power beyond opinion polls and to stimulate staff to be entrepreneurial and business seeking. One difficulty arising from the new approach is the image of trustworthiness. For example, in public opinion polls, banks were always placed as some of the most trustful institutions (over the Post Office, telephone companies and so on) in the mid-1980s in Denmark and elsewhere. In addition, insurance companies have a reasonably favourable image with the general public. In most financial centres including Denmark, the media invariably draw on 'experts' from the banks rather than independent academics to comment on national and international economic issues. This reflects a questionable belief that financial firms operate as quasi-independent (public) institutions rather than as bodies with a specific sectoral interest.

This belief stems partly from the fact that the central bank in most countries is a quasi-public institution established to regulate the financial markets for the nation as a whole. It is also reinforced by academic analyses which predominantly focus on the macro-economic role of the banks in the economic system (Cooper and Fraser, 1984; Gart, 1989) rather than on their commercial concerns of pursuing profitable exchanges (cf. Ingham, 1984).

In the light of the changing conditions of operation in which companies are forced to act even more as market-oriented business firms, media and academic treatments of financial institutions as quasi-public and of primarily macro-economic importance are becoming less valid.

A number of case studies in insurance companies and banks in Denmark (Sundbo, 1991a, 1992, 1996) show that business strategies within financial companies are more open and adaptive (cf. Quinn, 1980; Chaffee, 1985) than might be expected, given their formal bureaucratic nature. This seems to be a result of the absence of a tradition of strategic competition in the financial sector. Management therefore have little experience of formulating and implementing corporate and business strategies. Given the dynamic and uncertain nature of the market, this may be no bad thing since it enables companies to be more responsive than would ordinarily be the case in a machine bureaucracy (Mintzberg, 1979).

A major purpose behind most strategies of financial companies is to increase profitability either by cutting costs or building new markets. A common strategy for banks and mortgage corporations is to develop what are called bancassurance or allfinanz where there is an integration of banking and insurance activities and the latter marketed and sold to bank customers. Not all financial institutions have the capacity to integrate these activities fully so there is considerable variation in the type of model adopted (Knights *et al.*, 1993). We now discuss the various strategies in more detail. The criteria that we have adapted for selecting which elements to focus attention upon is their impact on consumers. Those which we consider of importance to consumers are as follows: (1) the cross-industrial products, mergers and cooperations across the borders of the traditional financial industry boundaries, (2) self-service as a production concept, (3) market segmentation and (4) a new price setting system.

FINANCIAL SERVICE STRATEGIES AND THEIR IMPACT ON CONSUMERS

New Cross-industrial Products and Multi-industrial Firms

In Denmark, there has been an increasing level of cross-integration between different parts of the sector involving mergers and strategic alliances (Ministry of Industry, 1987; SELFI, 1988). It began with insurance companies marketing banking services, either inside the insurance company or by establishing or purchasing a bank. However, banks, other financial service firms and even building societies are following the trend as they are affected by increasing competition and reduced margins. The examples are many. In the late 1980s the third largest insurance company (Topsikring) bought up a middle-sized Danish bank. The largest bank (Den Danske Bank) and the largest insurance company (Hafnia) formed an agreement where the bank sells insurances as a retailer and the insurance company remains the producer. These kind of arrangements generally known as bancassurance are advancing across the whole of Europe as banks are looking for new fee-earning products to distribute and insurance companies are searching for new distribution outlets and, in particular, those (for example, banks and building societies) that have a ready supply of potential clients. In the UK, however, the development has taken place primarily through banks creating their own insurance companies only among the building societies have cooperative arrangements or joint ventures developed with insurance companies. However, even here the larger building societies have established their own insurance companies in the same way as the banks. In addition, in Denmark a network of provincial banks created their own building society in 1991 and all the Danish building societies and most insurance companies today own estate agencies. This latter development also took place in the UK although a number of large institutions (for example, Prudential Assurance and Abbey National Building Society) have divested themselves of the estate agency chains because of huge losses following the collapse of the domestic housing market. In Denmark, insurance companies have also purchased travel agencies, salvage corps, automobile repair firms and so on.

One major idea underlying cross-industry mergers is the financial supermarket which has been much discussed in the international literature (for example, Arthur Andersen and Co., 1986, 1989; Muldur and Pastre, 1987; Gart, 1989). Although bancassurance is widespread (albeit unevenly between countries), the full-scale financial supermarket is slow to develop. A central purpose of these mergers is to reduce costs. As wages typically constitute 70 to 80 per cent of the expenses, this must logically mean reductions in the number of employees. In addition, it is believed that there is an oversupply in retail banking (OECD, 1987; Price Waterhouse, 1989) in all countries. Consequently, most banks have begun a programme of branch closures and staff redundancies and this has been easier to accomplish where mergers have taken place since the overcapacity is then made highly visible. So, for example, the merger of the two largest Danish banks (Den Danske Bank and Handelsbanken) in 1990 was followed by a statement from the general manager that the branches and staff numbers should be reduced by 10 to 20 per cent within two years. And this policy seems to have been followed.

New entrepreneurial firms offering specialist financial services have also emerged in Denmark. These new services are of a non-traditional nature and are disapproved of by the establishment in the financial sector partly because of the risks associated with them but also because they represent a competitive threat to the larger institutions. These new products are usually first introduced on the wholesale market and then increasingly to private customers. In the early part of the 1980s, products designed to reduce the taxes of wealthy citizens were introduced. More recently, products that relate to stock market investment and other dealings for mass market consumption have emerged. In Denmark the established banks and insurance companies have retaliated by setting up a series of new independent advisory firms similar to those available in the US and UK. This is part of the service society development (Gershuny and Miles, 1983; Riddle, 1986; Channon, 1987), where consumers are predicted to spend an increasing part of their income on services that they have not previously used (for example, investment advice) or which once were previously available free of charge (for example, credit cards and cheque accounts).

This has created new opportunities for private customers to improve their financial position both from investments and from more optimum purchases of financial service products. However, in their enthusiasm to sell new financial products such as unit trusts, advisers have not always stressed the risk or downside to consumers and sudden stock market crashes have left many of the new investors resistant to continuing their consumption of risky investment products. This erosion of confidence in equity-linked savings and investments was particularly marked after the stock market crash of 1987.

Self-service as a Production Concept

As already indicated, innovation in financial services has often just taken the form of introducing new products but there have also been several attempts to emulate the retail industry in such things as self-service distribution systems, direct mail and the use of special offers and free gift stimulants to consumption. In the early phase of the new competitive environment, product innovation was seen as the major weapon for securing strategic advantage. Consequently, considerable investments particularly in terms of information technology (IT) systems work have gone into product 'innovation' only for companies to find that the innovations are speedily emulated. So, for example, the innovations over the last few years such as credit cards, debit cards, smart cards, insurance product combinations and mortgage links are offered by almost all financial services companies. Another area where innovations have taken place is in service, in particular since this is now seen to be where strategic advantages can be secured that are not so easily copied.

The use of IT has always been central to certain aspects of service as it can readily increase the speed and efficiency of processing and provide novel means of distributing products. Self-service is clearly one of the latter which is particularly cost-effective. In money transmission, the automated teller machine (ATM) has been highly successful although there have been disputes about the levels of use required for profitability (Smith and Wield, 1988) and problems associated with the absence of the customers from the branches who would otherwise be available for selling additional products. The full range of banking facilities are also available through personal computers but have not generally been adopted on a mass scale largely, one suspects, because the cost is primarily borne by the consumer who has become accustomed to 'free' banking. As yet, apart from motor policies, insurance products are not readily distributed through IT systems largely because of consumer inertia with respect to these. However, there are examples of telephone sales distribution using IT to target customers speedily and efficiently through 'relational marketing' particularly in the field of health and medical insurance. In addition, IT expert systems can be applied to underwriting and other aspects of product design in insurance to ensure profitability and possible more customised products. The value of self-service to the producer is clearly one of passing on the costs of distribution directly to the consumer, as has occurred in other parts of retailing. The problem for the producers, however, is that there is a greater degree of consumer inertia in the field of financial services than in other retail areas. Consumers are generally satisfied with self-service where the benefit is convenience (for example, the availability of cash at any time of the day) and speed of delivery. Self-service can enable consumers to conduct their business in shops, in town centres and in their home at every hour of the day. The self-service system also allows the customer to explore the market – the prices and conditions of products – without the hassle of a sales clerk seeking to influence their decisions. In the Danish SELFI (1988) project, many interviewees declared that they preferred to study the products themselves rather than have a bank clerk or insurance agent as an adviser. They felt more free in that situation. The problem for the producers though, is that the inertia factor will frequently limit the number of sales except for those products where legal compulsion requires them to be purchased (for example, motor insurance).

Several surveys have predicted that the self-service system will result in cheaper and better financial services to customers (Arthur Andersen and Co., 1986; Batelle, 1986; FAST, 1986; Muldur and Pastre, 1987; SELFI, 1988). Earlier experience from the introduction of new technology and self-service or self-producing systems – foremost from the wholesale market (automated trading system at the stock exchange, automated stock-trade systems at the stockbrokers and so on) – show that the number of transactions increases exponentially (OTA, 1984). While there has been an increase in the use of self-service, the development has not been as fast as predicted. Interviews in Danish banks indicate that one explanation is the feeling that banks could become anonymous to customers if the delivery of services is exclusively through distribution systems. On the other hand, it has been claimed by some of the banks in the UK that self-service technologies 'free up' staff in the branches to sell additional fee-earning products such as insurance and investment. Bancassurance networks in the UK have begun to increase the number of staff responsible for sales and are devising various techniques for attracting targeted customers to come into the bank for the purposes of selling them insurance-related products. Accordingly, self-service on routine money transmission exchanges enables the banks to become more productive in the targeting of individuals and groups with new profitable products.

Market Segmentation

To increase profit and reduce costs, many financial firms in Denmark have adopted the focus strategy of Porter (1980) where they concentrate on particular groups of customers. One objective is for the banks and insurance companies to secure 'one-stop' shopping where a customer buys all their products from one provider. This limits the costs of administration and enables companies to earn income on additional services (for example, fees on family budgeting in combination with a bank account) to counteract loss-making activities (for example, standard bank accounts with numerous transactions and low balances). In the Danish study there have been indications that the banks would prefer to reduce the number of accounts which are exclusively money transmission on low balances. Although financial firms do not publish their strategy and, in particular, such sensitive parts of it, a few years ago this strategy was leaked out from one of the savings banks to the press. Internally, low balance money transmission customers were called 'time robbers' and bank employees were advised to get rid of them as customers in their branch.

New Price Setting System: Fees and Double Sales Strategy

In looking for new income, in Denmark, at least, the banks have begun to charge for peripheral or extra services. Although formerly free, the general manager of the largest bank predicts that, in the future, bank charges will be a more important source of income than interest on loans to retail banks. A number of banks in the UK (for example, Barclays Bank and Royal Bank of Scotland) have offered new bank accounts with a range of extra services and discounts on products but incorporating a monthly fixed charge on the account.

The fee system could contribute to the establishment of a more market-orientated system since there is a greater degree of price transparency through which consumers may assess comparative services. The paradox, however, is that 'free' banking services arose largely as a result of competition for retail customers between the banks and even though low balance–high transaction accounts may be unprofitable, it is often these types of customers who are potentially profitable clients for fee-based services. The banks, therefore, do not want to lose customers or their loyalty by imposing charges on services that have previously been free. Nonetheless, in the UK, credit card charges were recently added with little loss of custom. However, this is probably because all the larger credit card companies imposed similar charges or declared they would do so at about the same time and consumer inertia, plus uncleared balances, prevented a mass departure from credit card contracts. However, one of the smaller banks – the Cooperative Bank – benefited substantially at this time by offering a credit card that would be free for life.

A recent development that has sought to combine market segmentation and discounting strategies can help to encourage the 'one-stop' shopping practice within financial services. In short, the provider will segment the market of existing customers and identify particular needs and then offer discounts for these products. It is possible that other more specialist products are still distributed with better profit margins once customers have become loyal. Whether or not this is ethical, it is a practice in some Danish banks according to our research. Some banks in the UK (for example, the TSB) are also encouraging family loyalty by offering the highest rates of interest on deposits to all family members where at least one of them is entitled to such because of the size of his or her bank balance.

Summary

What we have seen from this analysis is that the old 'paternalistic' mutual relationship between financial firms and customers has begun to break down, to be displaced by market relations. Financial firms have, therefore, had to become more competitive and cost orientated. This could result in a greater degree of price and quality competition giving some advantages to consumers. This has not generally occurred because of various attempts to lock customers into a range of products through discount and product tie policies (for a criticism of this practice in the UK, see Eaglesham (1992)). The full impact of market competition has, therefore, been restrained by these policies together with the lack of transparency with regard to prices, charges and product complexity. Yet even if there were none of these obstacles, it is not clear that consumers would act as 'rational' market agents.

CONSUMER RESPONSES

On the whole, customers in financial services are passive rather than active buyers of many of the products but, in particular, those such as life assurance, pensions and investments which are seen as the most profitable means of expanding bank business (Knights *et al.*, 1993). One consequence of the sales-oriented nature of these products is that few consumers actively seek knowledge of comparable products but even when they do, the complexity of products, benefits and charges make such comparisons extremely difficult. The inertia factor also plays a part in customer retention, particularly in the field of banking where, in the UK, there have been many complaints about the service. One of the reasons for this customer inertia, however, is the belief that the banks are all fairly similar and that changing one's bank account would hardly be worth the effort, particularly since it also involves having to identify and rearrange all automatic transfer payments.

Only where products are bought as single non-renewable (for example, travel insurance) contracts or where, because of legal compulsion (for example, motor insurance) price sensitivity prevails is there much activity in the market, but even here the intermediary (that is, the broker) has often been the person stimulating the change of provider. In the UK and Denmark this has changed recently as a result of Direct Line offering competitive motor insurance and other products over the phone. Even in banking change has begun to occur as new innovative developments such as telephone banking (for example, First Direct in the UK) or computer banking (for example, Bank of Scotland in the UK) are attracting customers away from traditional banking arrangements. This is also occurring in Denmark partly as a result of a series of mergers amongst the larger banks. As many as 200000 customers moved their bank accounts in 1990 and this is developing quite rapidly. Foreign competition, however, has been of virtually no significance in the retail market as customers seem not to trust non-national banks (Price Waterhouse, 1989).

REGULATORY FRAMEWORKS

Economic deregulation has been a major feature of Western politics in the 1980s and 1990s (Cooper and Fraser, 1984; Muldur and Pastre, 1987) but in the field of financial services it has been accompanied by a series of new regulations, particularly in the UK where the Financial Services Act has been designed to curtail the excesses of life insurance and associated sales activities. At the same time, the EC is seeking to harmonise the rules between states so as to secure a single market in financial services. A more market-orientated distribution system within financial services demands some degree of protection for consumers, particularly since the general public are often ignorant of the products and vulnerable to manipulation and exploitation by sophisticated sales staff.

Re-regulation and the Consumer

There have been two shifts in the regulation system. First, the emphasis has moved from the supplier to the consumer side. Financial firms continue to be limited in their activities by traditional state departments which regulate the sector. However, regulation cannot force them to develop new products or become more competitive. A common development has been to try and provide more protection and greater transparency for the consumer. Thus, for example, most countries have introduced an ombudsman system for processing consumer complaints against the companies. This has generally meant a redistribution of regulatory responsibility away from formal state institutions and towards quasi-governmental bodies or industry-based self-regulatory organisations (SROs). With respect to the latter, the UK is the most advanced having established SROs for each of the main financial activities and distinctive distribution channels.

In Denmark, the focus in the regulation policy has changed from the governmental financial regulation department to an independent consumer ombudsman. The consumer ombudsman has been very active in removing the barriers to a 'free' market in financial services. Primarily he has fought the blurring of fees and the strategy of selling tied products which are not fully transparent. For example, in 1991 he forced the banks into an agreement wherein they promised to (1) notify each customer, every time a fee is created or changed, at least one month in advance and (2) drop the 'total customer' principle. However, there is still doubt about whether this will generate full transparency and encourage more market-based transactions.

Of course, the ombudsman does not have equivalent power to a governmental institution. Nonetheless, the ombudsman can take legal proceedings against banks, insurance companies and other business firms. In addition, the Consumers Association has become increasingly involved in this field in both Denmark and the UK and has been prepared to take up consumer complaints and press the regulators for tighter control (Knights *et al.*, 1993).

In terms of regulation at the point of consumption, the UK has taken the lead in Europe with the introduction of the Financial Services Act and a complex system of self-regulation by the industry. While the system continues to be on probation and is continually threatened by new state regulation, it has uncovered numerous financial scandals that may well have passed unnoticed prior to self-regulation. Moreover, the principle of financial compensation for consumers badly advised is now embedded in institutional practice even when it goes well beyond the legal requirements. Although self-regulation in the UK is far from perfect because of agency capture and may indeed eventually collapse in favour of the US model of state control, it currently serves as a model for the rest of Europe where regulation at the point of consumption is more limited.

Another consequence of the increasing interest in this field is that the media has become more interested in the relationship between customer and firm in the financial sector. The parliamentary law-regulation system has to some extent been replaced by a public system for business ethic setting where the media seek to set the moral standards. The media has taken up a series of mortgage cases on behalf of both private and industrial clients where some degree of malpractice or unethical behaviour has been involved.

CONCLUSION

The financial services are in a process of transition from a traditional paternalism toward more market-orientated and competitive strategies (Kerfoot and Knights, 1993). At present, however, competition is not having the effect of rendering products and prices transparent. Consumers, therefore, do not necessarily benefit any more than they did from the system where they were tied to a single provider through inertia and ignorance. While governments are encouraging an increase in consumer knowledge and discernment, many other factors obstruct this development. Two obstacles constrain the empowerment of consumers. First is the tendency for new and increasingly complex products to proliferate in ways that limit or prevent their transparency. Second and relatedly, is the continuation of passivity and inertia on the part of consumers. These clearly reinforce one another and deflect the potential benefits to consumers that could be derived from the marketisation and re-regulation of financial services. The question remains as to whether the additional impetus of the Single European Market for financial services will stimulate the kind of competition that results in benefits to consumers and to what extent pressures for consumer protection will secure more universal standards throughout the EC.

ACKNOWLEDGEMENT

David Knights assisted the author by adding in some comparisons with the UK.

Note

1. This chapter could be seen as the alter ego of Chris Grey's 'Suburban Subjects: Financial Services and the New Right' (Chapter 3) since it suggests that the regulatory changes in financial services in recent years, dramatic though they are, have not provided the conditions whereby consumers can exercise their rationality effectively in pursuit of their (suburban) economic self-interests, while recognising that consumers are being transformed into subjects who would think it 'normal' or obligatory to behave in such a way if only the conditions allowed it. This chapter in contrast to Grey, does not question the moral implications of the effects or the subjectivity of consumerism and competition in this field.

References

Arthur Andersen and Co. (1986) *The Decade of Change* (London: Lafferty).

Arthur Andersen and Co. (1989) *European Capital Market. A Strategic Forecast* (London: Lafferty).

Batelle (1986) *ATM's and Cash Dispensers; an International Survey and Analysis* (London: Batelle).

Chaffee, E. (1985) 'Three Models of Strategy', *Management Review*, vol. 10, no. 1, pp. 89–98.

Channon, D. (1987) *The Service Industries, Strategy, Structure and Financial Performance* (London: Macmillan).

Cooper, K. and Fraser, R. (1984) *Banking, Deregulation and the New Competition in Financial Services* (Cambridge, Mass.).

de Bandt, J. (1989) 'Can we Measure Productivity in Service Activities?', in A. Bressland and N. Kalypso (eds), *Strategic Trends in Services* (New York: Ballinger).

Eaglesham, J. (1992) 'Product Tie-Ins and Property Loans', *Consumer Policy Review*, vol. 2, no. 4.

EEC (1986) *Technical Tools for New Services*, FAST report No. 68 (Bruxelles: EEC).

EEC (1988) *The Cost of Non-Europe in Financial Services*, vol. 9 (Bruxelles: EEC).

Fifield, P. (1989) 'Consumer Financial Services', in P. Jones (ed.), *Service Industries* (London: Pitman), pp. 32–72.

Gart, A. (1989) *An Analysis of the New Financial Institutions* (New York: Quorum).

Gershuny, J. and Miles, I. (1983) *The New Service Economy* (London: Pinter).

Gronroos, C. (1983) *Strategic Management and Marketing in the Service Sector* (Cambridge, Mass.: Marketing Science Institute).

Gronroos, C. (1990) *Service Management and Marketing: Managing the Moments of Truth in Service Competition* (Lexington: Lexington Books).

Ingham, G. (1984) *Capitalism Divided? The City and Industry in British Social Development* (London: Macmillan).

Kerfoot, D. and Knights, D. (1993) 'Management, Masculinity and Manipulation: from Paternalism to Corporate Strategy in Financial Services', *Journal of Management Studies*, pp. 659–79.

Knights, D. (1988) 'Risk, Financial Self-discipline and Commodity Relations', *Advances in Public Interest in Accounting*, vol. 2, pp. 47–69.

Knights, D., Morgan, G. and Sturdy, A. (1993) 'Quality for the Consumer in Bancassurance?', *Consumer Policy Review*, vol 3, no. 4, pp. 232–40.

Knights, D. and Willmott, H. (1993) '"Its a Very Foreign Discipline" the Genesis of Expenses Control in a Mutual Life Insurance Company', *British Journal of Management*, vol. 4, no. 1, p. 1–18.

Levitt, T. (1972) 'Production-line Approach to Service', *Harvard Business Review*, vol. 49, pp. 41–2.

Ministry of Industry (Industriministeriet) (1987) *Brancheglidning i den Finansielle Sektor (Sectorial Sliding in the Financial Sector)* (Kobenhavn).

Mintzberg, H. (1979) *The Structuring of Organizations* (Englewood Cliffs: Prentice-Hall).

Muldur, U. and Pastre, O. (1987) *Europe and the Future of Financial Services* (London: Lafferty).

Norman R. (1991) *Service Management* (London: John Wiley).

OECD (1987) *Economic Surveys 1986–87. Denmark 1989* (Paris: OECD).

OTA (Office of Technology Assessment) (1984) *Effects of Information Technology on Financial Services System* (Washington: OTA).

Pastre, O. (1985) *La Modernisation des Banques Francaises* (Paris: La documentation Francaise).

Pinchot, G. (1985) *Intrapreneuring* (New York: Harper & Row).

Porter, M. (1980) *Competitive Strategy* (New York: Macmillan).

Price Waterhouse (1989) *Europa–Danmark. En Handbog for den Finansielle Sektor om det Indre Marked (Europe–Denmark. A Manual for the Financial Sector on the Single Market)* (Kobenhavn: Schultz).

Quinn, J. (1980) *Strategies for Change* (Homewood: Irwin).

Riddle, D. (1986) *Service Led Growth* (New York: Praeger).

SELFI (Project on Self Service in the Finance Industry) (1988) *Teknologivurdering af-Selvgetjeningsteknologien i Finanssektoren (Assessment on Self Service Technology in the Finance Industry)* (Roskilde: SELFI).

SEMA-METRA (1986) *Services to the Manufacturing Sector. A Long Term Investigation* (Bruxelles: EEC).

Smith, S.L. and Wield, D. (1988) 'New Technology and Bank Work: Banking on IT as an Organisational Technology', in L. Harris (ed.), *New Perspectives on the Financial System* (London: Croom Helm).

Sundbo, J. (1990) 'Innovation Organisation in Service Firms', in *Proceedings from International Conference on Technology Transfer and Innovation in Mixed Economies* (Trondheim).

Sundbo, J. (1991a) 'The Tied Entrepreneur', paper to the *RENT V conference*, Vaxjo.

Sundbo, J. (1991b) 'Market Development and Production Organization in the Financial Service Firms of the 1990s', *Scandinavian Journal of Management*, vol 7, no. 2, pp. 95–110.

Sundbo, J. (1992) 'Innovationsorganisation i Service' ('Innovation Organization in Service'), unpublished thesis, Roskilde University.

Sundbo, J. (1994) 'Modulization of Service Production', *Scandinavian Journal of Management*, vol. 10, no. 3, pp. 245–66.

Sundbo, J. (1996) 'The Balancing of Empowerment', *Technovation*, vol. 16, no. 8, pp. 397–409.

Sundbo, J. (1997) 'Management of Innovation in Services', *The Service Industries Journal*, vol. 17, no. 3, in press.

7 Stability or Transformation of Employment Relations in German Banking

MICHAEL MULLER

In comparison to Anglo-Saxon countries the German financial system is unique. Table 7.1 compares the main features of the financial systems in Germany, the UK and the US. This illustrates that the structure of the financial system and the role of banks are different in Germany. In the market-based UK and US financial systems, financial markets play a major role. They are highly developed. There is a large number of publically listed firms, options and futures exchanges are very liquid and widely used and the market for corporate control is relatively open. Another major feature is the traditional segmentation between commercial banking, investment banking and trust fund functions in the UK and US. There is also a relatively weak long-term relationship between the banks and firms.

TABLE 7.1 *A comparison of the German with the UK and US financial systems*

	Germany	UK/US
Type of financial system	Bank based	Market based
Development of financial markets	Underdeveloped	Highly Developed
Number of publically listed firms	Small	Large
Market for corporate control	Closed	Open
Types of services provided by banks	Universal banks	Segmentation of banks
Long-term relationship between banks and firms	Strong	Weak

SOURCES   Allen and Gale (1995) and Vitols (1995b, c).

In contrast to the UK and the US, Germany has a bank-based system in which intermediaries predominate. The financial markets are underdeveloped. There is only a relatively small number of publically listed firms in Germany. The market for corporate control is relatively closed, as banks are not only key shareholders in many joint-stock corporations, but also exercise a proxy vote for small shareholders. Furthermore, as shareholders controlling a

135

quarter of the voting stock can often block outside proposals, hostile takeover attempts are rare (Vitols, 1995c). Another difference is that there are close links between the banks and companies in Germany. Although there is a small number of banks that provide a narrow range of services, almost all German banks are universal banks. These banks provide all types of banking services including taking deposits, granting loans and mortgages and investing directly in securities (Allen and Gale, 1995).

THE GERMAN BANKING SYSTEM

German banks are usually categorised according to the sector to which they belong. The sector 'commercial banks', which accounts for almost one-third of the total banking sector assets, is dominated by the three major banks: the Deutsche Bank, Dresdner Bank and Commerzbank. It also includes 195 regional banks, 65 subsidiaries of foreign banks and 64 private banks. The public 'savings bank' sector consists of 624 savings banks owned by local authorities. At the regional level are 12 state banks (Landesbanken) which are owned by the federal states and regional public savings bank associations. The top tier consists of the national savings bank organisation. The public savings bank sector is the most important banking sector in terms of total assets accounting for 38 per cent of the banking assets. The 'cooperative bank' sector is the third largest with 15 per cent of total assets. Similar to savings banks it has a three tier structure with 2591 local cooperative banks, three regional cooperative banks and a central cooperative bank (Deutsche Bundesbank, 1996, pp. 106–7). In contrast to commercial banks, savings banks are publically owned and the depositors of cooperative banks are the shareholders. A further difference is that traditionally there is hardly any competition within the public savings bank and the cooperative bank sector, whereas commercial banks are in competition with each other and the other two groups (Vitols, 1995b).

Since the early 1980s, most Organization for Economic Cooperation and Development (OECD) countries have deregulated and liberalised financial markets. As a result, the banking systems have been restructured, often as the result of a financial crisis. In the US, for example, the competition for banks intensified after the liberalisation and deregulation of the financial service markets in the 1980s. This resulted in a significant 'bank disintermediation' Between 1980 and 1990 the 'bank intermediation ratio', that is the share of total assets of all financial institutions held by banks, sunk from 0.52 to 0.3 (Schröder Münchmeyer Hengst & Co., 1996). As a consequence a crisis of the US banking system developed and the banks had to reposition themselves strategically, merge or even close.

In contrast with the US and other countries there has so far hardly been any bank disintermediation in Germany. The bank intermediation ratio sunk only modestly from 0.84 in 1975 to 0.80 in 1985 and 0.75 in 1995 (monthly reports of the Deutsche Bundesbank). More detailed data about bank disintermediation is provided in Table 7.2. It gives an overview of the longitudinal development of the liabilities of non-financial companies in Germany. This shows that although equity capital has become more important over the last decade, bank credits are still the primary source of finance for German firms. There has also been no securitisation, that is the replacement of bank credits with bonds, such as happened in the US.

TABLE 7.2   *Development of non-financial company sector liabilities (housing companies excluded)*

	1975	1985	1995
Bonds	4.4	2.8	3.0
Shares in circulation	11.1	8.7	26.9
Short-term bank credits	20.3	18.9	15.3
Longer-term bank credits	35.4	31.3	31.1
Insurance company loans	3.8	4.2	2.3
Other liabilities	25.0	34.1	21.4
Total	100.0	100.0	100.0

SOURCE   Monthly reports (*Monatsberichte*) of the Deutsche Bundesbank.

Similar to the largest net debtor, the non-financial company sector, there has also been no radical disintermediation of banks in regard to the household sector, the largest net saver. Table 7.3 shows into which financial assets German households have channelled their savings. These data reveal the growing importance of insurance companies and bonds as savings channels. The loss of the market share by banks, however, is not as dramatic as it looks. Bank bonds account for more than 50 per cent of all bonds. Insurance companies deposit almost half of their assets with banks and a further quarter in bonds. Furthermore, whereas in the UK only approximately 20 per cent of investment certificates are sold by banks, in Germany these are 80 per cent. In addition, foreign investment funds only control a small part of the German market and almost all German investment funds are owned by banks (*Frankfurter Allgemeine Zeitung*, 1994, p. 28).

The relative stability of the German banking system in comparison to those of other countries is also shown by two other indicators. Firstly, whereas the profits of commercial banks in the UK and the US have fluctuated widely over the last decade, they have been relatively stable in Germany (see Table 7.4). German banks still earn approximately 80 per cent of their revenues from lending and other interest-based activities and only approximately 20 per cent from fee-based business (monthly reports of the Deutsche Bundesbank). In contrast, US banks generate more than 40 per cent of their revenues from fee-based activities (Keltner, 1995, p. 48).

TABLE 7.3   *Development of household sector savings channels*

	1975	1985	1995
Banks	59.8	48.4	40.0
Building societies	8.6	5.8	3.3
Insurance companies	16.2	20.3	21.3
Bonds	11.9	15.6	15.9
Investment certificates			7.6
Shares	3.3	2.0	5.3
Other assets	0.2	7.9	6.6
Total	100.0	100.0	100.0

SOURCE   Monthly reports (*Monatsberichte*) of the Deutsche Bundesbank.

TABLE 7.4   *Profit after tax as a percentage of the average balance sheet total of commercial banks in Germany, the UK and the US*

Year	Germany	UK	US
1985	0.38	0.60	0.69
1986	0.38	0.76	0.62
1987	0.29	0.06	0.08
1988	0.33	0.93	0.71
1989	0.32	0.06	0.47
1990	0.34	0.38	0.47
1991	0.30	0.23	0.51
1992	0.22	0.14	0.91
1993	0.33	0.48	1.20
1994	0.35	0.76	1.15

SOURCE   OECD (1996).

Secondly, until 1993 employment increased in the German commercial banks (see Table 7.5). This is different in the US and the UK. Over the last decade, the number of bank employees has been significantly reduced in the US and with a time lag even more in the UK.

TABLE 7.5   *Longitudinal development of employee numbers in commercial banks in West Germany, the UK and the US (1985=100)*

Year	Germany	UK	US
1985	100.0	100.0	100.0
1986	103.9	102.9	100.0
1987	105.5	110.2	99.0
1988	104.6	118.4	97.9
1989	104.6	121.8	98.1
1990	107.1	121.0	97.1
1991	109.2	117.6	95.3
1992	111.9	118.0	94.7
1993	111.3	109.3	95.6
1994	110.8	105.7	95.1

SOURCES   OECD (1996), Arbeitgeberverband des privaten Bankgewerbes, and the author's own calculations.

Various reasons are given for the relative stability of the German banking system. Firstly, the universal bank system has enabled the German banks not only to diversify the risks, but also to accommodate market changes. For example, the banks have reacted to the shift from traditional low interest deposit accounts to other forms of saving by offering more attractive alternatives such as bancassurance products, bank bonds and investment certificates (D'Alessio and Oberbeck, 1997). Secondly, over the last decade, the German banks have not abandoned the principle of customer cultivation. Instead of competing with a low cost volume-oriented strategy as banks in the US do, the German banks have tied their customers with a relationship-oriented strategy (Keltner, 1995). Thirdly, German banking regulations set clear quantitative standards. These prescribe, for example, minimum liquidity requirements and a diversification of risk. As competing financial institutions are even more regulated, it is difficult for capital to flow to less regulated sectors (Vitols, 1995a, pp. 10–12). Fourthly, German banks have access to long-term refinancing mechanisms that offer stable interest rates such as long-term customer savings and bank bonds. This has made it possible for them to avoid interest rate and liquidity risks (Vitols, 1995a, pp. 13–14). Fifthly, more than 50 per cent of the total banking assets are accounted for by the public savings bank and the cooperative bank sectors. Both have a federalist structure which enables group banks to cooperate horizontally with each other and vertically with their regional and national institutions. The latter have a regulatory function, help with liquidity management, refinance long-term loans and offer regional and national training courses and facilities (Vitols, 1995a, pp. 14–16). Finally, over the last decade there has been no significant deregulation of the German banking system that could have upset the financial system. In contrast to the US, where the interest ceilings on deposits were only removed in the 1980s, the interest rates in Germany were deregulated in the 1960s. Nevertheless, current attempts to reform the German financial system which aim to bring it more in line with Anglo-Saxon standards could increase its volatility. For instance, the introduction of new financial investment instruments could threaten long-term refinancing mechanisms (Vitols, 1995a, p. 18).

CHANGES IN GERMAN BANKING

Some changes in German banking can already be observed. Firstly, there is growing competition from non-banks. Table 7.3 shows that insurance companies have increased their share of household savings at the expense of banks and that bonds and investment certificates have grown in importance. Although some of these savings are channelled back into the banks, their refinancing costs have grown as a result of these developments. One reaction of the German banks to this trend has been to enter the insurance market with bancassurance strategies. Secondly, there is growing competition between the banks. As a result they compete with new products that offer higher interest rates such as money market funds or offer cheaper services such as direct banking. Thirdly, the liberalisation of the European banking market and the globalisation of financial markets has made it easier for foreign banks to establish a foothold in the German market. US investment banks in particular have become major competitors for German banks. The direct investment of leading German banks such as Deutsche Bank and Dresdner Bank in the UK and the US explicitly aims to strengthen their position in the markets for corporate banking and institutional investment (Schröder Münchmeyer Hengst & Co., 1996). As a result of all these developments, the margins in the core banking business are becoming smaller. At the same time there is greater pressure on the banks to provide a high return of equity and dividends (Fisher, 1996).

The concept of 'lean banking' has been prescribed as a solution to the above pressures. In Germany and other European countries lean banking is promoted by the US consultants McKinsey. Among the prescriptions are a more marketing- and sales-oriented approach to business, a bancassurance strategy, a segmentation of customers, a standardisation of products, the use of sophisticated technologies, the introduction of profit centres, outsourcing of service functions and performance-related pay (Bierer et al., 1992; Leichtful and Mattern, 1994). Some of the leading German banks such as Bayerische Hypotheken- und Wechselbank (Hypo Bank), Commerzbank and Deutsche Bank have been advised by McKinsey about the introduction of lean banking prescriptions. In addition, other consultants promote similar concepts under different labels (Sperling, 1996).

Since the early 1990s, German banks have implemented lean banking elements. By 1990, Deutsche Bank had already established business divisions with their own profit targets and operational autonomy. Since then several other major German banks have introduced a divisional structure and profit centres. They are also increasingly using electronic information technology (IT). Deutsche Bank, for example, increased the number of automatic telling machines (ATMs) in its German network from 700 in 1990 to 2500 in 1995. Between 1993 and 1995 the number of electronic fund transfer systems at the point of sale grew from approximately 2000 to more than 16000.

The banks have also started to segment their customers into wealthy clients and companies that generate high revenues and distinguishing them from the mass market of private customers. Whereas advisory and consultancy services are concentrated on the former, the business with the latter is automated as much as possible. Customer segmentation has not only been implemented in the existing branch network, but also outside. In 1992, Hypo Bank founded an independent subsidiary, the HSB, in former East Germany. This bank is offering a limited range of products to private customers only. Two years later, Hypo Bank established Direkt Anlage Bank, a discount brokerage. Customers who do not rely on advice and who do their bank business via phone, fax or computer are only charged modest fees. Following the example of Hypo Bank, several other German banks started to offer home-based direct banking, usually with legally independent subsidiaries. In 1995, Deutsche Bank was the first major bank to open a direct bank, Bank 24, that offers other banking services such as current accounts in addition to discount brokerage. Industry experts believe that direct banking will become a serious challenge for traditional branch banking (*Bank und Markt*, 1996). Another development is that in recent years German banks have set up legally independent firms for services such as telephone banking, private banking and consultancy.

What effects are the changing markets and business strategies having on employment relations in German banks? Assessments that compare employment relations in Germany with those in Anglo-American countries have argued that German practices are unique. However, current developments such as lean banking suggest that there may be a convergence towards UK and US employment practices in German banking. In contrast with Germany, the employment relations of US banks are characterised by unitary decision making, the absence of collective bargaining, performance-related pay, low investment in training, unstable careers and a high labour turnover (Benthien, 1991; Keltner and Finegold, 1996). Since the early 1990s, the UK banks have begun to follow the US example (Storey, 1995). In the following we will describe the traditional employment practices of German banks in the areas of consultation, pay, training and employment stability and then assess whether there is a convergence towards US practices.

The data presented are based on six case studies of German banks. Among them are three of the five largest commercial banks in Germany (Deutsche Bank, Dresdner Bank and Hypo Bank), a large state bank (West LB), a small savings bank (Kreissparkasse Borken) and a nationwide cooperative bank. The case study data were mainly collected in the years 1992–1994 and are part of a larger study of employment relations of indigenous and foreign-owned banks and chemical firms operating in Germany. In addition to the case study data, interviews with industry experts were conducted and industry data collected. A more detailed description of the sample and methodology can be found elsewhere (Muller, 1996).

This chapter examines the consultation practices in German banking. It analyses current practices and then assesses future developments. In the following sections, terms and conditions, training and employment stability are examined in a similar way.

CONSULTATION

Traditional Practices

The formal channels of consultation are of pivotal importance in German banks. All six German banks in the sample have works councils. This is not surprising, as surveys show that in Germany more than 90 per cent of banking establishments with more than 100 employees have such bodies (Mendius and Semlinger, 1991; Seelmann, 1992). Compared to similar institutions in other European countries, German works councils have a relatively high influence on organisational decisions (Gill, 1993; IDE, 1993). This enables them to play a crucial role whenever there are changes affecting the workforce.

Three observations from the sample banks should give a flavour of the potential influence of a works council. At a subsidiary, the management intended to subcontract the canteen. To obtain the agreement of the employee representatives, the bank had to give the canteen employees the choice between being transferred to other parts of the subsidiary or to continue employment in the canteen on the old terms and conditions. The central works council of another bank opposed the introduction of a development assessment centre for junior staff. The management originally intended to use this as a selection device so that only the successful candidates would be allowed to take part in a management development scheme. Eventually the works council only agreed to the introduction after the employer had promised to select the participants of the development scheme before the assessment is done. The third example is that in one of the banks, the management attempted to change a system of fixed bonuses into a performance-related system based on variable bonuses. As the works council opposed this change, the bank was not able to implement it.

In addition to its influence on organisational decision making, the law assures the works council an important role in employee communication. It not only stipulates that management shares information with employee representatives, but also gives them several means to communicate with the workforce. Whereas at the company level the central works councils negotiate with top management, at the establishment level the works councils deal with local line and human resource managers. The law also stipulates a frequent two-way communication between the works council and employees. An important instrument for this are works meetings. These are regularly held in the various establishments of the sample banks. Works meetings are held during working hours, called by the works council and conducted by its chairperson. All employees of the establishment are entitled to participate.

In contrast to indirect communication via employee representatives, direct communication between the management and employees has traditionally been less formalised. For a long time almost all the sample banks have had suggestion schemes and have informed employees with staff magazines and circular about new procedures, new products or other changes. Nevertheless, only recently has direct communication become more systematic. For example, in the early 1990s Deutsche Bank and Dresdner Bank established units within their central human resource departments that are responsible for focusing on employee communication. Attitude surveys have also become more widespread. Five of the six sample banks have conducted comprehensive or representative attitude surveys of the workforce. Three of these have only used this tool for three years or less.

Future Developments

The evidence presented so far indicates that over the last decade, the German banks have increased their direct communication efforts. This development does not threaten the legally guaranteed status of the works council. As the consent of the works council is needed for the introduction and operation of most direct communication techniques, the management has to involve works councillors in their design and operation. An illustrative example for such an incorporation is Hypo Bank's 'speaking out' scheme. The prospectus advising employees about the scheme contains information that grievances can still be raised with the works council. In addition, member of the works council are in a commission which supervises the operation of the scheme.

A development which could threaten the traditional system of consultation in German banking is the establishment of legally independent subsidiaries for services such as telephone banking, direct banking and private banking. So far almost all of these subsidiaries have no works councils. Although the law stipulates the existence of works councils in all establishments with more than five employees, there has to be an employee initiative before such a body is installed. Such an initiative is more likely the bigger and the older an establishment gets. As we have shown in more detail elsewhere (Muller, 1994), even US banks operating in Germany, some of whom have actively tried to stop the establishment of a works council, have not been able to do this. Therefore, one can expect that in the medium-term most newly founded banks will have a works council. Hence, in the absence of legal changes we do not expect that there will be a convergence towards unitarist US-type consultation practices.

PAY

Traditional Practices

Similar to employees in other German industries, most German banks are members of an employers' association that negotiates collective bargaining agreements on their behalf. In commercial banks, for example, approximately 98 per cent of the employees are working for banks that are covered by multiemployer bargaining (Arbeitgeberverband des privaten Bankgewerbes 1995; the author's own calculations). There are two industry-wide agreements, one for commercial banks, cooperative banks and some large public sector banks and a version of the public sector agreement for savings banks. Both agreements not only regulate wages but also define terms and conditions such as bonuses, weekly working hours, vacation days and sickness provisions. Regarding pay, the remuneration agreement for commercial banks determines the monthly payment for each of nine job grades. The grades are defined in terms of the knowledge and skills needed and examples of typical jobs are given. The formal qualification needed for a job, such as a vocational certificate, the type of job and length of service is important for the classification.

Although theoretically the agreements only apply for union members, in practice they are applied to non-union members as well. None of the firms in the sample offered a detailed breakdown of their wage and salary bill. Nevertheless, an indication for the wage drift is given in the annual reports of the employers' association of commercial banks. These show that tariff employees in commercial banks received annual salaries which in the 1990s were between 8 and 11 per cent higher than the minimal requirements of the collective bargaining agreement. However, the wage drift is higher than indicated by these statistics. Human resource managers and works councillors suggested that there are two other ways in which bank employees can obtain a monthly salary which is above the tariff. Firstly, they can obtain a job grade enhancement. The bunching up of individual jobs into a higher level of the grading structure (grade drift) (Brown, 1989, p. 260) is possible, as there are no detailed prescriptions for jobs covered by a certain wage group. For example, there are three grades according to which financial advisers are paid. In private banks there has been a significant grade drift over recent decades from the lowest to the highest grades. Between 1973 and 1995 the number of tariff employees in the three lowest grades decreased from 25.8 to 4.5 per cent. At the same time the percentage of tariff employees in the three highest grades increased from 16.8 to 45.1 per cent (Arbeitgeberverband des privaten Bankgewerbes, 1996, p. 33). By allowing this wage drift, bank employees have participated in productivity improvements without changes to the whole grading system. Secondly, each grade contains a seniority element, which means that an employee has to work for up to 11 years in a bank before the top wage for the grade is paid. Nevertheless, management can decide to pay a junior employee the top amount of a certain job grade, even if this person has not worked for the required period in a bank, to meet labour market requirements.

The German banks offer a range of additional benefits to the whole workforce. The two biggest German banks, Deutsche Bank and Dresdner Bank, for example, provide two-thirds of the contribution to a bank employee's pension fund, have a company pension scheme, give preferential terms in bank services, issue employee shares and pay a bonus for good examination results. All employees also get a bonus in the form of a half or one month's salary in addition to the salaries guaranteed by the collective agreement.

One of the most important conditions determined by multiemployer bargaining in Germany besides pay is the working hours. Currently, bank employees regularly work 39 hours a week. The collective bargaining agreement for commercial banks makes provisions for the introduction of flexitime arrangements. All sample banks use flexitime, though not in all establishments. Dresdner Bank have had flexitime arrangements since the early 1970s. A representative of the employers' association of private banks suggested that 50 per cent of bank employees are involved in flexitime arrangements (interview with Dr Sauer, 11 August 1993). At the time of the company visits, some banks were developing alternative models for flexible working hours. One option discussed was 'variable working hours' (*variable Arbeitszeit*). In contrast to traditional flexitime arrangements, this has no core period. The working groups themselves have to ensure the proper function of their units. Savings Bank Borken introduced variable working hours in the 1980s and Dresdner Bank and West LB in the mid-1990s.

Besides tariff employees, German banks also employ exempts (*Außertarifliche Angestellte*). These are all those employees who earn significantly more than the highest base salary prescribed by the collective bargaining agreement (in 1995 this was approximately 80000 DM per year). This group, which in commercial banks is approximately 20 per cent of the total workforce, is outside the scope of the central remuneration agreement. Hence, the employers have more autonomy in exempt pay. Nevertheless, in the early 1990s, only one of the sample banks, West LB, had an analytic job evaluation system for exempts. The other three large sample banks classified exempt jobs on the basis of the title of the job incumbent. This crude form of job evaluation has been typical for German banks and meant that highly qualified jobs could only be paid adequately if the incumbent had a title. Today this system is perceived as outdated, as titles and hierarchical levels have become less meaningful with more complex organisational structures. In addition, variable pay for exempts is relatively small in Germany in comparison to the US and the UK (Leichtfuß and Bonacker, 1992). Share option schemes for managers are also not common. There are indications that exempt pay is becoming higher and more performance related. In 1994, West LB was increasing variable pay for exempts and Deutsche Bank publicly announced making exempt pay more performance related. Hypo Bank was planning to introduce a more performance-related pay system for exempts in 1996. In 1996, Deutsche Bank was the first major German bank that offered a share option scheme for senior managers.

Future Developments

Whereas the involvement of works councils in organisational decision making is guaranteed by law, employers are not legally required to join an employers' association. There is some dissatisfaction among bank employers with the terms and conditions set by the collective bargaining agreement. In particular they are demanding a comprehensive flexibility of working hours which includes the possibility of opening on Saturdays, the complete lifting of working hours restrictions for financial advisers and the introduction of annual working hours and a more performance-related pay. According to employers this is necessary to accommodate increasing competition by non-banks such as insurance companies. Insurance sales persons, for example, are free to work on Saturdays (annual reports of the Employers' Association of Commercial Banks).

These restrictions that the collective bargaining agreement imposes on the banks could at least partly explain why, as far as can be discerned, none of the legally independent firms founded by the German banks for services such as direct banking, telephone banking and private banking is a member of an employers' association. The advantages from an employer's point of view are that employees can be paid below the tariff and that there are fewer restrictions on working hours, that is employees can work on Saturdays and Sundays. As the number of employees involved is relatively small, so far this has not led to a significant decline in the percentage of bank employees covered by industry-wide bargaining. This might change if new sales forms become more important. In turn this could exert pressure on banks with an extensive branch network to cut costs and become more flexible and might eventually lead to a breakdown of the system of centralised collective bargaining.

This scenario, however, may well be too pessimistic. The banking unions are relatively weak. The trade union density is only approximately 20 per cent in this industry. In contrast to other German industries, which are dominated by a German trade union congress (DGB) affiliated union, there are two unions with similar strength that are in strong competition which each other. Their main counterpart, the employers' association of commercial banks, is a highly organised association dominated by the big commercial banks (Müller-Jentsch and Sperling, 1995, pp. 236–7). The banking strike in 1992 showed that strike action can cause relatively little disruption. The relative weakness of the banking unions has held the tariff wages down. Employers have also been able to gain flexibility concessions in the collective bargaining negotiations. For example, the weekly working time of 39 hours is only an average that has to be achieved in a three-month period. Furthermore, with the explicit aim of saving jobs, since 1996 it has become possible for the management and works council to reduce them to 31 hours without a pay compensation (*Frankfurter Allgemeine Zeitung*, 1996). Although one can expect a decline in the percentage of bank employees covered by collective bargaining, a breakdown of the system of industry-wide bargaining is not imminent.

TRAINING

Traditional Practices

If one believes annual reports, mission statements and image brochures, the German banks invest a lot in training. These publications often contain commitments to the provision of training. For example, in the 1992 annual report of Hypo Bank it is stated that 'In the long run sophisticated services can only be offered with active and qualified employees. Customer orientation is our measure. To achieve this goal constant initial and further vocational training is necessary. Only in this way can a high service culture be achieved that ties customers' (translated by the author).

There are three different forms of training provided by the German banks. These are an initial vocational training, further vocational training qualifications and company-specific further training. Firstly, each year more than 20 000 school leavers start an initial vocational training as a bank clerk. Depending on the entrance qualification, this training usually lasts for a period of between two and two-and-a-half years. Similar to apprentices in other occupations, bank clerks are trained externally in the vocational school, as well as internally on the job and off the job. The time spent in each area is approximately 39, 45 and 17 per cent (Stiller, 1992, p. 138; the author's own calculations). Today, approximately 80 per cent of all bank employees have an initial vocational training qualification (Kreyenschmidt, 1995).

Secondly, building on initial vocational training there is a system of further vocational qualifications. The examinations are set by the Chamber of Industry and Commerce or the recognised bodies in the cooperative and savings banks groups. The employees are supported by their employers who usually pay the fees and a bonus after the successful completion of the course. In savings banks, for which a special version of the collective bargaining agreement of the public sector applies, it is not possible to enter certain job grades without further training qualification. This explains why almost one-quarter of the savings bank employees have a further training qualification. Although there are no such formal links in the other sample banks, vocational qualifications are pivotal for the career prospects of those who do not have a university degree.

Thirdly, each of the six sample banks offers job- or company-specific off-the-job training courses. These are usually distinguished in technical training which concentrates on the selling of bank services and non-technical training which includes courses for managers.

Comparisons of apprentice ratios (see Table 7.6) and training expenditure (Bundesministerium für Bildung und Wissenschaft, 1993, p. 119) between banking and other industries show that the banks invest well in excess of the average in industry as a whole on training. The German banks also invest more in initial and further vocational training than the banks in Spain, the UK and the US (Keltner, 1995; Quack, *et al.*, 1995; Iglesias Fernández and Muller, 1996; Muller and Dickmann, 1996).

TABLE 7.6 *Percentage of apprentices in relation to the total workforce*

	1980	1985	1990	1995
Commercial banks	8.0	9.0	8.0	6.3
Savings bank group	9.1	9.3	9.8	7.4
German industry	6.3	6.9	5.2	4.5

SOURCE Annual reports; Bundesministerium für Wirtschaft (1996, pp. 12 and 171) and the author's own calculations.

When conducting the case studies we observed several trends in the form and focus of the training offered by the German banks. Firstly, initial vocational training has become more company specific. The quality of the vocational schools is perceived as being poor (Stiller, 1992, pp. 161–3). In the 1970s, the sample banks therefore started to teach general technical knowledge in internal off-the-job courses in order to prepare their apprentices better for the examinations. Today, the emphasis has shifted to the provision of more firm-specific information as well as key skills such as analytical thinking, successful teamwork and sales abilities. In 1990, Deutsche Bank introduced behavioural training which uses video cameras and teamwork. In seminars apprentices perform tasks such as the reception of a customer, a telephone conversation and a sales talk. Secondly, regarding further training the problem of transferring knowledge from off-the-job courses to the workplace has been recognised. Some of the banks have redesigned training schemes to integrate on-the-job and off-the-job training more closely. Three of the six banks surveyed have introduced team training for employees working together in a department, branch or project. Most of the banks studied have also started to use computer-based training. There also seems to be a bigger emphasis on job rotation between functions. This is a significant change as until recently it was normal that an employee stayed for 10, 20 or 30 years in a position, gained more and more technical experience and then waited for the retirement of the immediate supervisor to take their place.

Future Developments

Three of the sample banks have published data about the money spent on training in their annual reports. These show that the percentage of the total wage and salary bill spent on training decreased from approximately 6 per cent in 1991 to approximately 4 per cent in 1995. However, these reports also show that during this time the number of training courses and training days per employee increased or remained constant. What has declined are apprentice ratios. More representative data presented in Table 7.6 show that the percentage of apprentices in commercial banks and savings banks has significantly declined since 1990. Although this trend can at least partly be explained by a stagnation of employment and a lower labour turnover of apprentices, there are serious threats to initial vocational training.

A particular challenge is the increasing segmentation of customers, as this is likely to lead to a segmented labour workforce (Sperling, 1996). In the front office there could be a polarisation between service jobs which only require basic skills and a minimal qualification and advisory jobs for which a comprehensive knowledge about the products as well as communication and sales skills are needed. For the former, bank clerks with an initial vocational training are overqualified. They may also be too qualified for jobs in direct and telephone banking. As only a few standardised products are offered, employees with sales skills are more important than those with a broad vocational qualification. Nevertheless, approximately 60 per cent of the employees of Deutsche Bank's direct banking subsidiary, Bank 24, that are in direct contact with customers have an initial vocational training qualification as a bank clerk (*UNI Magazin*, 1996, p. 42). The example of Citibank Privatkunden, which has for some time concentrated on the active selling of a limited number of bank products to private customers, could also indicate that bank clerks with an initial vocational training will still be needed. This bank has a significant apprentice ratio. It is also interesting to note that the percentage of tariff employees in the three lowest wage groups is still declining (Arbeitgeberverband des privaten Bankgewerbes, 1996, p. 33). As only employees that work in low skill positions for which an initial vocational training as a bank clerk is not a requirement are in these wage groups, this percentage would increase if the banks started to recruit a lower qualified workforce.

For highly skilled jobs, bank clerks with an initial vocational training are more and more in competition with banks clerks that have a university degree. Traditionally, only a few graduates were employed by the banks. In recent years, graduate employment in the banks has increased substantially. For example, the graduate percentage of Hypo Bank increased from 6.2 per cent in 1985 to 16.1 per cent in 1995. Over the last 25 years the ratio between the recruitment of apprentices and the recruitment of graduates changed from 40 : 1 to 8 : 1. Whereas in the past graduates were usually only recruited as junior managers, today they can also be found in non-managerial positions (Arbeitgeberverband des privaten Bankgewerbes, 1995, p. 28). Hence, it appears that the increase in the availability of other forms of education and training has an impact on apprenticeship uptake. Nevertheless, new sales strategies and a growing intake of graduates is unlikely to lead to a collapse of the system of initial vocational training in banks. At least publically employers and their organisations are still committed to it.

EMPLOYMENT STABILITY

Current Practices

A fourth traditional feature of social relations in German banking is employment stability. In the past, banking careers started at the bottom of the hierarchy with the initial vocational training. As external recruitment was rare, male employees in particular had a good chance of progressing to management positions. With the increase in graduate employment, there is an intensification of career competition. Nevertheless, as German banks are usually committed to internal promotion there are still opportunities to progress.

All the banks in the sample have a system of job posting and usually advertise all vacant positions in the establishment first. In addition, half of them have committed themselves in written documents to a policy of internal promotion. Deutsche Bank, for example, has done this in its management guidelines. There it is stated that 'through a systematic human resource development we aim to fill all vacant positions internally if possible' (translation by the author). In the three banks where such a commitment does not exist, I was also told about an internal promotion policy, albeit not noted in company brochures.

Besides providing career opportunities, the German banks have traditionally also offered employment security. Table 7.7 provides a breakdown of the average labour turnover of the more than 140000 tariff employees commercial banks employ in West Germany, according to reasons for leaving. It indicates that in German banks on average each year only 1 in 200 bank employees is dismissed and that the total labour turnover of tariff employees is normally less than 10 per cent. If exempts had been included, this figure would have been even smaller. In contrast, the labour turnover of banks in the US is approximately 22 per cent per year (Keltner, 1995, p. 57). The variation in labour turnover between 1991 and 1995 is mainly due to the different percentages of employees leaving of their own volition (see Table 7.7). This in turn is linked to labour market developments. In the early 1990s, German unification led to a serious shortage of qualified bank employees. Since then demand has decreased, so that supply meets demand more.

TABLE 7.7:   *Labour turnover of tariff employees (apprentices and exempts excluded) in commercial banks with breakdown according to reasons for leaving (in per cent, West Germany only)*

	1991	1992	1993	1994	1995
Redundancies	2.0	2.3	2.6	2.8	3.9
Of these dismissals (compulsory redundancies)	0.5	0.8	0.5	0.6	0.6
Of these termination agreements (voluntary redundancies)	0.8	0.8	1.1	1.1	1.9
Of these early retirement	0.7	0.7	1.0	1.1	1.4
Notice given by employees	7.4	6.2	4.9	3.5	3.6
Other reasons (for example attainment of age limit or deaths)	1.3	1.2	1.3	1.1	1.0
Total labour turnover	10.7	9.7	8.8	7.4	8.5

SOURCE   Annual reports of Employers' Association of Commercial Banks and the author's own calculations.

The institutional environment, at least in part, seems to ensure that the German banks follow a policy of employment stability. The labour law makes dismissals more difficult than in the UK and the US. In addition, works councils can demand an internal job posting and also have a say in recruitment and dismissal decisions. Thus, they exert at least some pressure on management to use internal labour markets. As the works council has only co-determination rights with respect to non-executives, the management could theoretically behave differently here. Nevertheless, the recruitment policy for executive positions suggests that most companies in the sample would follow such a strategy even without this external pressure. Hence, the system of initial vocational training may be a more important factor in explaining why companies operating in Germany prefer internal labour markets. They not only have an incentive to recover their investment by retaining apprentices, but the qualifications generated by initial vocational training enable them to follow a strategy of functional flexibility to adjust to fluctuations in employment.

Future Developments

Whereas so far careers and employment have been relatively stable, experts have forecasted that because of the increasing use of computer technology, the standardisation of products and home-based banking, a radical reduction of bank employment will occur over the next decade. By 1990 Cartellieri (1990), a board member of Deutsche Bank, had already predicted that the banking sector would become the steel industry of the 1990s involving massive downsizing and rationalisation. In 1994, the consultancy firm Arthur D. Little estimated that 100000 jobs will be lost in German banks and that there will be mass branch closures over the coming years. The predictions of trade unions are even worse (*Zeitschrift für das gesamte Kreditwesen*, 1996).

Until the mid-1990s, employment remained relatively stable in the German banks. Nevertheless, employment growth has come to a standstill in recent years and commercial banks in particular have started to reduce their German workforce (see Table 7.8). To achieve this reduction, voluntary redundancies and early retirement were used. Compulsory dismissals are still not common (see Table 7.7). Is this likely to change? Will German banks follow the US and the UK example and reduce employment levels drastically?

TABLE 7.8   *Development of employment in the three Banking groups in the early 1990s*

	Commercial banks	Savings banks	Cooperative banks
1990	211 700	290 750	162 600
1991	218 000	306 150	169 800
1992	222 700	316 350	174 750
1993	221 000	321 600	178 200
1994	220 400	324 500	182 400
1995	217 550	323 300	185 500

SOURCE   Arbeitgeberverband des privaten Bankgewerbes and the author's own calculations.

In contrast to the US banks, which follow a volume-oriented strategy, the German banks have a relationship orientation. They compete less with promises of lower prices and put a higher emphasis on the cultivation of the customer relationship. Customers have, for example, personal contact with knowledgeable staff. One outcome of this strategy is a high branch density. Whereas the UK and the US have only approximately 300 branches per 1 million inhabitants, West Germany still has more than 650. Even McKinsey consultants who have accused Germany of being overbanked, do not expect that this will change in the short-term (Leichtfuß and Mattern, 1994, p. 706).

Another outcome is the use of technology in German retail banking. Customer demands for high-quality services have led German banks to implement less computer technology in the front office than would have been technically feasible. Whereas in the front office computer technology was primarily introduced to support customer advising, in the back office it replaced human capital (Oberbeck and Baethge, 1989). Table 7.9 indicates that German banks were relatively successful with this strategy. Since 1985, the staff costs as a percentage of the average balance sheet total in German commercial banks declined almost year by year without major cuts in employment. In contrast, in the UK the massive downsizing of the 1990s was necessary to achieve similar reductions.

TABLE 7.9   *Staff costs as a percentage of the average balance sheet total of commercial banks in Germany, the UK and the US*

Year	Germany	UK	US
1985	1.45	1.86	1.56
1986	1.51	1.94	1.56
1987	1.46	1.92	1.55
1988	1.42	1.95	1.55
1989	1.33	1.89	1.55
1990	1.29	1.81	1.56
1991	1.29	1.82	1.59
1992	1.27	1.65	1.62
1993	1.21	1.54	1.64
1994	1.13	1.48	1.58

SOURCE   OECD (1996).

In sum it appears that although career opportunities have become more limited and although there will be more frequent job changes, there is no massive downsizing. There is still a considerable gulf between the rather unstable employment practices in US banking and the relative stable employment in the German banks. Employment stability combined with a highly skilled workforce are pivotal elements of a relationship-oriented business strategy. They offer a competitive advantage and have even a model function for US banks (Keltner, 1995).

CONCLUSIONS

The evidence presented in this article indicates that employment relations in German banks are changing. New forms of organisation, new sales strategies and increasing market pressures are resulting in significant changes in key employment areas. Many of the changes in business and organisation strategies are inspired by US business practices and there is some convergence towards US employment practices. There is more direct communication, less initial vocational training, more flexible terms and conditions and less employment stability. Nevertheless, these changes are less dramatic and progressing much more slowly than in financial services in other countries (see Morgan and Knights, 1997). In particular there has been no radical transformation of the traditional system of employment relations in the German banks along US lines. Employment relations in German banking are embedded in the German financial system and the German system of labour market institutions. As long as these systems do not change radically, one cannot assume that the development in German banking will automatically mirror that of Anglo-Saxon countries. It seems that in the foreseeable future, employment relations in German banking will still be characterised by a high investment in training, relatively secure employment, the involvement of employee representatives in organisational decision making and industry-wide collective bargaining.

ACKNOWLEDGEMENTS

For comments on earlier drafts, I thank David Guest, Swen Hildebrandt, David Knights and Horst Kolvenbach. I also acknowledge the comments of the participants of the workshop 'Restructuring Financial Services within and across Europe, Wissenschaftszentrum Berlin, October 1993' and of the ESF EMOT 'Workshop on Financial Services, Paris, October 1994' on earlier versions of this paper.

References

Allen, F. and Gale, D. (1994) 'A Welfare Comparison of Intermediaries and Financial Markets in Germany and the US', *European Economic Review*, vol. 39, pp. 179–209.
Arbeitgeberverband des privaten Bankgewerbes (1995) *Jahresbericht 1994/95* (Köln: Arbeitgeberverband des privaten Bankgewerbes).
Arbeitgeberverband des privaten Bankgewerbes (1996) *Jahresbericht 1995/96* (Köln: Arbeitgeberverband des privaten Bankgewerbes).
Bank und Markt (1996) 'Schwerpunkt Direktbanken', *Bank und Markt*, May, vol. 25 pp. 8–16.
Benthien, T. (1991) 'Kurzfristige Erfolgsorientierung und hohe Fluktuation: Personalwesen bei amerikanischen Banken', *Blick durch die Wirtschaft*, vol. 34, 10 December, p. 7.

Bierer, H., Fassbender, H. and Rüdel, T. (1992) 'Auf dem Weg zur "schlanken Bank"', *Die Bank*, September, pp. 500–6.

Brown, W. (1989), 'Managing Remuneration' in K. Sisson (ed.), *Personnel Management in Britain* (Oxford: Basil Blackwell), pp. 249–70.

Bundesministerium für Bildung und Wissenschaft (ed.) (1993) *Berufsbildungsbericht 1993* (Bad Honnef: Bock).

Bundesministerium für Wirtschaft (1995) *Wirtschaft in Zahlen 95* (Bonn: Bundesministerium für Wirtschaft).

Cartellieri, U. (1990), 'Überkapazität erzwingt Auslese', *Die Bank*, July, pp. 366–71.

D'Alessio, N. and Oberbeck, H. (1997) 'Development Tendencies in the German Banking Industry and Probable Consequences with Regard to Marketing Strategies, Rationalisation Concepts, and Personnel Policies', in G. Morgan and D. Knights (eds), *Deregulation and European Financial Services*, (London: Macmillan).

Deutsche Bundesbank (1996) *Bankenstatistik Juli 1996* (Frankfurt/Main: Deutsche Bundesbank).

Fisher, A., (1996) 'Institutions Face a Painful Transition Survey German Banking', *Financial Times*, Supplement, 29 May, p. iv.

Frankfurter Allgemeine Zeitung (1994) 'Bankvertrieb bleibt tragende Säule des Absatzes von Fondsanteilen', *Frankfurter Allgemeine Zeitung*, 9 November, p. 28.

Frankfurter Allgemeine Zeitung (1996) 'Banken, Stahl und Großhandel: Tariferhöhungen um knapp 2 Prozent', *Frankfurter Allgemeine Zeitung*, 20 June, p. 17.

Gill, C. (1993) 'Technological Change and Participation in Work Organisation: Recent Results from a European Community Survey', *The International Journal of Human Resource Management,* vol. 4, no. 2, pp. 325–48.

IDE (1993) *Industrial Democracy in Europe Revisited* (Oxford: Oxford University Press).

Iglesias Fernández, C. and Muller, M. (1996) 'Ausbildung bei spanischen Banken', *Die Bank*, vol. 7, pp. 435–7.

Keltner, B. (1995) 'Relationship Banking and Competitive Advantage: Evidence from the US and Germany', *California Management Review*, vol. 37, no. 4, pp. 45–72.

Keltner, B. and Finegold, D. (1996) 'Adding Value in Banking: An Innovative Human Resource Strategy', *Sloan Management Review*, vol. 37, pp. 57–68.

Kreyenschmidt, G. (1995) 'Der Bankkaufmann – Zahlen, Fakten, Tendenzen', *Die Bank*, February, pp. 87–91.

Leichtfuß, R. and Bonacker, M. (1992) 'Erfolgsorientierte Anreizsysteme', *Die Bank*, November, pp. 624–9.

Leichtfuß, R. and Mattern, F. (1994) 'Auf dem Weg zur Weltklasse im Retail Banking', *Die Bank*, December, pp. 700–7.

Mendius, H. G. and Semlinger, K. (1991) *Personalplanung und Personalentwicklung in der gewerblichen Wirtschaft* (Eschborn: RKW).

Morgan, G. and Knights, D. (1997) *Deregulation and European Financial Services* (London: Macmillan).

Muller, M. (1994) *Labour Market Institutions and Private German Banks: Acceptance or Challenge*, paper presented to the ESF EMOT 'Workshop on Financial Services', Paris, 30 September–1 October.

Muller, M. (1996) 'Unitarism, Pluralism and Human Resource Management in Germany: a Comparison of Foreign and German-owned Companies', PhD thesis University of London.

Muller, M. and Dickmann, M. (1996) 'Aus- und Weiterbildung in britischen Banken', *Die Bank*, February, pp. 121–5.

Müller-Jentsch, W. and Sperling, H. J. (1995) 'New Technology and Employee Involvement in Banking: a Comparative View of British, German and Swedish Banks', in C. Crouch and F. Traxler (eds), *Organised Industrial Relations in Europe: What Future?* (Aldershot: Avebury), pp. 225–48.

Oberbeck, H. and Baethge, M. (1989) 'Computer and Pinstripes: Financial Institutions', in P. J. Katzenstein (ed.), *Industry and Politics in West Germany: Toward the Third Republic* (Ithaca: Cornell University Press), pp. 275–306.

OECD (1996) *Bank Profitability, Financial Statements of Banks 1985–1994* (Paris: OECD).

Quack, S., O'Reilly, J. and Hildebrandt, S. (1995) *New Patterns of Recruitment and Training in German, UK and French Banks. An Examination of Tensions between Sectoral and National Systems* (Berlin: Wissenschaftszentrum).

Schröder Münchmeyer Hengst & Co (1996) *Deutsche Banken im Umbruch* (Frankfurt: Schröder Münchmeyer Hengst & Co).

Seelmann, A. (1992) *Arbeits- und Betriebsordnungen privater Banken* (Köln: Universität Köln).

Sperling, H. J. (1996) *Restrukturierung von Unternehmens- und Arbeitsorganisation-eine Zwischenbilanz: Trend-Report Partizipation und Organisation* (Bochum: Ruhruniversität Lehrstuhl Mitbestimmung und Organisation).

Stiller, I. (1992) 'Grundlagen für die Neuordnung des Ausbildungsberufs Bankkaufmann', in *Berichte zur Beruflichen Bildung* (Berlin: Bundesinstitut für Berufsbildung), p. 146.

Storey, J. (1995) 'Employment Policies and Practices in UK Clearing Banks: an Overview', *Human Resource Management Journal*, vol. 5, no. 4, pp. 24–43.

UNI Magazin (1996) 'Finanzdienstleister: Beispiel Bank 24', *UNI Magazin*, June, pp. 42–3.

Vitols, S. (1995a) *Are German Banks Different?* (Berlin: Wissenschaftszentrum).

Vitols, S. (1995b) *German Banks and the Modernization of the Small Firm Sector: Long Term Finance in Comparative Perspective* (Berlin: Wissenschaftszentrum).

Vitols, S. (1995c) *Financial Systems and Industrial Policy in Germany and Great Britain: the Limits of Convergence* (Berlin: Wissenschaftszentrum).

Zeitschrift für das gesamte Kreditwesen (1996) 'Ende eines Tabus', *Zeitschrift für das gesamte Kreditwesen*, vol. 49, pp. 140–1.

8 Marketing the Soul: from the Ideology of Consumption to Consumer Subjectivity[1]

DAVID KNIGHTS AND ANDREW STURDY

INTRODUCTION

It comes as no surprise to recognise that just as the physical sciences facilitated the control over and exploitation of nature for human purposes, so the social sciences have been massively implicated in the exercise of power in the management of populations and individual subjects. Foucault (1973, p. 345) drew our attention to the transition in nineteenth-century Western culture whereupon human beings transformed themselves from being merely the agents of knowledge to also being its object. However, the development of the human sciences was not just about adding another object to the scientific enterprise; the human subjects of its concern were already producing representations of the life, production and language by which their existence was governed. In short, the human sciences have as their object of knowledge beings who themselves have a prior claim to produce such knowledge for themselves in their everyday lives. Theories about human life are, then, second-order constructs or theories relating to everyday first-order theoretical representations (Giddens, 1979a, p. 12, 1984, p. 284; see also Mouzelis, 1993, p. 688).

This double hermeneutic (Giddens, 1979a, b) involves social science trading on the interpretations and representations of those it studies, the knowledge of which is then drawn upon pragmatically in the exercise of power by groups whose purpose is one of identifying, influencing or controlling the behaviour of populations. Whether in the form of broad classificatory statistics or more detailed behavioural propensities, populations are governed and subjects are managed through practices that are informed by knowledge developed not necessarily with such purposes in mind. The provision of 'apparatuses of security' (for example, welfare) for populations at large is one condition and consequence of this knowledge that may be seen as a peculiar modern version of government rationality or governmentality (Foucault, 1991, p. 104).

In this chapter we are concerned with one aspect of such governmentality that frequently lies outside of the state but is heavily imbricated with those apparatuses of security through which populations are governed. We refer to the field of financial services and, in particular, private insurances, pensions and savings. Our objective is to examine critically the development and use of certain knowledges for purposes of responding to but also reconstituting populations as comprised of a diverse range of 'sovereign consumers'. In particular, our focus is upon marketing knowledge relating to the techniques of segmenting the market and, we suggest, transforming individuals into particular kinds of consumer subjects. In contrast to the social sciences (cf. Baritz, 1960; Hollway, 1991), marketing knowledge is perhaps more explicitly instrumental and managerial in its design, often perceiving its role quite narrowly as one of providing managers with the tools that enable them to exploit the market more effectively (Willmott, 1993) albeit in the name of 'consumer needs' (Knights *et al.*, 1994).

Our argument, however, is that while the intentions of marketing may have such self-defined limits, its impact is one of contributing significantly to the reproduction of a society of increasingly individualised subjects whose personal identity is founded upon specific forms of consumption and associated lifestyles. In examining the ideology of the segmenters and the subjectivity of the segmented in this chapter, we attempt to draw together certain of the Foucauldian literatures concerned with governmental rationality and the typically distinct traditions of organisation theory and cultural studies of consumer society (Knights and Morgan, 1993; see also Du Gay and Salaman, 1992; Du Gay, 1993).

The chapter is organised as follows. First, we provide a brief introduction to the changing character of identity and individual concerns about security in consumer society. This leads on to a discussion of governmental rationality and its relationship to insurance as an important element of the 'apparatus of security' (Foucault, 1979) in modern society. In the third section, we begin to explore the way in which marketing, particularly within the financial services, has been facilitated by but in turn contributed to the provision of 'apparatuses of security' and governmental procedures for the management of populations and subjects. In particular, we examine market segmentation as a practice that seeks detailed 'knowledge' of consumers and selectively deploys it in the design, delivery and promotion of products and services. Here we provide a brief exploratory account of the historical emergence of market segmentation as a technology for the regulation of subjectivity. Drawing on Rose's (1989) work, in particular, the current form of segmentation practices and, therefore, also of consumer society is shown to be crucially dependent upon psychological conceptions of populations as aggregates of individual 'wills' or 'attitudes' and 'motivations'. Moreover, it is argued that segmentation comprises a combination of knowledges, each with its own governmental and constitutive trajectory. The focus is on a particular form of segmentation based on consumer 'lifestyles' but we do not believe that this is entirely a one-way process. There is a mutuality of conditioning insofar as producers of 'security' products are also able to transform their products and services to coincide with changing identity profiles and consumer cultures and, in the fourth section, we draw upon some fieldwork in France to illustrate the most recent developments of these segmentation practices or technologies. In the final section, we seek to provide a more analytical appreciation of how power, knowledge and subjectivity are linked in what we see to be the processes of both private and public modes of managing subjects in contemporary society.

IDENTITY IN CONSUMER SOCIETY

There is a wide and varied literature ranging from Bell (1970) to Beck (1992) documenting and assessing the post-war change in the social structure of Western 'class societies' resulting from or associated with increased individualisation. At the risk of conflating diverse perspectives, a common thread is evident: the decline of fixed status hierarchies ('status decay') and the emergence of a 'freedom' in 'choosing' from a range of shifting lifestyles whereby personal identity is increasingly associated with and dependent upon consumption (for example, Baudrillard, 1981; Bourdieu, 1984; Featherstone, 1987; Bauman, 1988). For example, Beck's (1992) recent account of German society[2] documents how changes in the labour market primarily have given rise to an increasing freedom from the constraints of 'traditional' social structures of class, family, gender and occupation. The distinctiveness of this form of individualisation compared to that of previous historical periods is that it involves *liberation* from traditional structures of dominance, *instability* in the sense of a loss of traditional security with respect to the behavioural and normative order, but yet a *reintegration* of individuals through commitments to new (albeit individualised) social identities (Beck, 1992, p. 128).

Liberation and instability may be seen as coalescing around three focal points at least in terms of the life situation or objective world of individuals[3] – the 'breakdown' of traditional status-based classes, family structures and forms of employment (Beck, 1992, p. 129). Class, family and employment do not, as it were, disappear so much as recede into the background as they are displaced by an individualised 'biographical life plan' that compels individuals to 'choose between different lifestyles, subcultures, social ties and identities' (Beck, 1992, p. 131). Rather than the image of individuals having regained control of their own lives, Beck (1992) argued that the autonomous individual becomes ever more dependent upon externalities (for example, fashions, economic cycles, power of consumption and the market). In effect, then, liberation coincides with a reintegration in the form of a compulsive pursuit of individualistic lifestyles which are dependent upon labour market position and personal consumption.

The link between consumption and identity is by no means a new development. Consuming exclusive or distinctive goods and services, at varying levels of conspicuousness, has always been linked with status because of the public visibility of objects of dress, property and leisure (Veblen, 1899; Weber, 1948). Recently, however, the search for a degree of distinctiveness through the consumption of highly differentiated products and services is both the condition and consequence of a multiplicity of social identities (Knights and Morgan, 1993). By subscribing to a given set of discourses and conforming to or complying with their imperatives, individuals feel less isolated and insecure, even though at another level, such behaviour is not free of tension because it violates a sense of self-autonomy – another bastion of modern subjectivity. This central ambiguity in the discursive formation of modern subjectivity means that behavioural conformity is no more predictable than resistance. Both are equally possible as individuals balance the conflicting pressures for a secure identity by 'fitting in' with others, on the one hand, and expressions of self-autonomy or freedom through claiming a unique or differentiated identity, on the other. However, the pursuit of material wealth offers both security and self-autonomy simultaneously since, in contrast to other practices, it promises social respect through conformity to the material and symbolic values of success at the same time as it frees individuals from the dependence on others for their survival. For this reason, if no other, financial security is a condition and consequence of the discursive formation of the individualised subject and the power relations in which modern subjectivity is embedded.

In a phrase these developments could be described as a transition from the ideology of consumption to consumer subjectivity. In the former situation, individuals had to be manipulated to consume so that an excess productive capacity and saturated markets did not undermine the economic miracle of capitalism – a phenomenon described by Marx (1976) as 'commodity fetishism'. In the latter, by contrast, individuals are continually seeking out commodities through which both to identify with and differentiate themselves from others in society – a phenomenon that could be described as identity fetishism.

Beck (1992, p. 90), on the other hand, described these social changes as a process of modernisation leading to the transition from the industrial to the risk society. His argument is that, whereas in industrial society risk could be the price society is willing to pay for the benefits of economic growth and wealth, the risk society demands that productive activity only takes place when it is comparatively risk free (Beck, 1992, p. 12). Taking on board almost unquestioningly the politics of the environmentalists, Beck (1992) transformed their constitution of ecological, global and high-tech risks into a sociological thesis. While few would question that 'everything is dangerous' (Foucault, 1984, p. 343), it is simply polemical of Beck to argue that risk has begun to determine economic production, particularly when the process of constituting risks is left unexamined and their 'objective' status taken for granted. Clearly the political and ecological magnitude of global risks in contemporary economies are important but they are neither a property of the objects to which they are assigned (Knights and Vurdubakis, 1993) nor are they incontestable. Moreover, despite the attempts of environmentalists to create a political furore around the claimed threat of contemporary civilisation to ecological systems, people in Western societies are still more preoccupied with *social* than biological survival. That is to say, despite the various risks with which our bodies are confronted (for example, AIDS, pollution, and Creutzfeldt–Jacob disease (CJD)), the daily preoccupations of people with their identity at work, in leisure, in consumption and at home are broadly more continuous and intense. For this reason, it is perhaps appropriate to examine those ways in which risk is constituted and managed that are neglected by Beck (1992).

For example, in France, post-war prosperity, social security provision and increases in average lifespans in the context of growing individualisation have combined, it is claimed, to shift people's definition of security away from a 'passive' form of 'risk' protection against potential 'hazards' towards a more 'active' security associated with individual autonomy and achieving 'life projects' (Foucault, 1988; Paitra, 1990; Mendras and Cole, 1991). Such changes are highly significant for private financial services companies as well as for public policy with respect to social security.

The insured is going to look for the best trajectories in his/her life-cycle – less something against bad luck, more the optimisation of well-being. To call on an insurer to manage a risk is no longer to guard against a chaotic succession of hazards but to optimise trajectories which have a relative certainty (Albouy and Ewald, 1990, p. 12).

Not only did former 'insecurities', such as 'dependency' upon relatives in old age, become ameliorated through financial independence as a result of lifetime savings and pensions, but the nature of security 'needs' in general changed dramatically, at least for the relatively affluent middle classes, in the post-war years.[4] The risk of losing financial security, then, began to assume a greater significance in the lives of large sections of the population. The other side of the equation here, of course, is the history of how individuals have been transformed into security seeking and financially self-disciplined subjects by a range of insurantial practices both public and private (Donzelot, 1979; 1980; Ewald, 1986; Defert, 1991; Knights and Vurdubakis, 1993). It is largely through their marketing and sales activities that private financial services institutions contribute to this constitution of the modern subject and shortly we will present a brief case study to illustrate the levels of activity directed towards managing the market and, thereby, the consumer. Before doing so, we further elaborate the genesis of such activities in the accumulation of knowledge of populations and individual subjects as a significant element in the development of modern governmental rationality.

GOVERNMENTAL RATIONALITY AND INSURANCE PRACTICES

Inspired by Foucault's (1979) analysis, a number of researchers began to elaborate the changing nature of governmental rationality throughout the last two centuries (see Donzelot, 1980; Rose, 1988; Burchell *et al.*, 1991; Knights and Vurdubakis, 1993). Although independently examining the historical developments of statistical probability and calculability, Hacking (1990, p. 217) also acknowledged his debt to Foucault's work in his own tracing of the displacement of deterministic beliefs by a recognition that chance could be tamed through the use of statistics and a theory of probability. More importantly for our purposes, he showed how the growth and use of statistics in the eighteenth and nineteenth centuries were the condition rendering it possible to manage and control populations (Hacking, 1991). For in collecting numbers there is an immediate drawing up of classifications or models of human types which come to define the boundaries of identity – the normal from the deviant, the good from the bad, the reputable from the disreputable (Foucault, 1982, p. 208). Social statistics establish a new language through which to shape our lives, our reality.

Many of the modern categories by which we think about people and their activities, were put in place by an attempt to collect numerical data ... The bureaucracy of statistics imposes not just by creating administrative rulings but by determining classifications within which people must think of themselves and of the actions which are open to them (Hacking, 1991, pp. 182 and 194).

In the same way, there is a literature showing how insurantial knowledges establish a new form of social ethics, one in which financial calculations are introduced into the process of subjective self-discipline (Ewald, 1986; Knights, 1988; Daston, 1990; Knights and Vurdubakis, 1993). It reflects a cultural, Western (Daniel, 1992) preoccupation with rendering the future calculable and knowable – a principle of objectification (Knights, 1988; Ewald, 1991). In this way, insurance itself, as a technique of rational calculation, produces risks (Knights and Vurdubakis, 1993, p. 3). As Ewald (1991) observed, 'By objectivising certain [familiar or "dreaded"] events as risks, insurance can invert their meaning: it can make what was previously an obstacle into a possibility' (p. 200).

Insurance practices produce a continuous elaboration and proliferation of risks that are capable of rational calculation according to actuarial rules on the basis of probability statistics. It clearly does transform what was an obstacle (that is, uncertainty about the future) into a possibility that facilitates planning and at least some control over unforeseen consequences. Insurance turns security into a calculable project and a rational collective accomplishment that makes of one's life an object to be managed (Miller, 1987). 'Each new measure of protection makes visible a new form of insurable insecurity' (Defert, 1991, p. 215).

By reinforcing and constituting insecurity and offering a solution to it – the material and existential security from, for example, claims payments and 'peace of mind' – insurance serves as a 'moral–political technology' (Defert, 1991; Knights and Vurdubakis, 1993). However, the security that insurance provides for citizens, employees and consumers also transfers to those who would seek to maintain social order since, as Hacking (1991, p. 184) noted, 'proletarian revolutions have never occurred in any state whose assurantial technology was working properly' (p. 184). Not surprisingly, then, governments have shown and continue to demonstrate great interest in insurance practices both supporting their private proliferation through various fiscal and legal concessions, as well as appropriating or transferring their technologies into the public domain (Knights and Vurdubakis, 1993). Like other forms of calculation and classification, insurance 'provides a general principle for the objectification of things, people and their relations'

(Ewald, 1991, p. 206). At one and the same time it has individualising and totalising effects.

> (insurance is) ... a scheme of rationality, a way of breaking down, rearranging, ordering certain elements of reality ... (it) individualises, defines each person as a *risk*, but the individuality it confers is ... relative to that of other members of the *insured* population – an average sociological individuality (Ewald, 1991, pp. 199 and 203, emphasis added).

There are some clear parallels between the practice described here and that of the market segmentation of financial service consumers discussed in our study of a French bank. For example one could substitute the words 'risk' and 'insured' with those of 'consumer type' and 'market' to account for the way in which individuals are located in relation to behavioural–psychological 'clusters'.

As we argue below, such parallels are by no means coincidental. Rather, they reflect how the history of knowledges of consumer subjectivity within financial services as elsewhere are often 'bound up with programmes which, in order to govern subjects, have found that they need to know them' (Rose, 1989, p. 5). Through this knowledge of subjectivity, populations are isolated and their characteristics selected, examined, inscribed and acted upon. We are not suggesting here that there is some overall grand plan emanating from a central state institution. As Foucault (1991) stressed, government is dispersed across a wide array of institutions and practices designed and developed for a diverse range of purposes. It is not necessarily in the intentions so much as the effects of exercises of power that populations become governed. In addition the exercise of power is not immune to its own internal contradictions and tensions nor to resistance from those subjects upon whom it is targeted.

In marketing, however, there is considerable energy and potential, through market research and focus groups, to determine which strategies will be effective in controlling consumer behaviour. In the following brief sketch, we seek to show how the emergence of programmes to govern the consumer through demographic and psychographic (lifestyle) segmentation may be seen as a combination and mutation of knowledges and practices that were themselves products of governmentality. For clarity of presentation, the account is organised into three subsections which broadly correspond to, albeit overlapping, historical periods and forms of segmentation – demographic, psychographic and their 'strategic' combination and application in contemporary financial services.

TECHNOLOGIES OF SEGMENTATION: A BRIEF SKETCH

The Social Survey

Although the 'methodological roots' of the social survey can be traced to the work of philanthropists and early government concerns with knowledge of the population in late nineteenth-century Britain (Downham *et al.*, 1956; Moser, 1958), its regular and more elaborate use did not occur until the 1930s (Abrams, 1951). Popular among social reformers such as Booth, Rowntree and the Webbs who sought to document the extent of poverty and hardship among the working classes, the social survey also provided essential data for government policy makers. Collecting statistics on populations, however, was first stimulated by governments following the work of the Dutch actuarial pioneer De Witt in 1671 (O'Donnell, 1936), and subsequently, private insurers in the eighteenth century (Knights, 1988) seeking to advance a more scientific approach to actuarial calculations for annuities and life insurance. Hacking (1990, 1991) charted the emergence of the science of statistics from the seventeenth century onwards as an 'avalanche of printed numbers' whereby attributes of the population (for example, age, birth, death, habitation and employment) were inscribed in a numerical and usable form for the calculations of those in power (see also Rose, 1988, 1989). Hacking (1990, 1991) also showed how the socioeconomic and other categories devised for purposes of measuring populations became meaningful labels and, we would add, the bases of contemporary demographic segmentation practices.

The market research literature builds on this tradition of collecting statistics on the population by philanthropists and government policy makers. While central government statistics and classifications of the population (for example, the Registrar General's classification) provided a basis upon which to conduct market research, the poverty studies of Rowntree (1901), Booth (1902) and Bowley and Burnett-Hurst (1915) and the town planning surveys of the interwar period lent legitimacy and credibility to the activity. Paradigms of inscription such as the family lifecycle (Rowntree) and the neighbourhood concept (Booth)[5] as well as the continued extension of quantification of behaviour (Booth), sampling and interview techniques (Bowley) and observation research (mass observation) were 'pioneered' (Moser, 1958).

Such innovations also informed and were subsequently developed in the accelerated expansion of government social surveys during the 'crisis' period of the Second World War. For example, the Food Survey was initiated in 1940, in the first instance to examine the diet of the urban working class. Similar national surveys followed in sickness and consumer expenditure –

the Social Survey began in 1941. As we discuss below, market research, which was little practised during the war, drew on and contributed towards the extension of the social survey in the post-war period. The Market Research Society was formed in 1947 at approximately the same time as university statistics (applied economics) and sociology departments (for example, the London School of Economics) were extending the social survey method to encompass national data on incomes, savings and social mobility. Much of this data was of value to market researchers in general but of specific value to financial services where savings and income statistics are the raw data upon which forecasts of business activity in the area of financial security products could be made.

Market research had now become established and by the mid-1950s employed approximately 2000 people with an expenditure level of £3 million (Downham *et al.*, 1956).[6] The inscription paradigms of demographic segmentation (for example, family and financial lifecycles) were being developed and extended (Clark, 1955) from prior and continued governmental concerns to measure the *material* well-being of populations. However, the market research literature of the time observed some scepticism from statisticians (typically trained in economics or sociology) towards the new developments which were beginning to focus more on the *psychological* condition of consumers – 'motivation research' (Downham *et al.*, 1956). We now turn to this new combination of knowledges in surveys and its significance for the regulation of the consumer society.

Subjectivity and Self-discipline

As Foucault (1980) suggested, securing and developing knowledge of populations through statistical data and classifications provides for an exercise of power over 'objectified' subjects. Marketing had traditionally relied upon such objective data and even segmentation only broke the market up into fairly crude categories. Developments were at this time taking place that sought to understand not just segments of the population but also the subjectivity of individual consumers although not always at the level of conscious intention. This subjectification of consumers involved entering the soul of individuals and targeting them with whatever encourages or promotes their own subjective self-discipline. Early attempts to establish such knowledge occurred within psychology and was concerned with the 'morale' of the population and the armed services during the Second World War (Rose, 1989). They represented a new focus of scrutiny for governments in the US and UK and when combined with the pre-war (and post-war) development of public (voter) opinion research conducted in the growing spirit of liberal 'popular democracy', led to a number of developments in psychological theory and practice. For example, in 1939 Likert's work on public opinion in the US Agriculture Department was redirected to enemy morale and soldiers' attitudes. The resulting Likert scale was to become one of the key tools for making *attitudes* quantifiable and meaningful. According to Rose (1989),

> Earlier psychological conceptions of the mass psychology of the mob ... gave way to a notion of the populous as an *aggregate of individuals* with views and wishes that could be investigated by precise techniques and communicated to government by experts. The new science of democracy also drew upon a new way of thinking about individual will. ... Individuals were moved by attitudes ... (which) thus bridged the internal world of the psyche and the external world of conduct (p. 27, emphasis added).

Similarly with the concept of personality, the use of psychiatrists in War Office Selection Boards saw their role change from the 'keepers of lunatics' to examiners of the 'normal' psyche and the resulting conduct of individuals. The wartime development of psychological research from 1939 led to tests (for example, 'Cattells 16 personality factors') which, as with intelligence and testing in the previous war, enabled personality to be visualised, calculated and administered (Rose, 1989, p. 46). In addition psychiatrists were employed in War Office Selection Boards to transfer their skills in managing the mentally ill to the field of recruiting normal individuals into the war effort.

These developments in the conceptualisation of 'personality' and 'attitude' produced new ways of calculating the link between subjectivity and administrative objectives in the workplace, the family, the consulting room and, we would add, the store or branch. It began to transform our very sense of ourselves – 'the ways in which we interact ... Our thought worlds ... our ways of thinking about and talking about our personal feelings, our secret hopes, our ambitions and disappointments' (Rose, 1989, p. 8). Such knowledge was not only applied to programmes directly concerned with governing populations through, for example, social policy with respect to children and families. The management of subjectivity also became central to organisations in pursuing increased productivity, harmony and 'enterprise' from employees (see also Hollway, 1991). Techniques that 'allow us' to construct, sustain and remodel the self, Rose (1989) argued, proliferated in the form of the 'expertise' of counsellors, social workers and personnel managers or, what he disparagingly terms, 'engineers of the human soul'. This new expertise became effective in governing subjectivity not merely through the formal institutions of the state but in a more indirect way in keeping with the liberal democratic ideas of the time. 'It achieves its effects ... by way of the persuasion inherent in its truths, the anxiety stimulated by its norms, and the attraction exercised by the images of life and self it offers to us' (Rose, 1989, p. 10).

This advance in psychological assessment and the 'measurement' of attitudes, aptitudes, personalities and even of lifestyles and their use in marketing and segmentation can be self-disciplinary – they 'make[s] persons amenable to having things done to them – and doing things to themselves – in the name of their subjective capacities' (Rose, 1989, pp. 7–8). Following the post-war reconstruction period, it may be argued that the development of capitalism had resolved many of the (technological) problems of production but not of consumption and the danger of excess productive capacity (Marx, 1976). Consequently, an increasing interconnectedness between work and 'non-work' was being forged in contemporary employment as 'the primary economic image ... [became] ... not that of the producer but of the consumer ... we are urged to shape our lives by the use of purchasing power' (Rose, 1989, p. 102). Rose's (1989) focus is not with marketing practices, but upon how rational economic and social concerns were displaced at work by the profile of employees seeking a 'maximised quality of life'.

Capturing the Consumer through Marketing

Paralleling the development of these technologies of subjectivity, this engineering of the soul was extended through the application of the concepts of personality and attitude into market research and segmentation. Such segmentation practices are seen by neo-Marxists (for example, Curtis, 1988; Goldman, 1992) primarily in terms of their power to exploit markets and manipulate consumers for the purposes of sustaining surplus value and/or control (see Sturdy and Knights, 1996) . Without necessarily endorsing such a view, it is possible to argue that the marketing demands of organisations are a condition (as well as a consequence) of the growth and development of contemporary psychological knowledge – reshaping its methods, form and foci (see also Hollway, 1991). Indeed, in some marketing literature, segmentation is seen to have emerged as a result of managerial 'needs' in responding to an external (market) environment rather than as the product of new ways of seeing that environment. For example, in some companies where we have conducted research, marketing departments seek ever-increasing budgets for market research partly, at least, to enhance the status and significance of their activities (see Knights and Murray, 1994).

Contemporary market segmentation, as will be illustrated shortly in our case study, is clearly founded on the view of a population as an aggregation of individuals whereby inscription paradigms can render (buying) behaviour predictable. In particular, increased competition (and/or market saturation), flexible production technologies and increased consumer sophistication and/or heterogeneity are typically cited as the conditions for a heightened marketing orientation.[7] However, competition was and still is the primary impetus for the use of ever-increasingly sophisticated marketing technologies of subjectivity that facilitate a capturing of the consumer. For example, in French insurance, the relevance of psychographics and other newly emerging marketing practices were discussed and promoted in industry conferences in the 1970s, but it was not until changes in regulation and a more competitive market in the following decades that such developments began to be practised (Philippe, 1992). The use of these sophisticated marketing technologies, however, is not simply a matter of measuring the psychographic characteristics of markets and segmenting them accordingly. The new competitive conditions have resulted in market segments being evaluated not just for their psychological compatibility with particular products and services but also for their cost–profit effectiveness.

Consequently, other knowledge such as accounting and strategic management are brought into the equation. However, such knowledge does not merely represent a tactical response to the market environment; both these discourses have been shown to have their own history in the constitution of 'markets' (for example, prices), consumers (for example, 'value') and 'competition' (Hopwood, 1987; Hoskin, 1990; Knights and Morgan, 1990). Similarly, in insurance there is a parallel between the long-established actuarial and underwriting techniques of risk assessment whereby individual risks are defined, measured and priced (or declined) and the market segmentation concept of matching (responding to) individual needs with 'personalised' product offers (and prices). Indeed, it has been claimed in the insurance marketing literature that the 'triumph of the individual' in contemporary society means that a more general application of the insurance principle of assessing risks (security 'needs') individually renders insurance and marketing a 'marriage of reason' (Anon, 1992).[8] Furthermore, in France and elsewhere in Europe, the growing practice of marketing and segmentation in security 'products' such as insurance, loans and savings, has coincided with what has been deemed a 'crisis' in existing security systems (for example, state pensions and health care).

For example, the neo-liberal demands for reducing public expenditure and demographic fears of a welfare crisis, particularly in funding pensions and care for the elderly, have led governments to pursue reforms, *in part* by encouraging individuals to save more with private institutions. In France, where government-supported occupational pension schemes operated on the basis of a 'pay-as-you-go' system in which employees'contributions were more or less directly transferred to pensioners within the same occupational scheme, a major problem of funding arose. This arrangement for governing the security of populations (and of governments) became threatened by demographic changes within occupations (for example, the decline in contributions from a dwindling community of farm workers) and then, more recently, nationally as the falling birth rate and ageing population reduced the ratio of contributors to pensioners (Sturdy *et al.*, 1997). Such changes, combined with other political and ideological developments, have resulted in a shift in emphasis away from the state and occupational retirement schemes and towards individual and employer pensions as in the UK.

As we have sought to indicate, marketing does not merely respond to individual needs or lifestyles, but is proactive in constituting and modifying them so as to render the production–consumption relationship less problematic. Marketing does this through playing on the anxieties surrounding subjectivity and reinforcing a culture of competing identities where the consumption needs may be seen to reside (Knights *et al.*, 1994). By examining segmentation in contemporary practice, we now elaborate this argument through the use of some fieldwork material to show how the combination of psychological and other knowledges is precisely targeted at constituting consumer subjectivity.

SEGMENTATION IN CONTEMPORARY MARKETING PRACTICE

Over recent years, the marketing literature has proliferated to identify, represent and reproduce the markets for goods and services as consisting of increasingly fragmented and individualised, fluctuating and transitory consumer 'needs' (see Du Gay, 1993; Knights *et al.*, 1994; Morgan and Sturdy, in press). Recognising that companies have begun to take account of the changes, the literature argues that further developments are required in order to take advantage of what has become known as the marketing concept – identifying and responding to needs profitably (see Hooley *et al.*, 1990, p. 7). In manufacturing industries in the US and then elsewhere, changes rendered product-led mass marketing and production and their associated technologies increasingly inappropriate.[9] An increasing variety of goods were produced in response (that is, 'tailored') to differentiated 'needs' (a market segmentation strategy) and/or, at least, delivery mechanisms and promotional messages for standard products were targeted according to different perceived requirements (a product differentiation strategy) (Smith, 1956).

A similar development was advocated and followed in the service sectors including, more recently, the financial services. Here, in both Britain and France it is currently claimed that a market orientation is being adopted and there are calls for this to expand by matching products and services to the more individualised 'needs' or demands of consumers (de Moubray, 1990; Philippe, 1992; Sturdy and Morgan, 1993; cf. Morgan and Sturdy, in press). Moreover, as has been suggested, financial services marketing is increasingly concerned with responding to and constituting consumers in terms of new security needs that are based on the realisation of specific lifestyles and the optimisation of subjective well-being (Knights, 1988). A significant part of this development takes place through the strategy of market segmentation.

In order to achieve market segmentation or even the tailoring of promotional messages, increasingly sophisticated market research and analysis has been used to identify the consumer characteristics and needs and their location within given populations. The marketing literature documents varying approaches and techniques used in market segmentation (see Speed and Smith (1992) and Beane and Ennis (1987) for reviews). In general, a market or population is divided on a basis or, typically, a number of bases which describe or, more often, can be related in some way to buying behaviour. Ideally, the market divisions or segments should each be homogeneous in terms of the factor(s) under consideration. In addition, they should be 'accessible', 'measurable' 'actionable' and 'substantial' or profitable (Kotler, 1988) so that products, sales approaches and other information can be targeted/tailored with respect to them. Identifying appropriate 'signs' of behaviour and classifying distinct groups to which they are related provides the data to facilitate the achievement of the marketing concept through an efficient channelling of resources (Schauerman, 1990).

A wide and ever-increasing range of factors are researched for use in segmenting the market. They are typically classified into three types: demographic, geodemographic and psychographic (see Joseph and Yorke, 1989). Demographics include age, sex, socio-occupational group, income and family type and stage. The latter, the 'family lifecycle' concept consisted of a number of stages from 'single' to 'retired sole survivor' and has been subsequently modified to incorporate some 'non-traditional' family forms (Murphy and Staples, 1979). Geodemographics relates to neighbourhoods and are derived from census data, with classifications combining variables including race and class (for example, A Classification of Residential Neighbourhoods (ACORN) groups in the UK). Psychographics refers to various personality traits and particular values, attitudes and behaviours or lifestyles (VALS) (Wells, 1975). As we discuss below, it is claimed that psychographics gets 'closer' to the nature and identity of individuals and supersedes socioeconomic groups in reflecting the changed social structure

In addition to the above three general categories, segmentations can be product/sector specific. Indeed, it is argued that this is the most useful application to marketers (Bowles, 1987). For example, a 'classic' French study in 1971 revealed two distinct behaviour groups related to saving and spending – 'les accumulateurs' and 'les jouisseurs', 39 and 61 per cent of the population, respectively (Zollinger, 1985, p. 15). Now, companies make and use sharper distinctions. Crédit Lyonnais Bank, for example, began to market products on the basis of seven different saving–spending motivations, five 'modern' and two 'traditional'. In addition, the 'banking lifecycle' is commonly used, charting periods of saving and borrowing against age for particular groups such as *cadres supérieur* and revealing a concentration of saving in the 45–65 years age group, for example. Finally, segmentations may be tailored to specific companies' requirements including 'micro-segmentation' – classifying existing clients. Frequently, companies will conduct or commission a number of studies and seek to combine their findings to provide a 'truer' reflection of the market. This concern parallels the view that the greater the range of methods used to 'observe' behaviour the more precisely it can be 'captured'.

Other concerns of practitioners, aside from cost and practicability, relate to the availability of data, how up-to-date it is and, in particular, the extent to which the bases or variables used are accurate predictors of the behaviour (for example, saving) in question. Banks, in particular, with their large and 'captive' client bases have the potential to collect massive amounts of information. Many are currently engaged in identifying and collecting customer information and transcribing it through information technology (IT) into a usable form, adopting what is called a strategy of 'relational marketing', where a multiplicity of data files on a given customer are integrated in order to facilitate an effective targeting of products (Curtis, 1988; Morgan, and Sturdy, in press). We now provide more detail of segmentation practices, particularly psychographics and their application in French financial services by use of a case study company which we have named Banque Francaise (BF).

Case Study of a French Bank

BF is a large and well-known and established retail bank with a large number and wide range of customers throughout France. Its relative success as a mainstream bank was attributed in the company to the 'capture' of a high proportion of the post-war 'baby-boom' generation as they reached adulthood in the late 1960s and, subsequently, satisfying their hitherto relatively 'homogenous' needs as they progressed through the banking 'lifecycle' (for example, loans, housing, investments, life assurance and savings for pensions). However, its large and diffuse organisational structure and concomitant IT was considered 'costly' which, combined with a predominantly 'conservative' client base, resulted in a low profitability in relation to other banks. As we shall see, recent strategies sought to address this perceived weakness. For example, its marketing was seen in the industry to be advanced, often acting as a leader, to be followed in product innovations for example. In this sense, it can be considered a leading rather than typical player in the field of marketing financial services and, hence, is most appropriate as a case study of emerging developments in this area.[10]

The bank, in common with some others, used the results of a psychographic study series on 'Eurolifestyles' carried out by an agency, the CCA (Centre of Advanced Communications). The study is seen by its users as comprehensive, citing the 24 000 interviews carried out in 15 West European countries (60 regions) with 700 questions providing a range of 3200 responses in each case. The questions and variables used are presented as covering or capturing the three elements of people's lives – opinions (rationality), feelings (emotion and dreams) and behaviour (habits) – which colloquially correspond to the head, heart and body. Thus, it is claimed, a much richer picture of individuals can be gained than with, for example, demographic studies relating spending/saving patterns with socioeconomic groups. Indeed, the Eurolifestyles study identified a number of subcategories of financial behaviour within the occupational classification of 'cadres'. 'One will understand better, for example, consumers of insurance by knowing what they consume in their leisure, on cars, how they raise their children, how they vote, what they believe' (Cathelat, 1991, p. 120).

Using a range of statistical techniques, (for example, cluster and multivariate analysis), the responses are analysed with a view to forming relatively homogenous and distinct groups or 'clusters' of shared characteristics – lifestyle types.

In this case, 16 European 'sociostyles' were created which were further grouped for practicality in commercial application into six 'mentalities'. Both sets of categories are identified and presented by their location on a pictorial map incorporating the measures of 'materialistic–moralistic' along north–south and 'dynamism–stability' along west–east[11] polar axes (see Figure 8.1). Each cluster or segment is given a common-sense name or 'descriptor' which summarises the nature of the characteristics shared. For example, in the 'north-west' quarter (materialistic–dynamism) the 'socioambitieux' ('go-ahead individualists') 'mentality' is located comprising around 25 per cent of the European population and three sociostyles – 'Eurodandies, Rockies and Business'. The latter are described as 'yuppies' seeking power and money. By contrast, in the 'north-east' the 'Europrudent' are located – 'resigned seekers of security' and so on.

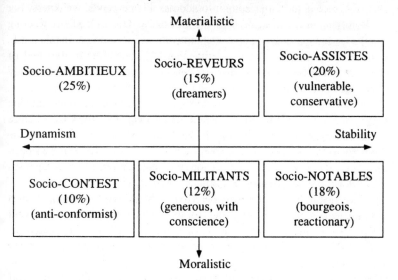

European Social Mentalities

Materialistic

Socio-AMBITIEUX (25%)	Socio-REVEURS (15%) (dreamers)	Socio-ASSISTES (20%) (vulnerable, conservative)

Dynamism ←————————————→ Stability

Socio-CONTEST (10%) (anti-conformist)	Socio-MILITANTS (12%) (generous, with conscience)	Socio-NOTABLES (18%) (bourgeois, reactionary)

Moralistic

FIGURE 8.1   Adapted from a BF marketing strategy document – original research by CCA, France. The percentages refer to the approximate populations across 15 West European countries.

The research on sociostyles is claimed to be dynamic as well as rich in that social trends can be identified by carrying out similar studies periodically, albeit with different interviewees. Indeed, the proliferation of differentiated groups with distinctive identities and behavioural characteristics is now clearly being seen as an important focus for market research. For example, it is claimed that in the 1950s there were only four or five sociostyles (and two mentalities), nine by 1970 and 14 (and five mentalities) in 1984. At the same time, apparently stable typologies exist across Europe which, for companies, highlights the possibility of marketing Pan-European products at target markets, regulations permitting (cf. Centre pour Reserche en Preyvoyance, CREP, 1991). For example, in France the insurers, GAN, developed a product for the same segment across the whole of Western Europe (Langlumé, 1992). The identification of such trends in social differentiation, particularly that of atomisation, is used to promote segmentation as a necessary marketing tool.

The CCA claimed that the sociostyles information was used by financial services companies to differing degrees. Most frequently, the messages in advertising and promotion (for example, product literature) are partly informed by such segmentation. To a lesser extent it was used in new product development, matching products with perceived 'needs' or risks and, increasingly, in distribution and sales training. For example, a training simulation computer package is available giving set phrases in response to signs from 'clients' in relation to their segment location or lifestyle (see Cathelat, 1991). BF's use of Eurolifestyles and other similar studies appeared to be relatively advanced, particularly in relation to insurance companies. The behaviours and orientations of different segments can be matched with ranges of risk types (for example, in relation to AIDS), available products, distribution channels/sales approaches, media (for promotions) and appropriate messages or images. Indeed, the ranges can be superimposed onto the 'polar' segment chart with, for example, the socioambitieux group particularly associated with distribution through the 'Mintel' (viewdata) network.

Clearly, existing services and messages could be better targeted using such techniques. More significantly, they could also be redesigned and changed to meet better the needs of groups of potential and existing clients (cf. Knights *et al.*, 1994). For example, the lifestyles analysis informed the development and launch of a new optional term savings account, with 17 options regarding, for example, the periods of deposits, interest payments and withdrawal penalties built into the contract. It was targeted in two main directions – conservative segments in the east of the chart and relatively young people located further west. A similar strategy followed the government's initiation in 1990 of a popular savings plan or PEP[12] with interest rates and fiscal benefits to encourage individual private saving for future security needs (Sturdy *et al.*, 1997). The bank adapted the basic product into six variations by combining it with other standard security products such as housing savings ('PEL'), passbook accounts, unit trusts and other investments.

Once again, this 'innovative' range of differentiated mixed products was designed to match the perceived range of savings needs (for example, security, rate of return, access and convenience) and to be targeted at different sociostyles or segments. For example, the two most conservative mentalities, both well-off (south-east) and more vulnerable and poor (north-east), were targeted through regular income and free access product features, respectively. By contrast, risk capital (high rates of return) products were positioned towards the less conservative groups. Other banks also repackaged their PEPs in a similar way, promoting them as being 'adapted to your objectives', and the product was hugely popular in terms of sales volume not least, in part, because of the climate of 'crisis' in public security systems.

BF also used sociostyles in its communications. For example, in line with a change in its corporate image, the company logo was changed to target those more 'dynamic' (and younger) segments to the west of the chart. In relation to products, the name PEP was changed to PEPS partly because of its perceived phonetic advantages ('like Pepsi'). In addition, each product was 'coloured' in promotion material to coincide 'psychologically' with the nature of the service and the target segments (for example, blue for the investment-related product and green for regular income). Again, similar practices were subsequently carried out by other financial services companies. One bank, for example, used different images for each of its PEPs – a dove, an hour glass, a country house, an abacus and a father and son/grandson.

BF's marketing was only partly informed by the sociostyles analysis. Other segmentations and tools were used in combination such as the family, banking and product 'lifecycles'. In addition, its existing clients were analysed in relation to their usage of bank services and numerous other available criteria. Again, typologies are established and labelled (see Zollinger, 1985). In addition to seeking simply to identify, respond to and target different segments, increasing attention was given to the costs in the strategic marketing plans which were formulated with the aid of consultants' analytical tools. A 'differentiated' strategy was seen as most appropriate for a large bank such as BF in an environment where consumer needs are increasingly diffuse. Such an approach was developed by the familiar technique of measuring the 'attractiveness' (profitability/risk) for the bank of each segment and product and comparing these measures with its perceived strengths and those of its competitors. One result was the hierarchical classification of clients' profitability for the bank into 'stars', 'dead weights' and 'leeches'. This partially informed a distribution strategy whereby it was considered that the latter category, of modest profitability, did not need to be actively 'courted', but had advantages for the bank in terms of contributing to the cash flow and economies of scale.

At the product level, the strategy was to develop three broad and segmented forms of distribution. Firstly, for simple, low 'added-value' (profitability) products which are 'bought' rather than sold, the distribution was externalised – telephone/home banking, mailing/phoning, mobile sales units and distribution alliances (for example, with retail stores). By contrast, the 'second level' is for high-profitability products sold by specialists in a 'made to measure' service closely matched to individual needs. Finally, the wide branch network was to be used to sell ranges of products, not distinguished technically (that is, between insurance or banking) but packaged and 'coloured' according to the needs of client groups. Thus, in summary, marketing and segmentation in particular became central to the activities in the BF as well as other financial services companies. As with earlier combinations of knowledges, such activities render a reformulation of subjectivity possible. We turn now to a closer analytical examination of the social processes of these emerging developments of consumer subjectivity.

CONSUMER SUBJECTIVITY REVISITED

So far we have reported on the techniques and procedures of governmentality whereby populations are regulated and subjects managed. We have sought to indicate, particularly in the field of financial services, where marketing has drawn upon and, in turn, contributed to these constructions of subjectivity. There is a danger that such an analysis, however, may be seen to treat human subjects as 'judgemental dopes' (Garfinkel, 1967; cf. Marcuse, 1964) who can be readily manipulated and labelled to meet the demands of public or private interests. In order to avoid such criticism we need to look more closely at the social processes through which individuals are transformed into consumer subjects. While it is clear that those exercising power in either a public or private capacity have definite intentions with respect to citizens or consumers, it is rarely the case that the effects of their actions coincide perfectly with these intentions. In this sense, subjectivity is a complex yet often unintended outcome of the exercise of power.

There are many reasons why individuals do not act in accordance with the intentions or formulations of those who exercise power over them. Intentions may not be clear or obvious, they may be communicated in such a way as to incline subjects to subvert them, they may be in conflict with the demands of other significant powers or with deeply internalised behavioural norms, they may be internally self-contradictory or inconsistent with previous demands or they may fail to reflect important changes that are relevant to the situation. Of course, subjects may also resist the demands made of them simply because they violate their sense of self-worth, dignity or material self-interests. For example, in the context of financial services, the efforts of life assurance sales forces are frequently unsuccessful. So much so that sales to call ratios are often as low as 1 : 100 where 'cold calling' (that is, no previous contact or recommendation) is employed.

More generally, despite the increased marketing activity and commentators' claims of the emergence of a more sophisticated and mobile financial services consumer, large sections of the population remain largely indifferent to and ignorant of new products and levels of service (Burton, 1994; Knights *et al.*, 1994). Moreover, resistance to the exercise of power can take subtle forms that are difficult to detect. For example, subjects may appear to conform to particular demands while in fact merely complying, and remaining relatively indifferent to the actual content of the demand. Finally, it has to be recognised that the exercise of power is usually neither unilinear nor one-to-one in its impact. Power is exercised in opposite directions or backwards and forwards simultaneously, has multiple sources and objects and is collective and therefore often indirect in its effects. The impact of power, then, is often a complex and unintended set of consequences that reflects a multiple and diverse range of often incompatible influences. Where power is exercised at a distance, as in marketing, these multiplicity of uncertain and unpredictable, intended and unintended effects are much in evidence. Consequently, no matter how sophisticated and scientific the segmentation and market research, consumers may resist or fail to comply with the consumer behaviour expected. This is because subjectivity can never be wholly captured and thereby controlled.

What it is crucial to recognise is that power is exercised not directly on subjects but on their actions (Foucault, 1982, p. 220) – actions that are frequently recalcitrant, intransigent and resistant to any exercise of power upon them. In the absence of such freedom of action, the notion of a power relationship would not exist since the behaviour of one could be determined by that of another (Foucault, 1982). Despite these multiple opportunities for non-conformity and resistance, individuals often do behave in accordance with the wishes or intentions of private and public bodies. As we have been suggesting throughout this chapter, citizens may identify with the mode of subjectivity that is a product of governmental action and consumers frequently buy what the marketers and sales people seek to sell them. This is particuarly so where what is being traded is security of some sort as in the case of insurance, investments and pensions. It may be argued that once individuals perceive themselves as an object to be managed (Miller, 1987), this will involve them in not only securing their life in the present but also in the future. This necessarily involves consuming financial services products that can transform future uncertainties into risks that can then be managed through various 'insurantial technologies' (Donzelot, 1980).

However, this concern with controlling the future is an almost inevitable extension from a situation of comparative affluence in the present where a large number of uncertainties have been transformed into risks that are manageable. It is reinforced by the effects of increasing individualisation where subjects are thrown back on their own devices and 'tied to [their] own identity by a conscience or self-knowledge' (Foucault, 1982, p. 212). Foucault (1982) did not go on to unpack this phrase nor to discuss identity in contrast to subjectivity in his work. Yet the phrase is a clue to the observed willingness of individuals often to accept the definitions of others and to subjugate themselves to their wills. For the anxiety and insecurity that resides in the freedom of action renders us highly vulnerable or suggestive to the demands of others, particularly when those others have a social status or presumed significance beyond our own.

This is intensified when, as a result of the decline of ascribed statuses and collective identities (Durkheim, 1947), identity can no longer be taken for granted. For in these uncertain and fragmenting conditions, the freedom of action is frequently directed narrowly towards practices which are seen to secure the recognition and social confirmation of significant others (Knights, 1990, p. 319). This is because the freedom to define oneself through significant others is a path strewn with pot holes and obstacles. Social confirmation or approval from significant others can never be guaranteed and the resulting uncertainty generates considerable anxiety and insecurity. Consequently, in the absence of having the resources or hierarchical authority to be in a formal situation of control, subjects will frequently seek to conform to others' expectations as a means of securing their social approbation. It is this suggestiveness that is the condition making it possible for individuals to be readily transformed into subjects who secure their identity, meaning and reality through engaging in (indeed being committed to) social practices that are the outcome of particular exercises of power (Knights, 1992, p. 518). Subjects then become self-disciplined in sustaining the practices that are supportive of a meaning or identity that promises some stability, order and security. When directly focused on security as in the private and public governmental domains which have been the subject of this chapter, a self-disciplined commitment to discourses and practices (for example, personal welfare and private insurance) designed to bring it about may well be the outcome.

SUMMARY AND CONCLUSION

Drawing primarily on examples from financial services, we have endeavoured to show how subjectivity has been constructed as both a resource and product of the search for security in modern Western society. Although noting the extent to which public institutions are involved in the provision of social security and the significance of this for financial services companies, our concern has largely been with the private sector and its development, distribution and sale of products designed and promoted to sustain the subjective well-being of clients rather than merely protecting them against risks. Focusing upon market segmentation, we have illustrated the growing use of psychographic or lifestyle classifications of consumer segments by French banks such as BF. The marketing view is that these practices are a *response* to changing social structures, in which 'traditional' and broad occupational and social class groupings are no longer the most significant source of social identity. The understanding that society is more fragmented and individualised means that producers have to adapt to a differentiated range of identities. Within financial services, this involves providing products that can satisfy consumers' security needs but in a way which relates to their achieving life projects rather than merely minimising 'hazards'.

As was reported earlier, Beck (1992) believed that we are in transition from a modern to a risk, not post-modern, society. While sympathetic to this view, we argued that Beck's (1992) global approach to risk as primarily connected with the scientific and technological exploitation of nature was limited in its understanding of the social construction of risk. We suggested that risk is increasingly being constituted in more positive ways to represent social realities that can be managed to advance the security and psychological growth of subjects. Much of this attention to subjectivity is both an intended and sometimes unintended outcome of the marketing and distribution practices of financial services (and other) companies, which locate particular meaning systems and the identities of subjects as the basis for providing the means of sustaining or reinforcing them.

Crucial to these developments has been the conception of populations as aggregates of individuals with capacities that can be measured and acted upon. In addition, we have suggested that the practice of market segmentation in financial services represents a combination and mutation of strategic, accounting and other financial (for example, insurantial) knowledges with those of the human sciences each of which has been historically developed in governing or producing subjectivity. For instance, marketing practices elaborate and reinforce long-established insurantial technologies in the classification of risk and constitution of 'security' needs and, thereby, of consumers.

The disciplinary *potential* of market (for example, lifestyle) segmentation in financial services is exercised in helping to define the boundaries and content of identity, particularly in relation to consumption and in reinforcing the discipline associated with insurantial technologies and the consumption of security products. In accounting for the extent to which segmentation and related practices and messages shape behaviour and identity, power has been conceived as enabling as well as repressive of subjectivity. For example, segmentation can be seen to constitute the 'norm' and facilitate the formation of the self as a particular sort of subject – a consumer of security products and, more specifically, a particular type (cluster) of consumer (for example, a risk taker).

This is not, of course, to argue that subjects use the precise labels of segmentation to describe themselves. Indeed, such a practice would conflict with a sense of distinctiveness and individual freedom. The 'willingness' of subjects to adopt identities of this form lies, as Curtis (1988) intimated, in the existential anxiety of individualisation processes whereby individuals come to seek a sense of 'belonging' or identification with a larger whole but, at the same time and sometimes paradoxically, emphasise their distinctive and unique character as autonomous individuals. For example, the marketing of 'personalised' financial services clearly appeals to the latter while the use in advertising and promotion of familial images or those representing aspirations may also heighten the former.

Equally there are paradoxes in the marketing of financial services where security products not only respond to the anxieties and insecurities of subjects but also produce these self-same insecurities in order to trade on them. The internalisation of such messages is not a straightforward process however. Firstly, there is a tension implicit in seeking to belong to a group (collective identity) and yet to be autonomous, different and unique (individual identity). Secondly and relatedly, it has been noted how marketing and sales messages and practices are periodically resisted or ignored, particularly in financial services. This reflects the way in which they may confront rather than appeal to prevailing or localised identities and insecurities (for example, fear of hazards in relation to insurance). However, even in such dynamic circumstances, power continues to be exercised in the constitution of identities, firstly through the incorporation of themes of resistance in subsequent and modified marketing messages and practices where previous negative images can be countered (Goldman, 1992; Sturdy and Knights, 1996) and, secondly, through taking the act of resistance (for example, environmental protests) as the basis for new products/identities.

Our account has been exploratory in nature. Further research is required to explore empirically and in more detail how knowledges have come to be combined, transformed and applied in governing the consumer. For example, Rose (1989) noted the frequently *ad hoc* nature of interventions in the development of psychological innovations (see also Hollway, 1991). In addition, the correspondence of the observations of social scientists, such as Beck (1992), of an increasing plurality of lifestyles with similarly constituting marketing practices requires further research. More generally, other than in relation to advertising, the ways in which marketing practices and knowledges constitute consumer needs and identities have not been a focus of research attention. Such gaps in the literature may partly reflect the way in which knowledge itself has come to be segmented so that we have difficulty learning from one another's disciplines (cf. Knights and Morgan, 1993; Du Gay, 1996). This chapter is clearly concerned with promoting inter-disciplinary possibilities in the narrow sphere of developments in financial services (cf. Burgoyne *et al.*, 1997). Nevertheless, there remains considerable scope for further critical study of marketing discourses.

ACKNOWLEDGEMENT

The authors acknowledge the Financial Services Research Centre for the funding enabling this research to be conducted.

Notes

1. An earlier draft of this paper was delivered at the 11th European Group for Organisation Studies (EGOS) Colloquium, Paris, 6–8 July 1993 and parts of the empirical field data have been published in Palmer and Clegg (1996).
2. Beck (1992) disclaimed the applicability of his thesis to France and the UK. However, similar observations have been made of these countries (for example, Featherstone, 1987, 1991; Mendras and Cole, 1991).
3. Beck (1992, p. 128) distinguished between the objective life situation which he discussed at length and the subjective consciousness–identity aspects of individualisation which he admits would require a book-length thesis all of its own. This dualism between the 'subjective' and the 'objective' is wholly problematic except at the purely analytic level which Beck (1992) claimed to go beyond (see Giddens, 1979b; Knights and Willmott, 1983, 1985, 1989). In particular, it renders his project overly abstract and disembodied.
4. A clear example of this shift is the way in which life assurance products have been promoted and have become principally savings products rather than solely an insurance against financial losses on death (Knights, 1988). At a broader level, however, American consumer society provides the best example of how risks have been reconstituted to encompass a whole range of items not ordinarily considered to be hazards but simply occasions for the maintenance of subjective well-being.
5. This was further developed in town planning surveys (for example, Lock *et al.*, 1947) and, later, in geodemographic market segmentation.
6. These authors claim that given the different level and scope of economic activity between the UK and the USA, their market research activity was equivalent at this time.
7. See Smith (1956) for its emergence in the consumer goods markets and Ennew *et al.* (1990) for its later development in financial services (cf. Morgan and Sturdy, in press).
8. While this individualistic approach of 'to each according to their risks' reflects the actuarial side of insurance, it also conforms to an increasing reluctance of consumers to share risks once discriminatory opportunities are available (for example, non-smokers and life assurance). However, it conflicts with the principle of mutualising risks. It is more of a mutualisation of *groups* (or segments) of risks (Roche, 1990; Rothmann, 1990). Moreover, it also conflicts with solidaristic values, which both compete and co-exist with individualism (Mendras and Cole, 1991, p. 117), because certain groups/individuals are

excluded by, for example, the companies selecting only the most profitable segments. It is claimed that this 'segmentation–selection' tension may lead to a crisis of legitimacy for the insurance industry (Albouy, 1992).

9. The change in production technologies towards greater flexibility and its wider context has been widely discussed elsewhere not least in relation to Piore and Sabel (1984) (for example, Wood, 1989). Genetic testing could be a further problem here since it may mean large-scale discrimination against those with genetically predicted life risks.

10. The material used in the following account is drawn largely from internal sources (for example, interviews, company documents and presentations) (see also Zollinger, 1985; Cathelat, 1991). This, combined with the paper's focus on formal marketing techniques, means that little attention is given here to those practices that are likely to limit the possibilities for 'rational' and 'systematic' management such as organisational 'politics'. However, such neglect is not thought to detract from the arguments presented.

11. Other axes can be used including the addition of a third dimension such as an 'imaginative–serious' scale.

12. This is not to be confused with the personal equity plan (PEP) in the UK which, in contrast to its French counterpart, attracts a tax-free status both on income and capital returns.

References

Abrams, M. (1951) *Social Surveys and Social Action* (London: Heinemann).

Albouy, F-X. (1992) 'A Chacun selon ses Risques', *Directions* (CAPA), no. 19, pp. 88–94.

Albouy, F-X. and Ewald, F. (1990) 'Le Client', *Risques*, no. 6, Octobre, pp. 11–23.

Anon (1992) 'Marketing et assurances, un mariage de raison', *L'Assurance Française*, no. 648, pp. 11–14.

Baritz, L. (1960) *The Servants of Power* (New York: Wesleyan University Press)

Baudrillard, J. (1981) *Towards a Critique of the Political Economy of the Sign* (St Louis: Telsos).

Bauman, Z. (1988) *Legislators and Interpreters* (London: Polity Press).

Beane, T.P. and Ennis, D.M. (1987) 'Market Segmentation: a Review', *European Journal of Marketing*, vol. 21, no. 5, pp. 20–42.

Beck, U. (1992) *Risk Society – Towards a New Modernity* (London: Sage).

Bell, D. (1970) 'The Cultural Contradictions of Capitalism', *Public Interest*, vol. 21, pp. 16–43.

Booth, C. (1902) *The Life and Labour of the People of London* (London: Macmillan).

Bourdieu, P. (1984) *Distinction – A Social Critique of the Judgement of Taste* (London: Routledge).

Bowles, T. (1987) 'Does Classifying People by Lifestyle Really Help the Advertiser?', *Admap*, May, pp. 36–40.

Bowley, A.L. and Burnett-Hurst, A.R. (1915) *Livelihood and Poverty* (London: King).

Burchell, G., Gordon, C. and Miller, P. (eds) (1991) *The Foucault Effect – Studies in Governmentality* (Hemel Hempstead: Harvester Wheatsheaf).

Burgoyne, J., Knights, D. and Willmott, H.C., 1997 editors' introduction, *British Journal of Management*, (in press), Special Edition on Interdisciplinary Research, 8/1, pp. 1–2.

Burton, D. (1994) *Financial Services and the Consumer* (London: Routledge).

Cathelat, B. (1991) 'Marketing et Société', *Risques*, no. 7, pp. 119–27.

Centre pour Reserche en Preyvoyance (CREP) (1991) *Money as they Like It – Europeans' View Vis a Vis Financial Products* (Paris: Openers Secodip).

Clark, L.H. (ed.) (1955) *Consumer Behaviour Volume II: The Life Cycle* (New York: New York University Press).

Curtis, T. (1988) 'The Information Society: a Computer Generated Caste System?', in V. Mosco and J. Wasko (eds), *The Political Economy of Information* (Wisconsin: University of Wisconsin Press), pp. 95–107.

Daniel, J-P. (1992) 'Boudda et Confucius, Même Combat Contre Sainte Barbe?', *Directions* (CAPA), no. 12, pp. 24–5.

Daston, L. (1990) 'The Domestication of Risk: Mathematical Probability and Insurance 1650–1830', in L. Kruger, L.J. Daston and M. Heidelberger (eds), *The Probabilistic Revolution Vol. 1* (Cambridge, Mass.: MIT Press), pp. 237–60.

de Moubray, G. (1990) 'Le Consommateur Recherche une Securité Emotionelle', *Le Moniteur des Assurance*, no. 1095.

Defert, D. (1991) '"Popular Life" and Insurance Technology', in G. Burchell, C. Gordon and P. Miller (eds), *The Foucault Effect – Studies in Governmentality* (Hemel Hempstead: Harvester Wheatsheaf), pp. 211–33.

Donzelot, J. (1979) 'The Poverty of Political Culture', *Ideology and Consciousness*, no. 5.

Donzelot, J. (1980) *The Policing of Families: Welfare Versus the State*, London: Hutchinson.

Downham, J.S., Shankleman, E. and Treasure, J.A.P. (1956) 'A Survey of Market Research in Great Britain', in F. Edwards (ed.), *Readings in Market Research* (London: British Market Research Bureau), pp. ix–xxxvi.

Du Gay, P. (1993) *Markets and Souls*, paper presented at the *Re-thinking Marketing Conference*, Warwick Business School, University of Warwick, 1–2 July.

Du Gay, P. (1996) *Consumption and Identity at Work* (London: Sage).

Du Gay, P. and Salaman, G. (1992) 'The Cult(ure) of the Customer', *Journal of Management Studies* , vol. 29, no. 5, pp. 615–33.

Durkheim, E (1947) *The Division of Labour in Society* (Glencoe, IL: Free Press).

Ennew, C.T., Watkins, T. and Wright, M. (eds) (1990) *Marketing Financial Services* (Oxford: Heinemann).

Ewald, F. (1986) *L'Etat Providence* (Paris: Grasset).

Ewald, F. (1991) 'Insurance and Risk', in G. Burchell, C. Gordon and P. Miller (eds), *The Foucault Effect – Studies in Governmentality* (Hemel Hempstead: Harvester Wheatsheaf), pp. 197–210.

Featherstone, M. (1987) 'Lifestyles and Consumer Culture', *Theory, Culture and Society*, vol. 4, pp. 55–70.

Featherstone, M. (1991) *Consumer Culture and Postmodernism* (London: Sage).

Foucault, M (1973) *The Order Of Things: the Archaeology of the Social Sciences* (London: Tavistock).

Foucault, M.(1979) 'Governmentality' (transcribed and edited by Pasquale Pasquire), *Ideology and Consciousness*, vol. 6, pp. 5–21.

Foucault, M. (1980) *Power/Knowledge* (edited and translated by Colin Gordon) (London: Tavistock).

Foucault, M. (1982) 'The Subject and Power', in H. Dreyfus and P. Rabinow (eds), *Michel Foucault: Beyond Structuralism and Hermeneutics* (Brighton: Harvester Press), pp. 208–26.

Foucault, M. (1984) in P. Rabinow (ed.), *The Foucault Reader* (Harmondsworth: Penguin).

Foucault, M. (1988) 'On Power' and 'Social Security', in L.D. Kritzman (ed.), *Foucault ... Interviews and Other Writings 1977–1984* (London: Routledge), pp. 121–34.

Foucault, M. (1991) 'Governmentality', in G. Burchell, C. Gordon and P. Miller (eds), *The Foucault Effect – Studies in Governmentality* (Hemel Hempstead: Harvester Wheatsheaf), pp. 87–104.

Garfinkel, H. (1967) *Studies in Ethnomethodology* (Englewood Cliffs, NJ: Prentice Hall).

Giddens, A. (1979a) *Studies in Social and Political Theory* (London: Hutchinson).

Giddens, A. (1979b) *Central Problems in Social Theory* (London: Macmillan).

Giddens, A. (1984) *The Constitution of Society* (Oxford: Polity Press).

Goldman, R. (1992) *Reading Ads Socially* (London: Routledge).

Hacking, I. (1990) *The Taming of Chance* (Cambridge: Cambridge University Press).

Hacking, I. (1991) 'How Should We Do the History of Statistics', in G. Burchell, C. Gordon and P. Miller (eds), *The Foucault Effect – Studies in Governmentality* (Hemel Hempstead: Harvester Wheatsheaf), pp. 181–95.

Hollway, W. (1991) *Work Psychology and Organisational Behaviour* (London: Sage).

Hooley, G.J., Lynch, J.E. and Shepherd, J. (1990) 'The Marketing Concept – Putting Theory into Practice', *European Journal of Marketing*, vol. 24, no. 9, pp. 7–24.

Hopwood, A. (1987) 'The Archaeology of Accounting Systems', *Accounting, Organisations and Society*, vol. 12, no. 3, pp. 207–34.

Hoskin, K.W. (1990) *Using History to Understand Theory: a Re-consideration of the Historical Genesis of 'Strategy'*, paper delivered at the EIASM Workshop on Strategy, Accounting and Control, Venice, October.

Joseph, L. and Yorke, D. (1989) 'Know Your Game Plan: Market Segmentation in the Personal Financial Services Sector', *Quarterly Review of Marketing*, vol. 15, no. 1, pp. 8–13.

Knights, D. (1988) 'Risk, Financial Self-discipline and Commodity Relations: an Analysis of the Growth of Life Assurance in Contemporary Capitalism', *Advances in Public Interest Accounting*, vol. 2, pp. 47–69 (New York: JAI Press).

Knights, D. (1990) 'Subjectivity, Power and the Labour Process', in D. Knights and H. Willmott (eds), *Labour Process Theory* (London: Macmillan), pp. 297–335.

Knights, D. (1992) 'Changing Spaces: the Disruptive Power of Epistemological Location for the Management and Organisational Sciences', *Academy of Management Review*, vol. 17, no. 3, pp. 514–36.

Knights, D. and Morgan, G. (1993) 'Organisation Theory and Consumption in a Postmodern Era', *Organisation Studies*, vol. 14, no. 2, pp. 211–34.

Knights, D. and Morgan, G. (1990) 'The Concept of Strategy in Sociology', *Sociology*, vol. 23, no. 3, pp. 475–83.

Knights, D. and Murray, F. (1994) *Managers Divided* (London: Wiley).

Knights, D. and Vurdubakis, T. (1993) 'Calculations of Risk: Towards an Understanding of Insurance as a Moral and Political Technology', *Accounting, Organisations and Society*, vol. 18, no. 6, pp. 1–36.

Knights, D. and Willmott, H. (1983) 'Dualism and Domination', *Australian and New Zealand Journal of Sociology*, vol. 19, no. 1, pp. 33–49.

Knights, D. and Willmott, H. (1985) 'Power and Identity in Theory and Practice', *Sociological Review*, vol. 33, no. 1, pp. 22–46.

Knights, D. and Willmott, H. (1989) 'Power and Subjectivity at Work', *Sociology*, vol. 23, no. 4, pp. 535–58.

Knights, D., Sturdy, A.J. and Morgan, G. (1994) 'The Consumer Rules? The Rhetoric and Reality of Marketing in Financial Services', *European Journal of Marketing*, vol. 28, no. 3, pp. 42–54.

Kotler, P. (1988) *Marketing Management Analysis, Planning, Implementation and Control*, 6th edn (New York: Prentice Hall).

Langlumé, P-M. (1992) 'Fidéliser, Segmenter, Globaliser', *Directions* (CAPA), no. 19, pp. 61–3.

Lock, C.M. *et al.* (1947) *The County Borough of Middlesborough Survey and Plan* (Middlesborough: Middlesborough Corporation).

Marcuse, H. (1964) *One-dimensional Man* (London: RKP).

Marx, K. (1976) *Capital* (Harmondsworth: Penguin).

Mendras, H. and Cole, A. (1991) *Social Change in Modern France: Towards a Cultural Anthropology of the Fifth Republic* (Cambridge: Cambridge University Press).

Miller, P. (1987) *Domination and Power* (London: Routledge and Kegan Paul).

Morgan, G. and Sturdy, A.J. (in press) *The Dynamics of Organisational Change* (London: Macmillan).

Moser, C.A. (1958) *Survey Methods in Social Investigation* (London: Heinemann).

Mouzelis, N. (1993) 'The Poverty of Sociological Theory', *Sociology*, vol. 27, no. 4. pp. 675–95.

Murphy, P.E. and Staples W.A. (1979) 'A Modernised Family Life Cycle', *Journal of Consumer Research*, vol. 6, pp. 12–22.

O'Donnell, T. (1936) *History of Life Insurance in its Formative Years* (Chicago: American Conservation Co.).

Paitra, J. (1990) 'De la Securité Passive à la Securité Active', *Risques*, no. 3.

Palmer, G. and Clegg, S. (eds) (1996) *Constituting Management – Markets, Meanings and Identities* (Berlin: De Gruyter).

Philippe, M-A. (1992) 'La Saga de la Distribution', *Directions* (CAPA), no. 19, pp. 46–51.

Piore, M. and Sabel, C. (1984) *The Second Industrial Divide: Possibilities for Prosperity* (New York: Basic Books).

Roche, P. (1990) 'Stratégie des Sociétés d'Assurance: Segmentation ou Selection', *Risques*, vol. 6, Octobre, pp. 146–51.

Rose, N. (1988) 'Calculable Minds and Manageable Individuals', *History of the Human Sciences*, vol. 1, pp. 179–200.

Rose, N. (1989) *Governing the Soul – the Shaping of the Private Self* (London: Routledge).

Rothmann, J-M. (1990) 'Assurance et Solidariteé – le Point de Vue des Consommateurs', *Risques*, vol. 6, Octobre, pp. 85–8.

Rowntree, B.S. (1901) *Poverty: A Study of Town Life* (London: Macmillan).

Schauerman, J. (1990) 'A New Basis for Segmenting the Corporate Banking Market', in R. Teare, L. Motinko and N. Morgan (eds), *Managing and Marketing Services in the 1990s* (London: Cassel), pp. 170–83.

Smith, W.R. (1956) 'Product Differentiation and Market Segmentation as Alternative Strategies', *Journal of Marketing*, vol. 20, July, pp. 3–8.

Speed, R. and Smith, G. (1992) 'Retail Financial Services Segmentation', *Services Industry Journal*, vol. 12, no. 3, pp. 368–83.

Sturdy, A.J. and Knights, D. (1996) 'The Subjectivity of Segmentation', in G. Palmer and S. Clegg (eds), *Constituting Management – Markets, Meanings and Indentities* (Berlin: De Gruyter), pp. 73–93.

Sturdy, A.J. and Morgan, G. (1993) 'Segmenting the Market – a Review of Marketing Trends in French Retail Banking', *International Journal of Bank Marketing*, vol. 11, no. 7, pp. 11–19.

Sturdy, A.J., Morgan, G. and Daniel, J-P. (1997) 'National Management Styles – a Comparative Study of Bancassurance', in G. Morgan and D. Knights (eds), *Deregulation and European Financial Services* (London: Macmillan), pp. 154–77.

Veblen, T. (1899) *The Theory of the Leisure Class* (New York: Macmillan).

Weber, M. (1948) *Selected Writings* (London: RKP).

Wells, W.D. (1975) 'Psychographics – a Critical Review', *Journal of Marketing Research*, vol. 12, pp. 196–213.

Willmott, H. (1993) *Paradoxes of Marketing: Some Critical Reflexions*, paper presented at the *Re-thinking Marketing Conference*, Warwick Business School, University of Warwick, 1–2 July.

Wood, S. (ed.) (1989) *The Transformation of Work?* (London: Unwin Hyman).

Zollinger, M. (1985) *Marketing Bancaire* (Paris: Bardas).

9 The Japanese Main Bank Relationship: Governance or Competitive Strategy?

MARK J. SCHER

This article explores the nature of the main bank in its roles as the major creditor and lender of last resort to its clients within Japanese banking's cultural, historical and institutional context, and in relation to governmental institutions that strive to foster economic development through the main bank system. In so doing it discloses some of the myriad formal and informal systems which the main bank uses to structure a profitable and lasting relationship with its client firms, the nature of the direct rewards sought by the banks, and how their needs are served by the main bank relationship.

In general, the literature to date has tended to emphasize the benefits of the main bank relationship to the corporate enterprise, particularly in terms of the efficiency of capital or when a firm is in financial distress, as well as its benefits to the economic development of society, particularly in times of scarcity of capital. Some agency theorists have proposed the bank as corporate governor and monitoring agent, not only on behalf of other creditors, but also for other shareholders in the client firm. Such interpretations ignore the bank's own institutional reasons for promoting the relationship. Treating the bank as a "black box", the literature has largely overlooked how the bank itself benefits as the "main bank" and the control it wields in determining the limits and terms of the relationship.

THE PURPORTED MAIN BANK RELATIONSHIP

The purported benefits of the main bank relationship to the firm and society have generally been classified in the following three areas: (1) efficiencies of capital derived from the delegated cost of monitoring, the so-called signal function, (2) main bank assistance to firms in financial distress, the so-called rescue function and (3) the main bank role in corporate governance.

Nakatani (1983, 1984) first put forward the notion that one of the functions of Japanese industrial groups is risk sharing among their members, the chief mechanism of that risk sharing being the group bank's long-term implicit

189

contractual role as risk insurer for the group member firms. Furthermore, he proposed, the main bank provided a continuous signal of the creditworthiness of its client firms to banks and financial institutions outside the group. Almost immediately, however, the credibility of this hypothesis was questioned by scholars in Japan who had been studying the main bank system. In particular, they questioned the existence of such benefits, the efficacy of the relationship, and the actual role of the group's main bank in risk sharing (Horiuchi and Fukuda, 1987, Horiuchi *et al.*, 1988; Horiuchi, 1989; Oba and Horiuchi, 1991; Okazaki and Horiuchi, 1992; A. Horiuchi, 1995); at least one scholar has even questioned the existence of the main bank itself (Miwa, 1985, 1991).[1]

Agency theorists have emphasized the role of the main bank in "rescuing" companies in financial distress (Sheard, 1989, 1991, 1994) and have asserted that through reciprocal monitoring among members, chiefly by the main bank, there is a reduction of agency costs (Hoshi *et al.*, 1990a, b, 1991). These economists place heavy emphasis upon the information-gathering role of the industrial group's main bank. Aoki (1994) focused upon main bank monitoring and corporate governance, Sheard (1989) upon bank team monitoring, the transfer of bank executives to clients firms in financial distress,[2] and purported main bank rescue; and Hoshi *et al.* (1990a, 1990b) upon lower agency costs by means of the so-called "signal function" which presumably results in efficiencies of corporate finance to the firm. Although these assumptions have been challenged in a number of Japanese studies, for example, those of Horiuchi, R. Okazaki (R. Oba), and Miwa, these studies, however have been seldom acknowledged, let alone responded to, by agency theorists.

This article will show that corporate executives generally see the main bank relationship as lacking the benefits it purportedly accords the firm (Fuji Sogo Kenkyujo, 1993; Omura, 1993). This view is shared by the banker practitioners in our data who also dismiss ideas of such benefits to the firm. We will then show, however, that the main bank relationship exists, is stable, and is part and parcel of some very traditional expectations coming from traditional ideas of relationships. Furthermore, although the benefits of the relationship may be doubtful to the client, the bankers believe the relationship is quite beneficial to the profitability of the bank.

As we have briefly described, many economists have analyzed different details and presumed attributes of the main bank system, extrapolating those pieces into theories of the whole, mainly agency theory. Our research revealed contradictions of fact underpinning these theories. These conflicts presented us with two critical tasks. First, the need to test the "stylized facts" which were used in constructing agency models. This included testing the following propositions: Do banks monitor for corporate governance? Do they send a signal to other creditors and to other investors? Is the correct signal always sent? Do they really "rescue" firms in financial distress? If so, under what circumstances? Are agency costs lower for group firms when compared to non-group member firms? If not, then for what purpose do main banks "monitor"? For what purpose do banks transfer their retired bank executives to client firms? If bank–client relationships in Japan are fixed according to principles of governance and are by nature long-term, why then are banks so highly competitive? What are the benefits of the relationship to the bank?

In agency theories the main bank is a black box, its character and role deduced chiefly from the perceived effects of its actions. The second task was to uncloak that black box and scrutinize the banking system itself: What are the forces that drive competition among banks? Is the competitive pressure among banks undervalued by agency theorists? Does the main bank system even exist?

During the course of our research, interviews were conducted with 71 Japanese respondents who consisted of executives at seven city banks, including the top six *kigyo shudan* (enterprise group) affiliated banks and a former specialized bank; two of the three long-term credit banks; three regional banks; two trust banks; one foreign-owned bank; and a government-owned bank. In addition, interviews were conducted with officials from the Ministry of Finance (MoF), Ministry of International Trade and Industry (MITI), the Postal Savings Bureau of the Ministry of Posts and Telecommunications, and six other regulatory and bank service organizations. These interviews were conducted during a three-and-a-half-year period between 1992 and 1995, in addition to the numerous but less formal interchanges with additional respondents in the course of the author's professional activities as Senior Research Fellow at the Kinyu Zaisei Jijo Kenkyu-kai (Institute of Financial Affairs).

A great amount of data was needed in order to get as complete a portrait as possible, since there was very little literature as to how the main bank relationship with its clients was actually managed. The highly stylized economic models were of little help. Alltogether there was a total of 192 formal interviews (251.25 hours) with 71 respondents, each interview totaling 1 hour, 18 minutes, on average. Among the major institutions included in the study, (city and long-term credit banks), 106 interviews were conducted with the 38 respondents in these major banks. Although the case-study method is rarely used in finance, my experience suggests that it can be a highly useful methodology, if not a necessity.[3]

THE MAIN BANK RELATIONSHIP AND SUTTON'S LAW:
THE PROFITABILITY MOTIVE

In the course of attempting to define the bank's role within the Japanese industrial group relationship, it became immediately apparent during the preliminary interviews with the bankers that they viewed the main bank relationship quite differently from the prevailing academic interpretation, which many bankers thought was in fact a rather naive view of main bank practices. To my first general question, 'Why the main bank relationship?', I frequently received what could be called the Willie Sutton response. When that infamous American bank robber of the 1940s and 1950s was asked by a reporter why he robbed banks, Sutton replied, 'That's where the money is!'

Only a few scholars have noted in passing the pecuniary forces central to main bank strategy and organization. For example, the Horiuchi–Packer–Fukuda (1988) hypothesis, which focused on information asymmetries, took for granted that banks continue their relationship with their client firms for only as long as the knowledge they gain is profitable and exceeds the cost of their risk in supporting the firm. Sheard (1991) conceded that the main bank would be unlikely to shoulder the costs of a corporate rescue, either in terms of administration or increased risk-bearing, without the expectation of being able to maintain close transactional ties with the firm in the future.

Our research found that by their own accounts the bankers overwhelmingly regard the main bank relationship as the source of their greatest profitability. Whereas in earlier years banks had prioritized increasing the volume of lending as their chief strategy, in the postwar regulatory regime of fixed interest rates lending profits were all but guaranteed. However, profitability had become a key concern by the early 1990s. Pressure on the banks to improve their profitability had escalated in the face of interest rate deregulation and narrowing spreads on lending, the Bank for International Settlements (BIS) capital/assets ratio requirements, and the rapidly deteriorating quality of bank assets which resulted from underperforming real estate-related loans. By common definition, main bank status signifies that the bank is the largest lender to the client corporation among all of the banks with which the company conducts its banking business. This status confers major rewards on the bank way beyond the current rewards of corporate lending. These rewards include receiving the main depository accounts of the firm, non-interest-bearing compensating balance accounts (formerly called *ryodate* accounts), low-interest time deposit accounts, and a disproportionately large share of the client's commission and fee-based business. These rewards have gained even greater importance since the liberalization of Japanese financial markets which has led to narrow lending margins and diminished profits from large corporate lending.

Depository and Compensating Balance Accounts

From the bank's viewpoint, the [main bank] relationship is a major source of profit. Because of interest rates and the need to keep a compensating balance, clients must keep money in their transaction account, and not a small amount. These accounts are non-interest-bearing ... [or low-interest-bearing].[4]

The true importance of depository and compensating balance accounts is understood only when it is also understood that these accounts reflect not only deposit taking but the transaction-fee generating aspects of a large-sized firm's relationship among several banks.

The respondents typically emphasized the connection between profitability and depository accounts and often reported as least profitable the lending side of the business, that is, the return on assets (ROA).

Respondent: The main bank is usually in the most profitable position because they get the largest share of a company's deposits as well as [the largest share] of its other profitable business, such as foreign exchange.

Question: Then the unprofitable parts ...

Respondent: are the loans, because what we are talking about is return on assets, right? We are talking about the management of banks under the new BIS regulations.[5]

Lending is regarded as a "loss leader" in the portfolio of financial services provided by the main bank. The lower cost of loans is rationalized not by their lower risk but by their use as a competitive vehicle in merchandising more profitable banking services to the client.

Fee-based and Commission Banking

With lending diminished in profitability, the banks have increasingly turned to fee-based banking, which requires no commitment of funds. Fee-based banking has expanded enormously in recent years and is seen by most Japanese bankers as one of the best ways to observe the BIS regulations because there are no assets behind the transaction.[6] Fee-based products include foreign exchange transactions, letters of credit, and exchanging foreign currency.[7]

When extending credit, the bank considers whether the loan transaction will lead to expanding the amount of the company's deposits in the bank, or its fee services, or to increasing employee salary deposits. If a company seeks to increase its borrowing from other banks, then its main bank will often apply pressure upon the company for an increase also and to receive a greater share of the company's other business. The bank typically expects an increased share of the company's loans, foreign exchange, transfer payments to public utilities, and other fee-based services. However, severe competition means each bank will try to get as much as possible, and as a result, the main bank can never get it all. Although the main bank of a company in its *kigyo shudan* will almost never change, it is possible through competition to get independent companies to change their main bank, or at least change the second and third position banks.[8]

Employee Accounts

The personal accounts of employees of client firms represent perhaps one of the bank's greatest rewards to the main bank in the relationship. The bank and the company predicate much of their ensuing relationship on these accounts. Companies will "request" all of their personnel to open accounts at the main bank for the direct deposit of their salary. Furthermore, the identification of the bank with the company also encourages employees to conduct their personal business with the bank. How successfully a bank wins over this captive client base depends, at least in part, on how strong a group consciousness exists at the company.

> The percentage of employees [who comply] often depends on the size of the company. Usually, in smaller and medium-sized companies there is more of a family type of atmosphere, *ie ishiki* – family consciousness – among all the people at the company, its managers and employees, particularly if the branches of the bank are convenient to their own households. The level of compliance relates to the level of *ie* consciousness.[9]

Employees' personal accounts also become an important source of cheap funds by which the bank, through intermediation, can recycle employee savings back to the client company. In exchange for these benefits, the bank provides the corporation with a credit safety net and main bank services.

Group member companies usually get better credit terms. They also don't have to put up as large a compensating deposit. But, in return, of course, the bank expects to receive more of the transactions from a group company – as their main bank. For example, all the employees of the core Mitsui group companies put their deposits in the Sakura Bank ... It's direct deposit now. Ten or fifteen years ago it was given out as cash. But for large companies now it's almost all direct deposit and they use it for other services as well. All the employees put all of their deposits into the Sakura Bank, and if they need a housing loan they receive priority at the Sakura Bank. It's a captive market.[10]

Employee accounts generally bring other benefits. A large base of employee accounts means a significant amount of business for the bank in the retail sector, normally a high profit-margin area. The bank is rewarded with a large volume of consumer transactions, in the form of electronic transfers, consumer lending, personal lending, credit card, mortgages, and so on.

The main bank relationship provides a safety net for its companies. A very large bank has a very large commitment to its customer, like Mitsubishi Bank to Mitsubishi Corporation. When things get rough, the Mitsubishi Corporation can always go back to the bank, or to Meiji Life, which is in the same group. Having a main bank behind it lowers the risk for the company, and for the bank it means a very large percentage of all types of transactions of the client are concentrated in the bank. Considering all the Mitsubishi companies together, they have hundreds of thousands of employees with accounts in the bank. Whenever an individual has to make a transfer, he has to pay ¥300–400, and that represents a very large amount of revenue for Mitsubishi Bank. ¥300–400 for an electronic transfer – that's really exorbitant compared to the cost of [personal] checks in the US.[11]

As the emphasis on profits increases, it is not surprising that the extent of the main bank's efforts to maintain its relationship with the client firm is often directly proportional to the size of the captive employee base. The focus has shifted away from volume corporate lending and towards emphasizing business relationships with retail customers.

What we do is no different from any other bank. We are aiming to use the main bank position not only for firms, but also for individuals and households, providing housing loans, credit cards, other settlement services, such as utilities, card loans, everything. By their concentrating those transactions in us, we are giving them some benefits, such as lowering some interest rates on loans. Many other city banks are doing the same thing.[12]

Of course, having a profitable relationship depends not only on the company but also on having a banking relationship with that company's employees. So, taking all those factors into account, we think that it's profitable but sometimes difficult to analyze those type of transactions.[13]

Competition for Profits Among the Lead "Main" Banks

Although the highly-coveted status of the main bank is hard to displace, the status of second and third bank also provide desirable opportunities for them to receive substantial business, and these positions are much sought after by competing lending banks. These second and third "main" banks are often significantly involved in the day-to-day financial dealings of client firms.

A typical large company may do business with some 20 to 30 banks but use only three to five of the lead banks for most, if not all, of its fee-based transactions, such as foreign exchange, swap transactions, underwriting, or leasing by the bank's affiliated securities and leasing affiliates or overseas subsidiaries. Although the top five banks may supply less than 50 percent of their client's borrowing needs, they will receive nearly 100 percent of its fee-based business. The opportunity for banks below the top five to acquire profitable business with the client outside of lending has become quite remote, principally because corporations themselves are attempting to rationalize their relations. Therefore, a bank which has an unprofitable relationship with a company will first attempt to improve its fee-based business with the client before it seeks to recall its loan.[14]

The distribution of expected fee-based transactions from the client corporation to the top five lending banks is not strictly based on the bank's percentage of the client's loans. A company usually concentrates most of its fee-based business in its main bank, and next in its second and third lenders. The following is a case in point offered by an officer of the second lead bank of a very large, established company. Dai-Ichi Kangyo (DKB) is the company's main bank. The respondent's bank is in second position. The company has six major banks: DKB, the respondent's bank, the Industrial Bank of Japan (IBJ), Mitsubishi, Fuji, and one other. Of those, five account for 50 percent of the company's borrowing. DKB has 16 or 17 percent, while the respondent's bank has approximately 8 percent. Together DKB and the respondent's bank receive in the range of 40–50 percent of the company's fee-based business; the remaining 50–60 percent is divided among the other four banks. In this case, the main bank will receive more than twice its loan percentage in fee-based business, and, by supplying 50 percent of the company's loans, the top six banks receive 100 percent of the fee-based business.

> We want to be in the stable number two position, but the other banks also are competing for that spot. If we are number two we will always be the co-lead manager on bond issues. Our bank is not a member of any *kigyo shudan* (enterprise group), but we are in a good position with our clients. If a company borrows from ten banks, number one is their main bank, but we usually are the second, third, or fourth bank. That puts us in a good position to promote a lot of business with that client. If we were very low [in the hierarchy], then we would not have the opportunity to do foreign exchange business for that client. But if we are positioned very well, then we can get that type of business. We would try to be promoted from fourth to third, or third to second position.[15]

Bankers at some leading institutions see the decrease in the main bank's lending to their clients as an opportunity to increase business through bank-facilitated access to the money market. They view Japan as a whole as still achieving so-called oversaving, despite the current tight money economy, and therefore still having plenty of funds. While a number of large corporations are claiming that some of the major city banks are limiting their lending volume because of the BIS regulations, these bankers deny any such problems and point to increased bank-assisted financing through the straight bond market, both domestically and internationally by the bank's overseas subsidiaries,[16] and since 1994 by domestic bank-owned securities underwriting subsidiaries.

Bankers acknowledge that a particular bank's capabilities and expertise to meet a company's need may be determinative in the placement of its fee-based business, outweighing the influence of the percentage of lending supplied by its lead banks. The bank that can offer the most types of services clearly has an advantage. Despite ranking order, the type of transaction a company is seeking will usually decide which bank gets that portion of its business. As in the case of bond market underwriting, a company will tend to go to the bank which specializes in the desired financial service. Therefore, a company's collateral banking business is not all destined for its top banks in strict hierarchical order. The arrangement is often much looser and dependent on the needs of each company and the capabilities of each bank.

> The percentage of transactions are just one criteria. Decisions are not based solely on the amount of lending. When it comes to Eurobond issues, for

example, some other banks might not have our capabilities. It depends upon each company and each bank, and the type of transactions. It is not fixed. There is a loose relation but it's not well defined.[17]

Although the exact percentage of distribution of each fee-based service is not precisely defined and is highly dependent upon the individual capabilities of each bank, the hierarchy among the lending institutions is strictly observed by the firm and a variety of devices are employed by the client corporation to preserve the relative standing overall among the lending institutions. There is a tacit understanding that, no matter what, the corporation will make sure that its main bank comes out on top at the end of the fiscal year. This is true even when only a single percent of lending separates the first and second banks. That additional 1 percent is almost impossible to overcome until the top management decides to change their policy as to which is their main bank.[18]

A corporation will go to great lengths to maintain the relative ranking of its lenders and to protect its relationship to that bank. This includes the disguising of transactions and borrowing patterns so that the firm's financial statement reflects the established hierarchy. Foreign-owned banks, which lack the established long-term client relationships of Japanese banks, are customarily excluded from the role of main bank. However, even loans from foreign banks and from domestic insurance companies that are not part of the company's industrial group are managed in such a way as to prevent public disclosure. For example, such loans are timed to terminate before the end of the fiscal period so that they will go unreported in the firm's annual statement.

COMPONENTS OF THE BANK–CLIENT RELATIONSHIP

Competitive Strategy

In a sense, every bank and every company has a group. Being a member of a group, whether a large *kigyo shudan* or a small regional grouping, will give the bank a competitive advantage over non-group financial institutions.[19] Although it is improbable that the main bank will be displaced from its lead position by another bank, it is virtually impossible if the client corporation and its main bank are members of the same *kigyo shudan*.[20] The rare case of a change in lead lending status is usually the result of a temporary increase in lending in some year by the trust bank member of the same group for some capital expenditure, such as a construction project that may be beyond the lending capabilities of the firm's leading main bank.

Nevertheless, it does sometimes happen that a company changes its main bank for good reason. This occurs most typically in a small- or medium-sized company. One commonly cited reason is that the company president simply gets angry with the bank.[21] This is a virtually impossible outcome for a large company and its main bank because of the number of temporarily transferred or retired former bank employees at the company. Most typically, it happens when a small company outgrows its current bank, usually a regional bank from which it is said to "graduate". For example, a very small, domestically-oriented company, whose sales have gone from ¥10 million to ¥4.5 billion in just five years, wants to go abroad. Dissatisfied with the limited capabilities of its current bank, the company goes out to find a banker with a more long-term perspective and a bank with extensive international experience. The company has also become large enough so that a major bank will be seriously interested in doing business with it.[22]

Despite the fact that a regional or second-tier regional (former *sogo*) bank might have more branches in a given local area than a large city bank, the city bank nonetheless has a competitive advantage because the interest on its loans is lower and its total amount of funds is larger. And, most importantly, the larger city bank has available to it much more information and a wider range of business contacts useful to the client company. By contrast, the second-tier regional banks do their business in local areas because they take higher risks and have easier credit standards.[23]

When banks compete against each other for the same client, each bank tries to ensure that it gets at least the full share to which it is entitled of the company's business. Thus, if a company wants to increase its borrowing from one of its lending banks, that bank will expect the company to increase its ancillary business with the bank proportionately, or even more. This business includes several groups of services: foreign exchange, transfer payments to public utilities, and other fee-based services. With each bank striving to get as much as possible, the main bank never gets 100 percent.[24]

The Kansai Style of Competition

Some of the banks, notably those which were historically based in the Kansai (Osaka) region, have developed a reputation for an innovative and aggressive style in pursuing relations with clients and potential clients that goes well beyond the usual excesses of the "bubble period". The key elements to their approach include a willingness to skirt around customary guidelines and to employ adventurous tactics described by the bankers themselves as "hara-kiri". The banks are also noted for their ability to target potential growth companies, regardless of any group affiliations. Once a company is targeted, the bank tries by any and all means to become its main bank.

Traditionally Japanese banks tend to think on a long-term basis when acquiring new customers. A client's initial business is only an opening to the future. To gain that entry, an interloper bank will sometimes employ what they call a hara-kiri strategy to win clients, usually offering up some Euro-issue or other item at a loss to the bank. The bank's act of "hara-kiri" in taking a loss it can otherwise ill afford must be covered up on their books by shadow accounts or other similar tactics.[25]

Officers of Tokyo-based banks often displayed disdain for such aggressive tactics, citing in particular the two leading Kansai banks for their frequent refusal to cooperate with other banks in assisting a mutual client firm, despite press reports to the contrary, thus leaving those client firms in the lurch. One Tokyo banker referred to these two banks as "rivals trying to surpass each other in rudeness".[26]

Responsibilities of the Lead Main Bank – Purported Rescue Function

First among the perceived responsibilities of the main bank, according to the conventional view, is its obligation to provide rescue and a safety net to the client firm in trouble. Although often only informally acknowledged, the responsibilities of the main bank to resolve its client's problems are said to bear the full weight of duty and obligation.

> When a business goes bankrupt here, usually the main bank leads the rescue, or becomes the leader of a settlement, something like a [bankruptcy] trustee in the US. I think in the US if there is some problem, the biggest lenders will quickly withdraw, but here in Japan the situation is different in that the main bank has to solve the problems of the business corporation and mitigate the social impact in many other areas.[27]

In actual practice, however, bankers concede that this obligation is generally balanced against considerations of profitability. If a client's circumstances are deemed too bleak or irretrievable, even its main bank will not step forward to mitigate the situation.

> I don't think the banks felt obliged to do that kind of operation, even in the 1950s and 1960s. Banks will act if they believe they can earn profits through the rescue operation and because it will also strengthen their relationship with the customer. If the customer can be bailed out and then prospers, the customer will depend upon the bank, and the bank can then

grant it further loans and take their deposits. But if there is no potential for recovery, then banks will not undertake the rescue operation.[28]

The degree to which the rescue function exists is more a matter of perception on the part of the client than contractual. Bankers report that they are loath to make even an implicit commitment. The actual existence of the rescue function is decided case by case on its merits. Bankers also report that often the most significant factor beyond the particular merits for the bank is the "suggestion" by the MoF that the bank support an enterprise or industry whose demise the government deems will have repercussions upon the social and/or strategic economic fabric of the nation. Implicit in the bank's willingness to provide funds to a sunset industry is the understanding that the MoF will reward the bank by granting it some concession in another area.

In good times the basic task of the main bank is to meet the needs of that company's development, help the company raise its annual earnings, develop its resources, expand its transactions, and so on. However, the overriding characteristic that distinguishes the main bank from the second and third banks is that it is by custom the creditor of last resort for the firm in financial distress. The main bank is expected to initiate any rescue plan among the other banks. It is presumed that the main bank's status as the company's largest lender and its access to superior information would normally alert it to problems and enable it to determine whether the company's problems were due to a temporary liquidity crisis or to more fundamental problems of insolvency.

When the company is having difficulty, the main bank's task is to reconstruct, reform, or financially support the company as much as possible to achieve a rescue. The bank will send some of its employees to work within the company. It is quite possible that in the near final stages the task of the main bank will be to ask some member company of their *kigyo shudan* to take over the company or find some other enterprise to merge with the troubled company.[29] The typical response of the other lead banks to a company in trouble is not to commit more funds. The percentage of loans by the main bank increases as a consequence. If the second, third, and fourth lead banks had provided extremely large loans, the main bank would not be able to take over these liabilities and a meeting of the bank creditors to resolve the situation would be required.[30]

This problem became particularly acute after the loose monetary conditions of the "bubble economy" of the 1980s. The banks had continually increased their number of customers and expanded their opportunities to make loans. Along with this growth, the traditional bank practice of frequent client interviews and visiting customers became very loose; the opportunity for the corporation to give the bank up-to-date information was reduced. In some cases, the bank did not find out about a company's trouble until the very last moment.[31]

The Bank Team – Monitoring or Sales Function?

The primary vehicle for carrying out the main bank relationship is the bank team assigned to large client firms. The team typically consists of a lending officer, foreign exchange officer, and may number four or more officers, depending on the size of the client and the nature of the client's transactional business with the bank. They visit the client's business premises and other points of operation on a daily basis, interacting with the financial officers of the corporation, as well as collecting receipts, advising and consulting on specific issues, and generally acquiring useful information as to current operations and what future plans are under consideration. The team is considered the most effective way of doing business and maintaining the close contact required by the main bank relationship. The second and even the third banks of a major corporation will also assign teams to service a larger client.

The bank team will often visit the various units and locations of the client firm. Frequently, they will also be called upon not only to consult with the financial officers and the accounting department there but sometimes to attend to the private banking affairs of the employees.[32] Such attentiveness, however, comes at a price, which is sometimes very high. Banks therefore tend to take a pragmatic approach, estimating profit from overall corporate and employee transactions versus cost. If too much cost is associated with employee services, then the allocation of the time of the banking team is reprioritized to reflect those estimations.[33]

The main bank relationship works quite differently when applied to small- and medium-sized businesses than to the major corporations, usually defined as those listed on the Tokyo Stock Exchange. A medium-sized company may only have one person assigned to it at the bank's branch office, and that person may service/monitor as many as ten to twenty, or more, such companies. Small companies scarcely receive any attention. Such an overload of clients means that the banker's primary activity becomes promoting new business among these companies, encouraging them to increase their deposits and persuading them to join the credit loan system, or to join the bank's direct transfer system. At the same time the banker is supposed to inquire about how the client is doing and review their monthly balance, but such attentions can only be cursory at best.[34]

By the early 1980s most banks had abandoned their credit analysis sections. It was quite apparent from the interviews that the bank team's function was not monitoring but rather that of a sales team. Indeed, senior- and middle-level bank management reported that a generation of young bankers recruited during that period received no training in evaluating client creditworthiness and only recently has senior management taken remedial steps to train them belatedly in these skills.[35]

Shukko Relations – Trimming Bank Costs and Supplying the Client with Expertise

An established way of providing clients with financial expertise is through the transfer of bank employees. The process of sending out or transferring bank workers to client firms and government agencies, known as *shukko*, may involve junior or senior employees, each for quite different purposes.

In the past, a typical scenario would begin when a bank is asked by its client to send a senior banker for the number two position in its corporate finance department. The firm is anticipating the retirement of its own department head and provides informal assurances that the banker will eventually become a director within the company. The bank will then transfer an experienced and able senior employee who is not on the track for its own board of directors.[36] Thus, a vice-president of the bank is likely to become at least a vice-president of a major corporation or president or chairman of one of its direct subsidiaries. In this manner the practice of *shukko* serves the bank by cementing a close bond between executives of the client firm and the bank who are now the firm's employees.

This one-way ticket *shukko* functions primarily as an outplacement mechanism within Japan's lifetime employment system. Although people are usually retired in their mid-50s, the bank must find jobs for them after their retirement, at least until they are 60. A common pattern is for the bank to transfer out an employee in his 50s for a series of short-term assignments at different companies until he reaches the compulsory retirement age of 60, when he retires permanently to a position at a client company.[37]

Changes in the economy have upended the expectation that employees will be able to move up and out. Slower economic growth coupled with the creation of fewer new subsidiary companies, which in the past have served as locations to farm out employees, have led many corporations to become top heavy and to begin rationing the sharply reduced number of available directoral positions formerly reserved for their bank's retirees.[38] This problem for the banks has been particularly acute where bank mergers have occurred, which further limit the positions available in client companies and bank subsidiaries for an excessive number of redundant bank employees.[39]

As Japanese firms continue to downsize in the 1990s there are fewer and fewer positions available in client firms for retirement *shukko* from the banks. Another result of the "bubble economy" of the 1980s was the hoarding mentality of the most prestigious firms, including banks, which led to the overhiring of new college graduates. Now banks must outplace their mid-career employees at increasingly younger ages, either to client companies or to bank-owned subsidiaries with a cut in their pay.

The Shukko *Employee's Conflict of Interest: Insider Versus Outsider*

Any inherent conflict of interest brought about by the *shukko* system is rarely acknowledged. Since *shukko* facilitates the flow of information back and forth between the client and the bank, sometimes inside information is revealed to the bank. Senior bankers stated that they saw no conflict since the information "was harmless if kept strictly between the bank and the client". Bankers said that *shukko* is seen as an expression of loyalty and commitment to a long-term relationship, which helps to build bonds of reliance and confidentiality between the company and the bank, and declared the main bank–client relationship non-competitive.[40]

However, loyalty to the bank can appear to supersede acting in the client's best interest. For instance, a former bank employee now at the client firm may find it difficult not to accept a loan offer at a rate higher than the going rate because it is being made by his former bank. Companies, particularly small- and medium-sized firms, are willing to trade off such conflicts of interest against the experience and skills they acquire by hiring bank retirees.[41] Although the bank may get an inside man in the retiree, the company, for its part, expects the assurance that the bank will provide the company with continued support no matter how bad it gets. One banker sardonically referred to the *shukko* employee as being "held hostage" by the client firm.[42]

On the other hand, those former bank employees who have been "seconded", sent on a one-way ticket *shukko,* must quickly transfer allegiance to their new firm or otherwise be isolated as a *soto* – an outsider– not an *uchi* – an insider. The covert resentment of fellow employees to the outside appointee is particularly common when the outsider is seen as coming in at the expense of an insider's advancement. Identity within the group and indeed within the context of the society at large is defined by issues of *soto* versus *uchi*. The strongest personal imperatives of the seconded employee will be to cross the lines from *soto* to being *uchi*, because it will determine his future within his new firm, and whether he will be isolated from knowledge of sensitive matters and effective participation in the decision-making process. Any hint to his co-workers of divided loyalties between the firm and the former bank would be of the greatest detriment to his future career. For this reason alone, the longevity of his usefulness as an information conduit to the bank is quite limited, according to one former bank director, "a couple of years at most".[43]

Nevertheless, the *shukko* system tends to influence the bank–client relationship in such a way that it becomes virtually impossible to displace the main bank from its position. A rival banker from the client's second bank lamented that a practically insurmountable hurdle is created when the main bank "has sent over the years 50 to 60 people to a company, many of them executives in a position to exclude other banks".[44] With such intimate personal ties at so many levels between the bank and its client, it becomes extremely problematic for a client firm even to contemplate a change of main bank. For this reason, Japanese banking is said to be a "skin-to-skin relationship".[45]

The relationship between the main bank and its client firm must remain sufficiently flexible and responsive so as to meet the needs of both the bank and the firm. Both sides are aware that each must first and foremost satisfy the other's expectations. The nature of those expectations is defined by what each provides to the other. The firm provides its main deposit and compensating balance accounts as well as access to its employees through their personal accounts and their related and highly profitable consumer banking services. The bank provides a stable source of funding, which in the case of larger firms has come to mean their corporate bond underwriting facilities, and a whole host of business introductions and client advisory services. On the other hand, as we will now see, the firm considers the main bank an outsider when it comes to issues of monitoring. Likewise, the bank will coldly examine its own position when the firm is facing solvency problems and is in need of life-saving financial support.

PURPORTED MAIN BANK GOVERNANCE

The "Monitoring" Function of the Main Bank Relationship

Among the most scrutinized questions regarding the main bank system is the purported governance role of the main bank in relation to its client firm. Monitoring of the client firm by the bank team is often cited as one evidence of the existence of such an external governance function. As the bankers reported, the bank works hard to maintain close bank-to-client relations. In the case of a large corporation, a bank team, typically headed by a relationship manager, is intimately involved in the affairs of the client, visiting the firm's offices and other facilities on a daily basis. This team is solely dedicated to that one assignment. Our respondents revealed, however, that the nature of the team's mission is essentially sales oriented. The team's purpose is to try and obtain information about the firm's future plans in order to promote the bank's services. According to our respondents, a bank's ability to exercise any form of outside governance arises exclusively from its position as a major creditor and only when there are no other options for the client firm to access other banks, outside money markets, or internal sources of funds. However, given the competitive nature of the banking industry, other banks competing with the firm's main bank are usually only too eager to grant a new loan in an effort to improve their position in the relationship hierarchy and the increased access that it affords.

The main bank's leverage is therefore quite low over firms listed in the First Section of the Tokyo Stock Exchange (generally large capitalized firms) and even for Second Section firms (generally large to medium capitalized firms), because the firms in both categories have direct access to money markets and thus can circumvent the need for bank finance. Indeed, it is difficult for banks to monitor the activities of many such firms due to these firms' large scope of operations, business locations and the multitude of other banks a firm may deal with.

When firms are of mid- to small-size and are unlisted (Over The Counter-publicly traded firms and privately held firms), the banks are most often unable to provide the scrutiny required to monitor them because of the insufficient numbers of bank personnel assigned to service this category of firm. The often closed nature of privately held firms, which are usually controlled by the firm's founder and family, also precludes bank monitoring. As reported by our respondents, in such smaller sized firms, unless the president–owner comes to the bank for additional credit assistance under distressed circumstances, the bank is often unaware of any current, undisclosed problems. At this point, the bank must make the judgement of whether a workout is worthwhile or even possible from the business perspective of the bank. Unlike the case of a large firm in which the bank may have a greater stake as a creditor, for small-sized and privately held firms the possibility of rescue by the main bank does not exist and the best the firm can hope for is some bank-arranged takeover by another firm. Aware of such consequences, the head of such a distressed closely-held firm typically loathes the bank's interference and often tries to cover up or forestall the reporting of difficulties. Only if the bank has been monitoring for abnormalities in the cash flows of a firm's deposit accounts might it be able to catch any hint of trouble, but by this time any corrective action or even the bank's withdrawal of lending could be too late. In those cases it simply becomes a race by the bank to seize the firm's collateral before other creditors get wind of the impending failure.

Purported "Signaling" Function of the Main Bank

According to agency theorists, other creditors take their cues by observing the "signals" of the main bank's actions, stemming from its position as the firm's largest creditor (Sheard, 1989, 1991; Aoki, 1990; Hoshi *et al.*, 1990). This of course begs the question, as our interview data revealed, whether the signal "sent" was necessarily an accurate representation of the client firm's actual internal affairs. Often the signal is distorted by the main bank's own strategic considerations and needs in maintaining a particular client relationship. Sick patients can be very profitable (higher interest rates, increased guarantee fees and so on); dead patients not at all. However, any hint of trouble, signaled by a decrease in lending by the firm's main bank, would indeed be noted by the other creditors, typically setting off a chain reaction of retreat by those banks which benefit least from their relationship with the ailing firm.

The bankers reported that the main bank was often the lender of "last resort" to a firm only because the other creditors had been able to accomplish a rapid retreat, thereby increasing the burden of the main bank(s). Main banks were therefore very keen on *not* sending any signal which would lead to the collapse of the firm's lending syndicate. That is why competing banks prudently make their own independent credit assessments – *caveat creditor*.

Main Bank Governance through Cross-shareholding?

Cross-shareholding between the bank and the client firm is another often-cited evidence of the main bank's governance function. Agency theorists have paid most attention to the cross-shareholding relationship between firms and financial institutions, specifically ascribing the central role in governance to the main bank (Sheard, 1991, 1994). Other shareholders are then able to "free ride" on the main bank's alleged monitoring activities. However, the questionnaire data (Fuji Sogo Kenkyujo, 1993; Omura, 1993) further support the reports of our banker respondents that any presumed free-riding action by other cross-shareholders is irrelevant. The results of the two questionnaire surveys, which studied the firms' perspectives on their main banks as reported by corporate executives, clearly demonstrate that non-financial company managers do not regard mutual stock ownership in investment terms but more often as mutual security and non-aggression pacts. The nature of cross-shareholding is such that in most situations the other cross-shareholders are neither free to sell their shares nor free to exercise ownership rights over recalcitrant managers (agents) of the other firm because cross-shareholding arrangements in general have *anti*governance, rather than governance, expectations built into them. Indeed, they themselves (as agents) in their own firms have made a non-interference pact with those very same managers of the other firms to protect their own incumbency.[46]

The Omura (1993) data further revealed that the only firms which valued their cross-shareholding relationships with financial institutions more than with non-financial shareholding partners were those firms that were highly dependent upon banks. This category of firm was indicated by such negative factors as: a relatively small size of capital; low efficiency of capital ratio (pretax income/total capital); low capital/assets ratio; low capital growth; large losses in the firm's stock price; and low concentrations of ownership. Another key bank dependency factor reported by Omura (1993) was the general negative health of the particular industry to which the firm belonged, for example, publicly traded companies in such ailing industries as iron and steel and, to a lesser degree, machine tools, electrical machinery, trading firms, and the services industries. The healthy (at the time of the survey) high cross-shareholding automotive industry respondent companies saw cross-shareholding relations with financial institutions as much less beneficial than those with their own *keiretsu* or "group"-affiliated companies.

SUMMARY AND CONCLUSION

Our findings begin with a fundamental redefinition of the main bank relationship. Some commentators predict that the main bank system will ultimately disappear in Japan as a result of the liberalization process of financial markets, which presumably would undermine the close-knit ties inherent in those relationships. Proponents of that view cite the fact that bank lending to large corporations has decreased, now that the corporations have direct access to and are able to raise funds more cheaply in domestic and international money markets. However, as our most recent set of respondent interviews indicate (November–December 1995), the banks themselves, with the establishment of their own securities subsidiaries, have assumed this role, displacing all but the top Big Four securities firms (Nomura, Daiwa, Nikko, and Yamaichi) as the leading underwriters of corporate bonds.

The respondents in our study reported that, rather than corporate lending, the main bank relationship *itself* is the bank's greatest source of profits. Indeed, the liberalization of interest rates in recent years has made large corporate lending the least profitable aspect of the banking business. Similarly, the competition between bank securities subsidiaries in underwriting corporate bonds has proven to be a low profit area, and likewise is considered by bankers as a "loss leader" necessary in maintaining client relationships. By contrast, the respondents reported, a bank will ordinarily receive many lucrative benefits from its status as lead main bank to a company. The bank expects to be given the main deposit accounts of its client, and it will require, as well, that the client firm hold a standing low- or non-interest compensating balance account (formerly called *ryodate* account). The client may also be expected to maintain low-interest-bearing time deposits at the bank for some off-balance sheet favor such as a business introduction. In addition, the bank receives a disproportionately larger share of fee-based transactions such as transfers, foreign exchange, and derivative products, an important area of bank profits, than the other banks in the client firm's lending hierarchy. Finally, whether the client is large or small, the bank also expects to receive the advantage of the company's employee pool as its customers and with it the opportunity to supply a host of lucrative retail services to this captive client base. A single large company can lead to many hundreds, if not thousands, of personal accounts and employee customers for such bank services as personal loans, home mortgages, credit card, consumer lending, bill payments, and account transaction fees. These retail banking services are among the highest profit centers for banks today.

Our research suggests that the main bank system is no longer driven by large corporate bank borrowing. It has found new fuel in a host of bank products and services so that a main bank's relationship with its large clients remains quite profitable – for the main bank and for the second, third, fourth, and even fifth bank in the lending hierarchy as well.

On the other side of the picture, the interview respondents reported that firms, for their part, recognize the benefits gained from the mutual relationship and will also go to great lengths to maintain it. Firms expect to be able to rely on the bank's good offices to supply business information, consulting services, and, especially for the medium-sized firms, the ever-important bank introductions to prospective clients or suppliers. The bankers reported that the client corporation will go to extraordinary lengths to protect the hierarchical standing of its lead main bank but that the practices associated with relationship banking are not restricted nor exclusive to the lead main bank and its client. The second and third lending banks of that company will attempt to provide similar services, as will even the fourth and fifth banks in the lending hierarchy, which may be composed of upwards of 20 to 30 banks if the corporation is large. The preservation of that hierarchy in a highly competitive environment is of paramount importance to the main bank, particularly since it receives a disproportionately large share of profits from the client than the other institutions in the hierarchy. In fact, when the top five lending banks typically supply only 50 percent of the firm's borrowed funds, they can still expect to receive almost 100 percent of the firm's fee-based transactions, such as foreign exchange, letters of credit and other trade- or business-related credit guarantees, leasing and underwriting to their non-bank financial subsidiaries.

As we see it, the misplaced assumptions of agency theorists relating to main bank monitoring by the bank team stem chiefly from the failure to understand the nature and abilities of the bank team, particularly as to its overriding sales function, that is, to promote new business. During the "bubble period" of the 1980s the mission of the bank teams was primarily to boost bank assets by issuing new loans, which were often used for speculative purposes by the client. This lending/sales function was in obvious conflict with agency theory notions of monitoring a client firm's creditworthiness, which the bank could do only to a very limited extent in any case. Furthermore, today, as in the past, only the largest corporations merit their own bank teams. Medium- and small-sized firms receive only the occasional attentions of already overburdened junior officers whose ability to monitor their client firms is often limited to tracking the cash flow into the client's main deposit account.

The agency assumption of firm monitoring by former bankers, the so-called *shukko* process, is similarly flawed. As discussed, *shukko* reflects the primarily fiscal necessity of the bank to find early retirement positions for high-salaried senior bank executives and only secondarily may operate to influence a client firm's management. In our study, bankers readily acknowledged that their continued influence over their former employees was extremely limited, if not nil, when a conflict of interest arose between the bank and its client firm. The necessity to retire senior bank employees has accelerated in pace since the overhiring of junior personnel during the "bubble period."

In considering the role of banks in corporate governance, we conclude that banks are not acting as monitors in the agency sense, that is, as agents for fellow shareholders, since the bank's own credit exposure to the client far exceeds its own equity position in the client firm. Even from a creditor's standpoint, the bank's ability to monitor is limited. The current banking crisis in Japan has painfully revealed the banks' less than minimal ability to evaluate the creditworthiness of clients when money was lent to pursue land and stock speculations in the 1980s.

Another key agency assumption of bank governance are the so-called bank rescues. Our evidence reveals that they generally have been effected only when the bank determined that a client's difficulties were a result of a liquidity problem rather than a solvency crisis – and then it acted out of its own interest, if not just for its own profit. However, as a number of bank officers reported, they were often the last to know of an imminent financial crisis when the client firm was intent on evading bank oversight. If the main bank rescue function really did exist, such calculated evasion by failing client firms would have been pointless at the very least, if not counter-productive. In cases of insolvency, "rescue" most often means overseeing the dissolution of the firm's assets and the distribution of collateral to its chief creditors, namely, the banks. Only in those limited cases deemed by governmental authorities to be in the interest of the nation's welfare does the Ministry of Finance "request" a main bank to deliver a rescue package.

The main bank relationship is rooted in the history of the postwar reconstruction of the Japanese economy, and prior to that in the role of the bank within the prewar *zaibatsu* groups. Indeed, much of its present-day practices stem from that history and also bear within them a strong component of traditional group relationships endogenous to Japanese society.[47] Nonetheless, we cannot escape the fact that the functionalist practices of the main bank relationship are to seek competitive advantages in a system in which the relationship itself is a key source of bank profits.

In the ever-rising economy which had been characteristic of Japan in the postwar era, the validity of agency assumptions of internal corporate governance, issues of "self-governance" and the main bank's "rescue function," implicit or otherwise, had not been seriously tested. Now, as Japan suffers its first profound postwar recession, questions of corporate efficiency are being starkly confronted. In a sense this recession can be and with increasing frequency is being characterized as a "governance recession". For shareholders, the return on investment is no longer being satisfied by capital gains. Furthermore, the banks and other financial institutions are no longer able to rely on the size and growth of assets as reliable indicators of the soundness of their institution. Rather, for banks return on assets and the quality of assets have become the watchwords of the "post-bubble economy".

Notes

1. For a review and analysis of these studies, see M.J. Scher (1997).
2. Testing the concept of banks as corporate monitors, some researchers suggested a statistical correlation between firm performance as measured by stock prices and the appointment of former bankers as outside directors to the cross-shareholding firm's board (Kaplan and Minton, 1994) although Kang and Shivdasani (1995) found no such correlation. The selection of methodological approach, in particular, was critical because it appeared that many of the conclusions propounded by agency theorists may well have been the result of inadequacies in their research methodologies. For a more detailed review and critique of the shortcomings of these agency theorist's methodologies, see M.J. Scher (1997).
3. For a detailed account of the multiple case-study approach used in this fieldwork, see M.J. Scher (1997).

4. Respondent 1 at bank I: an officer of a long-term credit bank.
5. Respondent 2 formerly of bank H: a former officer of a long-term credit bank.
6. Respondent 1 at bank C: an officer of a top six city bank.
7. Respondent 1 at bank C: an officer of a top six city bank.
8. Respondent 1 at bank D: an officer of a top six city bank.
9. Respondent 1 at bank D: an officer of a top six city bank.
10. Respondent 1: president of bank services organization.
11. Respondent 1: president of bank services organization.
12. Respondent 1 at bank B: senior officer of a top six city bank.
13. Respondent 1 at bank B: senior officer of a top six city bank.
14. Respondent 1 at bank B: senior officer of a top six city bank.
15. Respondent 1 at bank I: an officer of a long-term credit bank.
16. Respondent 1 at bank A: an officer of a top six city bank.
17. Respondent 1 at bank H: an officer of a long-term credit bank.
18. Respondent 2 formerly of bank H: a former officer of a long-term credit bank.
19. Respondent 2 at bank O: senior officer of a government-owned bank.
20. Respondent 1 at bank P: an officer of a foreign-owned bank, formerly an officer of a top six bank.
21. Respondent 1 at bank B: senior officer of a top six city bank.
22. Respondent 2 formerly of Bank H: a former officer of a long-term credit bank.
23. Respondent 1 at bank D: an officer of a top six city bank.
24. Respondent 1 at bank D: an officer of a top six city bank.
25. Respondent 1 at bank P: an officer of a foreign-owned bank, formerly an officer of a top six bank.
26. Respondent 2 at bank B: an officer of a top six city bank.
27. Respondent 1 at bank H: an officer of a long-term credit bank.
28. Respondent 2 at bank I: an officer of a long-term credit bank.
29. Respondent 1 at bank D: an officer of a top six city bank.
30. Respondent 1 at bank D: an officer of a top six city bank.
31. Respondent 1 at bank D: an officer of a top six city bank.
32. Respondent 1: president of bank services organization.
33. Respondent 1 at bank C: an officer of a top six city bank.
34. Respondent 1 at bank D: an officer of a top six city bank.
35. Respondent 6 at bank D: an officer of a top six city bank.
36. Respondent 2 formerly of bank H: a former officer of a long-term credit bank.
37. Respondent 1 at bank D: an officer of a top six city bank.
38. Respondent 1 at bank C: an officer of a top six city bank.
39. Respondent 1 at bank C: an officer of a top six city bank.
40. Respondents 1 and 2 at bank B: officers of a top six city bank.
41. Respondent 1 at bank C: an officer of a top six city bank.
42. Respondent 2 formerly of bank H: a former officer of a long-term credit bank.
43. Respondent 1 at bank G: a retired senior officer of a former specialized city bank.
44. Respondent 1 at bank I: an officer of a long-term credit bank.
45. Respondent 1: senior officer of a banking association.
46. See M.J. Scher (1997) for a detailed account of cross-shareholding practices, particularly in regard to main banks.
47. See M.J. Scher (1997) for a detailed description of these historically-based groups and traditional firm–bank relationships.

References

Aoki Masahiko. (1990). "Toward an Economic Model of the Japanese Firm," *Journal of Economic Literature* 28(March): 1–27.

—— (1994). "Monitoring Characteristics of the Main Bank System: An Analytical and Developmental View," in M. Aoki and H. Patrick, eds. *The Japanese Main Bank System: Its Relevancy for Developing and Transforming Economies*. New York: Oxford University Press.

Fuji Sogo Kenkyujo. (1993). *'Main bank system oyobi kabushiki' ni tsuite no chosa*, (An investigation regarding the influence of shareholding on the main bank system). Research report. Tokyo.

Horiuchi Akiyoshi. (1989). "Informational Properties of the Japanese Financial System," *Japan and the World Economy*, 1 (3): 255–78.

—— (1995). "Financial Sector Reforms in Postwar Japan." Unpublished paper October 1995.

Horiuchi Akiyoshi, and Fukuda Shin'ichi (1987). "Nihon no mainbank wa dono yohna yakuwari wo hatashitaka" (What Was the Role of the Japanese Main Bank System?), Nihon Ginko Kinyu Kenkyujo *Kinyu Kenkyu* 6 (3): 1–28.

Horiuchi Akiyoshi, and Okazaki Ryoko. (1992). "Capital Markets and the Banking Sector: The Efficiency of Japanese Banks in Reducing Agency Costs." Discussion Paper 92-F-6 Research Institute for the Japanese Economy, Faculty of Economics, University of Tokyo.

Horiuchi Akiyoshi, F. Packer, and S. Fukuda. (1988). "What Role Has the Main Bank Played in Japan," in *Journal of the Japanese and International Economies*, 2, 159–80.

Hoshi Takeo, A. Kashyap, and D. Scharfstein. (1990a). "Bank Monitoring and Investment: Evidence from the Changing Structure of Japanese Corporate Banking Relationships" in R. Glenn Hubbard, ed. *Asymmetric Information, Corporate Finance, and Economic Development*. Chicago: University of Chicago Press pp. 105–26.

—— (1990b). "The Role of Banks in Reducing Costs of Financial Distress in Japan," in *Journal of Financial Economics*, 27: 67–88.

—— (1991). "Corporate Structure, Liquidity, and Investment: Evidence from Japanese Industrial Groups," *Quarterly Journal of Economics*, 106: 33–60.

Kang Jun-Koo and Anil Shivdasani. (1995). "Firm Performance, Corporate Governance, and Top Executive Turnover in Japan" *Journal of Financial Economics* 38, 29–58.

Kaplan, Steven N. and Bernadette A. Minton. (1994). "Appointments of Outsiders to Japanese Boards: Determinants and Implications for Managers" *Journal of Financial Economics* 36, 225–58.

Miwa Yoshiro. (1985). "Mainbank to sono kinou" (The Function of Main Banks) in Y. Kosai and S. Nishikawa eds. *Nihon Keizai Sistemu*. Tokyo: University of Tokyo Press, pp. 170–99.

—— (1991). "Mainbank to Nihon no shihon shijo" (Main Banks and Japanese Capital Markets) Zenginkyo *Kin'yu*, August 11–19.

Nakatani Iwao. (1983). "Kigyo shudan no keizaiteki imi to ginko no yakuwari," (The Economic Significance of the Enterprise Groups and the Role of Banks) *Kin'yu Keizai* 202: 51–75.

—— (1984). "The Economic Role of Financial Corporate Grouping" in M. Aoki ed. *The Economic Analysis of the Japanese Firm*, 227–58. Amsterdam: North-Holland: Elsevier.

Nomura Sogo Kenkyujo. (1992). "Nihon kigyo no corporate governance" (Corporate Governance of Japanese Companies), *Zaikai Kansoku*, Sept.

Oba Ryoko, and Horiuchi Akiyoshi. (1991). "Honpo kigyo no mainbank kankei to setsubi toshi kodo no kankei ni tsuite" (On the Relationship Between Our Country's Corporate Main Bank System and Capital Expenditure Behavior), Nihon Ginko Kinyu Kenkyujo *Kinyu Kenkyu* 9 (4): 23–50. December.

Okazaki Ryoko, and Horiuchi Akiyoshi. (1992). "Kigyo no setsubi toshi to mainbank kankei" (The Relationship Between the Main Bank and Corporate Capital Expenditure) Nihon Ginko Kinyu Kenkyujo *Kinyu Kenkyu* 11 (1): 37–59. March.

Omura Kei'ichi. (1993). *Kabushiki mochiai no ishiki kozo* (How Companies Consider Cross-Shareholding) Report of International Finance Group, Keiei Academy, Tokyo.

Scher, Mark J. (1997). *Japanese Interfirm Networks and Their Main Banks*, London: Macmillan.

Sheard, Paul. (1989). "The Main Bank System and Corporate Monitoring and Control in Japan," in *Journal of Economic Behavior*. 11: 399–422.

—— (1991). "The Economics of Interlocking Shareholding," *Ricerche Economiche*, 45: 421–48.

—— (1994). "Interlocking Shareholdings and Corporate Governance" in M. Aoki and R. Dore eds. *The Japanese Firm, Sources of Competitive Strength*, New York: Oxford University Press, pp. 310–49.

Acknowledgments

I would like to express my profound gratitude to the seventy-one Japanese banking practitioners without whose help my research would not have been possible. Regretfully, discretion requires that their names and institutions remain anonymous. I am also most grateful to Tokyo Keizai (Economics) University where I was Visiting Research Fellow and, in particular, to Prof. Yoshiaki Jinnai and the Accounting Faculty Seminar.

I am also most appreciative of the assistance of my colleagues at the Institute for Financial Affairs and the staff of the Fuji Sogo Kenkyujo. I would also like to thank the following people for their comments on earlier drafts of this article: Prof. Shoichi Asajima, Dr. Penelope Ciancanelli, Prof. David Knights, Prof. Kei'ichi Omura, Prof. Hugh Patrick, Dr. C. Tait Ratcliffe, Prof. Adrian Tschoegl, Prof. Juro Teranishi, and especially Prof. Akiyoshi Horiuchi for his continuing encouragement of my research. Needless to say, this article's outlook and shortcomings are solely my responsibility.

Index

AA, insurance underwriting, 26n
Abbey Life, 9
Abbey National Building Society,
    conversion to bank, 7
accountability, of personal bankers (NZ),
    22–3, 104–5
accounts: compensating balance (Japan),
    192, 193, 209; depository (Japan),
    192, 193; Japanese employee, 194–6,
    209
ACORN (geodemographic segmentation),
    172
advertising: to create demand, 72–6;
    insurance, 10; and normalising
    subjectivity, 49–50; psychology in,
    88–9nn; and suburban subjectivity, 55,
    65n
agency theory, in Japanese main bank
    system, 190–1
American Bankers Association, 35, 45
AMEX (American Stock Exchange), 21, 32
apprentice ratios, in German bank system,
    148, 149, **149**
Arthur Andersen & Co., 121
ATMs (automated teller machines), 15–16,
    94
attitude, conceptualisation of, 168
Auckland Savings Bank, 94
Australia and New Zealand Bank, 93–4
Australian banks, and New Zealand
    deregulation, 93–4
autonomy, employees', 111–12

bancassurance, 2, 11, 19; in Denmark, 124;
    in Germany, 140; Lloyds Bank, 9
Bank Holding Companies Act (1956) (US),
    39, 40
bank intermediation ratio, Germany, 136–7,
    137
Bank of New England, collapse, 44
Bank of Scotland: computer banking, 16,
    130; in New Zealand, 94
Banking Act (1933) (US) *see* Glass–Steagall
    Act
Banking Act (1935) (US), 36
banks: and competitive change, 13–15;
    cross-industry mergers in Denmark,
    124–6; culpability for Wall Street
    Crash, 34–5; employment levels, **139**,

149; face-to-face access to customers,
    16; and Financial Services Act, 5;
    financial services from, 5, 11; interna-
    tionalisation of, 40; mortgages from, 6,
    15; professional image of, 8, 9, 13;
    relations with building societies, 6, 8;
    relations with insurance, 2–3, 7–8,
    9–10; role under Glass–Steagall Act,
    36; role of universal German, 135–6;
    and use of computer technology, 16,
    see also Germany; Japan; New
    Zealand; profitability
'Banque Francaise' psychographic
    segmentation case study, 173–8
Barclays Bank, insurance company, 9
Barlow Clowes, 65–6n
Barron's journal, 28
Baudrillard, J., 49–50
BCCI, collapse of, 26n
benefits, for German bank employees, 145
'Big Bang' (City of London), 3, 4–5
BIS (Bank of International Settlements),
    regulations, 192, 193
Black Horse Life, agency network, 9
Blair, A., New Labour, 50–1
Boetsky, Ivan, junk bond dealer, 28
bonds: junk, 28; for savings in Germany,
    137
Bradford & Bingley Building Society, 6
'brand imperialism', 84
brand marketing, 11, 54, 118
Britannia Building Society, 12
building societies: and competitive change,
    13–15; conversion to banks, 12;
    Denmark, 124; and Financial Services
    Act, 5–6; and insurance business, 8,
    11–12; in New Zealand, 94; and
    protection of borrowers, 59–60;
    restructuring, 6–8; US, 36
Building Societies Act (1986), 3, 6; and free
    market theory, 57, 59
Bush, George, administration, 43–4, 45

capital form, and labour as commodity, 31
capital market, in Marxist analysis, 31
capitalism: instabilities of, 31–2, 41;
    Marxist analysis of, 29–33; popular
    (New Right), 61–2
Certificate of Deposits (CDs), 40

215

Index by Auriol Griffith-Jones